GET
YOURS!

GET YOURS!

Amy DuBois Barnett

How to Have Everything You Ever Dreamed Of and More

BROADWAY BOOKS

NEW YORK

BROADWAY

Copyright © 2007 by Amy DuBois Barnett

All Rights Reserved

Published in the United States by Broadway Books, an imprint of
The Doubleday Publishing Group, a division of Random House, Inc.,
New York.
www.broadwaybooks.com

A hardcover edition of this book was originally published
in 2007 by Broadway Books.

BROADWAY BOOKS and its logo, a letter B bisected on the diagonal,
are trademarks of Random House, Inc.

LIBRARY OF CONGRESS CATALOGING-IN-PUBLICATION DATA
Barnett, Amy DuBois.
    Get yours! : how to have everything you ever dreamed of
and more / by: Amy DuBois Barnett.—1st paperback ed.
        p.   cm.
    "A hardcover edition of this book was originally published in 2007
by Broadway Books. It is here reprinted by arrangement with
Broadway Books."
    1. African American women—Life skills guide. 2. Self-actualization
(Psychology) 3. Success—United States. I. Title.
    E185.86.B3744 2008
    646.70084'220973—dc22
    2008005126

ISBN 978-0-7679-2509-9

PRINTED IN THE UNITED STATES OF AMERICA

10 9 8 7 6 5 4 3 2

This book is dedicated to my mother,

MARGUERITE ROSS BARNETT,

an extraordinary woman

who showed me how to dream big,

love hard, and make every day an adventure.

CONTENTS

GET
YOURS!

FOREWORD

By Angela Burt-Murray,
Editor-in-Chief of *Essence* magazine

I've always been a behind-the-scenes kind of person. The sister who's willing to do neighborhood committee work, but never leading the charge. The one who would make the calls to raise funding for a charity, but then gladly let someone else announce the results. The one who would come up with a groundbreaking idea at work, but then give the team all the credit for the execution. I always played background. You know, more like Kelly or Michelle than Beyoncé. That was where I was most comfortable.

Then one day everything changed: I learned that *Essence* magazine was looking for a new editor-in-chief. The opportunity to run the premier magazine for black women had long been a dream of mine, but one I wasn't quite sure I'd ever achieve. After all, this was a highly coveted job that many qualified people wanted just as much as I did. I had worked as an editor for the previous ten years at various magazines and had a reputation as a hard worker, creative thinker, and strong manager. But I'd heard that some industry people weren't sure I was the "right material" to run *Essence*. Suddenly a nagging inner voice of self-doubt was the only thing I could hear. *Maybe I should pull out of contention.*

It was during that time that I went into my then-boss Amy DuBois Barnett's office, threw myself down on her couch, and poured out my problem. Amy and I had worked together for a long time (starting as editors in *Essence*'s fashion and beauty department seven years before!). We made such a good team that when she got the job as editor-in-chief of *Honey,* she hired me as her executive editor. And then, when she was hired to run *Teen People,* she brought me onboard as the executive editor there as well. After working side by side for so long, she knew me better than anyone—and certainly as a successful editor-in-chief she knew what it took to get this job.

Also, I had always been inspired by Amy's drive, determination, and seemingly effortless confidence. Both *Honey* and *Teen People* were extremely challenging brands to run, yet Amy never hesitated in taking them on. Her infectious enthusiasm for facing what others considered to be insurmountable odds was what had kept me working for her at three different magazines.

In three words: Amy was fearless!

After listening to me complain about the things that people were saying about me and watching me wring my hands in confusion over what I should do, Amy gave me some of the best advice of my career. "This job is yours to lose. You've been preparing for this your entire life, and there's no one better for the position," she said. "I know it, but if you don't *really* know it then you'll never get the job. You've got to make them feel your passion and your purpose. Make them see your vision the way we do." And Amy told me that while she knew that I was scared, that was actually a good sign. It meant that I was stretching and going outside my comfort zone. That was a test, Amy said, that she often used on herself to know that she was pushing herself to the next level. Fear, she told me firmly, is good.

I went home that night and thought about what Amy had said and came to the conclusion that she was absolutely right. If I didn't believe in myself and my vision for *Essence,* how could I expect someone else to? I decided right then that I wasn't going to let another person's misguided opinions or my own fear keep me from the job of my dreams.

And now I'm proud to say that I silenced that nagging inner voice of self-doubt, went for the job, and became the Editor-in-Chief of *Essence* in 2005. While I'd love to claim that I'm completely confident in every situation every single day, there are still times when I get nervous as I face a new challenge. But I remember Amy's advice to trust that my apprehension just means I'm realizing my full potential and to keep pushing forward. And it's working!

Happily, there's nothing I treasure more about my dream job than having the opportunity to be a cheerleader for millions of women just like you as you reach for goals that you may have thought impossible—

just as Amy did for me! And thankfully so many of you are reaching your goals. Our success stories are everywhere: Liberian President Ellen Johnson Sirleaf, Pulitzer Prize–winning *Washington Post* journalist Robin Givhan, Tony Award–winning Broadway actress LaChanze, Secretary of State Condoleezza Rice, cable and radio tycoon Cathy Hughes, *Grey's Anatomy* creator Shonda Rimes, Atlanta Mayor Shirley Franklin. From the boardroom to the White House to the television studio, you're running things, girlfriend!

And while we all have that nagging voice of self-doubt, we have to look inside ourselves to move past paralyzing fear to reach our dreams.

Amy's brilliant new book *Get Yours! How to Have Everything You Ever Dreamed Of and More* will be the personal guidebook you need to help you identify your passions, prioritize your happiness, and take on your next big challenge. Within this book, you will find the inspiration to stretch beyond self-imposed limitations, embrace your fear, and use it to realize your goals. Amy's "get yours" philosophy helped me achieve my dream, and I know it will do the same for you!

I am one of the happiest people I know. My husband of three years is a good man, I recently gave birth to a healthy baby boy, and we live in a beautiful penthouse apartment in New York City with a tree-lined deck and huge windows that bathe our home in light all day long. I've traveled the world, hung out with celebrities, partied in the most exclusive VIP rooms, and, through it all, maintained a group of girlfriends who are like my sisters. I've also had wonderful professional success— as the Editor-in-Chief of *Honey,* the first-ever magazine devoted to the lifestyle of young urban women, and as the chief editor of *Teen People,* where I became the first black woman in this country to run a major national mainstream magazine.

Before you start rolling your eyes and looking for something to throw in my general direction, please know that although I do consider myself to be blessed, I had to work for all I achieved. The life I live today was not handed to me on a silver platter. It took me years not only to gain the "things" I have but also to become the confident, outspoken woman I am today. I can say without hesitation that I am happy— but for way too long I was miserable, afraid to pursue what I truly wanted in life, hesitant to speak my mind, and eager to please everyone, except myself.

It all began with my strange, nomadic childhood. After my parents separated, then divorced when I was eight, my mom and I moved from town to town, never staying long enough to get to know any one place, much less make good friends. For chunks of my childhood, my dad, though consistently loving toward me, was too busy fighting his own demons to see how hard it was for me to be so rootless. By the time I applied to college, I'd already lived in seven cities on three different continents.

Just after I graduated from college, my mom was diagnosed with a vicious form of cancer that killed her within five months. Shortly after, my stepfather tried to take some of the money my mother left me, forcing me to sue him to get it back. After being devastated by my mom's death, my maternal grandmother succumbed to Alzheimer's, stopped recognizing me, and had to be moved into a nursing home. During this time I was working at a job that I hated, living in a dingy basement apartment, and dealing with the fact that my first great love—my boyfriend of several years—had cheated on me.

Were my hardships the worst in the world? No, of course not. Others have suffered far worse, and I'm well aware of how truly fortunate I am. But I do know that the happiness I feel now was hard-won—and if I can figure out how to turn my life around, *anyone* can. Don't get me wrong—I'm not saying I have all the answers, because I'm still figuring this whole life thing out, just like everyone else. But during the dark period following my mother's death, I adopted a personal philosophy—seven simple rules that ultimately saved my life:

- Embrace fear as growth.
- Be true to yourself.
- Realize your value and demand the best.
- Put into the universe what you want to get back.
- Have integrity.
- Stay independent.
- Do something meaningful every day.

In other words, I developed what I like to call the "get yours" school of thought. By "get yours," I don't mean be selfish and grab your slice of pie before everyone else. I mean: *Get the absolute most out of this life that you possibly can.* Figure out what your real passions are and who you want to be—and stay true to that always. Push yourself toward your best life every single day in every single area—health, career, family, friends, and relationships. Commit to your dreams: Know that realizing them won't be easy, but that the satisfaction you will feel after having worked toward something important will be as fulfilling as achieving the goal. And understand that energy is real and the universe is more sensitive than you think. Be generous and patient and kind—not only because it is your responsibility as a citizen of the world, but because you will receive tenfold what you give in return.

Embracing this philosophy paid me back big-time. It gave me the power to envision the life I truly wanted, make a plan to change my circumstances, and put together the pieces of the happiness I have now.

And now I'd like to share my knowledge. It was as editor of *Honey* that I first realized one of my major callings was to help other women "get theirs." I had a very close relationship with my readers (maybe you were one of them!) through "Personal Space," my monthly column. In it, I shared stories about my moments of confusion and clarity, embarrassment and triumph. I wrote about lessons I'd learned through my trials and tribulations, adventures I'd taken, people I'd met, and the success or failure I'd had in trying to actualize my dreams.

Clearly my words struck a chord; I would receive tons of e-mails and letters each day. Since the tone of these messages was always so intimate, I read every single one. Usually, they started with "I'm so grateful you wrote about that . . . I thought nobody felt that way but me," and went on to relate their own similar episodes. Sometimes, though, they'd ask for unrelated advice. Should they leave their man, change careers, move across the country, apologize to their girlfriend . . . ? I was constantly moved by the number of my readers who wanted and needed help to create a better life. For generations, women of color—particularly black women—have led our families, but apparently we still hadn't figured out how to value ourselves and live the lives we truly desired.

This book is the culmination of the mission that began for me at *Honey* magazine. In each chapter, I will share with you my story—things I've been through as I've carved out my own space in this world. I will also ask you to really look at yourself—honestly explore where you are right now, and where you want to go. Then I will give you strategies that work for setting and achieving goals, and for ensuring that the rest of your life will be all it can be. I've also asked some well-known achievers to weigh in at the end of each chapter with their own stories of happiness and success, personal insights and tips for continued fulfillment. At the end of each chapter, I include a "promise page." I want you to use it to define your dreams and make a plan for realizing them today, this year, and for the rest of your life. I cannot overstate how important it is for your happiness and success to make serious commitments (to yourself and to others), and then to keep them. *Do what you say you are going to do.*

I'm not expecting you to do what I do. If I've learned one thing, it's that life is a DIY project. I'm just hopeful that my story will inspire you. Motivate you. Help explain a few things you've been curious or unsure about. Assure you that someone else has been there, cried over that, and moved on. If so, then I will know my mission was successful, and that yours—whatever it is—will be, too.

When I left *Teen People* to write this book, people told me I was insane to give up a high-powered, lucrative job for the uncertainty that being an author brings. And I told them what I always say when someone questions a risk that I'm taking to follow a dream: I'm sure it seems crazy now, but I just *know* that this will lead to a better life.

I honestly believe that if you're comfortable with who you are, decent to those around you, go after your passions, and make room for adventure, the same will be true for you, too, girlfriend! All I want is for you to go out and get yours!

1

GET HAPPY

The first and most important step to getting yours is figuring out what truly makes you happy. And this, girlfriend, is way harder than it seems—mainly because most of us have been conditioned to believe that our happiness is based on how much we can chip off our to-do lists in a day. We're so used to bearing a disproportionate amount of household responsibility, and having people ask and not give in return. Society at large expects us to be plow horses that don't need praise or even rest. No wonder we see every aspect of our lives as work! We don't appreciate the good things we may already have and we certainly don't value the experience of adversity and the strength it gives us to make the life we truly want. I know because it took the most horrible event of my life, my mother's death, to finally teach me how to truly live and be happy.

Growing up, home was not a place, it was one person: my mom. Because we moved around so much, people used to ask me if I was an army brat. After a while I began to identify myself as an "academia brat." Both my parents were college professors, so we would move from university to university. Most of my friends reminisce about growing up in Dallas or Oakland or Detroit. But I never think about towns; instead, I recall Princeton and Howard and Columbia universities, the look of the campuses, my parents' colleagues, being passed from student to student while my mom or dad taught a class. Throughout my childhood I was constantly adjusting—to an unfamiliar environment, a new school, a different bunch of kids.

The way I managed to function within our wandering way of life—to make my passage easier and to develop new relationships quickly—was simply to give everyone else the upper hand, all the time. I kept my head down, my defenses up, and my expectations low. In my teens, I rarely made demands on a friendship, volunteering to be the designated driver, fake-ID holder, term-paper writer. I was the new girl everyone turned to but no one truly liked (let's face it, no one actually *likes* a suck-up).

Fortunately, I had my mom. While I didn't have a lot of extended family, she was the one person I could always count on to be there, the stable force. Despite my confusion, I knew at my core I was valuable and talented because my mother instilled those feelings—even when I wavered, she believed in me. While I was at college, still unsure how to stand up for myself and make my own way, Mom became the president of the University of Houston, earning her place in history as the first black woman in the country to head a major research university.

" Be you always. "

I was so lucky to have her as a role model, a smart, ambitious, funny, and loving woman who prioritized family but still managed to achieve every goal she set out for herself. Still, for years her example and words of wisdom couldn't penetrate my shell of insecurity. I spent so much time catering to everyone else, I had no idea who *I* was. I let my friends and boyfriends and, even though she meant well, my mom tell me what to eat, what to wear, what classes to take, whom to hang out with.

In college, I majored in political science because my mom was a political scientist. And even though I'd fantasized about editing a magazine since I was a teen, I decided to be a lawyer. I hated my classes, but didn't switch my major. Boyfriends were unfaithful to me and I didn't leave them. Some of my friends took and never gave, but I was always there for them.

I graduated from college and got a job in finance. I hated it from day one, but figured I'd stick it out for a couple of years, then apply to law school. Every morning, I trudged to the subway, and rode a cramped, sweaty half hour to my deadly dull job as a low-level number cruncher in the corporate finance division of a huge Wall Street bank that was so conservative, women were forbidden to wear pants or skirts without pantyhose. Yeah, girlfriend, it was *that* bad. Quitting time meant going home to the only apartment I could comfortably afford on my own: a tiny one-bedroom in a run-down neighborhood that I shared with a kooky woman whose matted weave and holey clothes belied her claims to be a singer with a hit single in Japan.

I felt trapped and miserable.

Then one evening, Mom called me from Houston. "Don't tell your grandmother the truth," she began strangely. "Tell her it's the flu."

"Um, okay," I said slowly. "What *is* the truth?"

"That I have cancer and it's serious," Mom told me, her words a rush.

I had just turned twenty-two. Even though I still felt like a kid, there was no time to regress. Mom's cancer was aggressive, and after five blurry months, she was dead.

Because I identified so strongly with my mother, without her I had no real sense of self. I was petrified of facing the world alone and had no idea where to even begin my journey. For a year after she passed, I forced myself awake every day, and dragged myself to work wearing clothes that, increasingly, felt like a costume. My few friends faded away as it became apparent that I was unable to give, and for once needed help from them. My boyfriend at the time lived in a town a few hours away, and he barely visited me. Every night, I ordered Chinese food at ten o'clock, which I ate while watching bad sitcom reruns. Gaining twenty pounds was as easy as asking for extra pancakes with my moo shu pork.

One evening, as I sluggishly sorted laundry in my room, I stopped to stare at a framed picture of me and my mom that I kept on my cluttered dresser. I was still for a long time, waiting for some moment of revelation I instinctively felt was coming.

And then I knew. All of a sudden I realized that this was *my* life. No one could crawl inside my skin and live for me. No one was coming to rescue me from my unhappiness—no Mom, no man, no guardian angel. This was it. This particular day was never going to happen again, so what the hell was I going to do to make it worthwhile? I remained standing where I was as a flood of my mom's words and deeds flowed through my mind. I realized with relief mixed with cold fear that only I had the ultimate power over what I did, where I went, and who I spent my time with. I *owned* my life.

It was weird, but after those intense few minutes, I felt like a completely different person. I saw with new clarity how sad and lonely I was making myself by living someone else's idea of what would be best for me and not being open to new adventures and possibilities. Right then, I resolved to create a different life for myself—one in which I made every single day count. And from that day on, I took charge.

I quit my miserable job, dumped my crappy boyfriend, and moved out of that nasty little apartment. I started exercising five days a week, lost weight, and gave away all the clothing I didn't actually enjoy putting on. I also got a tattoo on my right ankle—a design from one of my mom's favorite scarves—as a tribute to her and as a mark that would forever show through the pantyhose any job would ever force me to wear.

Somehow, in clearing out all that held me back, I was removing the layers that had been hiding the real me all that time. I followed my long-standing interest in fashion to Parsons School of Design, where I studied fashion merchandising for a year. My days took on a completely different new rhythm. I'd go to Parsons all day, then head to the gym or to a dance class at night. I was exploring a whole new side of me; finally, I had a creative outlet, and I discovered a love for visual art that I never knew I had. And I was pushing my body in new ways, becoming strong and lithe and confident.

Almost instantly, I became a magnet for good luck. I met great new people, and reconnected with old friends I didn't get to know well enough because I'd moved away. My life was an open window—opportunities flew in. I got a job as an assistant buyer at Lord & Taylor, but after a year I realized I didn't love it (my new criteria for everything in my life). No longer afraid to honor my true passions, I quit to pursue my love of writing. I ended up moving to Ireland for a year to study writing and literature, supporting myself by tutoring students in English and essay writing (okay, so there was a guy involved in that decision . . . more on that later!). I lived in a cozy house in a suburb of Dublin called Goatstown. I got a yellow labrador puppy, went for long walks, dated hot foreign guys, and drank many a pint of beer at the local pub. It was, put simply, an adventure.

While there I applied to creative writing programs at various graduate schools, and was accepted at Columbia University back in New York. I packed up, moved home, and, with the money my mom had left me, bought a small apartment in Brooklyn to settle into. Over the next few years I wrote, decorated my apartment, and fell in and out of love—with men, with hairstyles, with skirt lengths. I was throwing myself into the world and having a blast.

As I finished my master's degree, I began freelance writing for various Web sites, eventually settling into a position as an editor at FashionPlanet.com. I got to write short stories and edit fashion features while living in an apartment I loved with my awesome dog, who made me feel like queen of the world every night when I got home. True happiness is not superficial pleasure—it's the development of strength and the fulfillment of purpose. For the first time in my life, I was *truly* happy because I'd created this life for myself.

In a weird way, I almost feel like my independence and happiness were my mother's final gifts to me. She was my best friend, but it took losing her for me to figure out who I really was and how to welcome joy into my world. It took me years to realize that I was wasting precious time by doubting myself. At the end of the day, you are who you are. I mean, you could drop a few pounds, switch your hair color, and get a new gig, but the core of who you are stays the same. And girlfriend, you might as well fall in love with that core, because it's all you've got.

"Do something meaningful every day."

When you fall in love with who you really are, it's that much easier to be *you,* always. Trust me, it's so much better to walk through the world with confidence in yourself than trying to be what other people think you should be. You'll attract more people (yes, men!) by sincerely enjoying yourself, you'll have a much clearer view of the world, and, best of all, you'll be able to make decisions that honor your passions.

Being yourself will automatically make you feel calmer—life is less stressful when you don't front. But it's important to love yourself completely, to not just accept but be grateful for *everything* in your life, the good and the bad. Living a full life is actually experiencing the entire range of emotions we have. Life doesn't just occur when you're feeling fine. Life is happening all the time—and it's impossible to really feel the good without the contrast of the hard and painful. I know it's difficult—especially when you're right in the middle of a rough time—but being able to understand challenges as experiences in one long adventure will change your whole attitude. It will enable you to extract the positive from the negative, to not get paralyzed, and to appreciate all you do have in your world.

Ultimately, life is what you make it, and no one can live it for you—

not your parents, not your friends, not your man. So take ownership and get out there; think about what's really going to make you happy and get yours!

Quiz: ARE YOU FEELIN' IT?

To get the life you want, it helps to enjoy the ride and take pleasure in the process. Take this quiz to focus on your current satisfaction level—you may find that you're closer to living your dream than you think!

1. Your company restructures and you lose your job in the process. You consider this

a. a chance to tell your loser ex-coworkers exactly what you think of them.

b. an opportunity to chill for a while and figure out what you want to do next.

c. the worst failure of your life, and wonder how long you'll be able to put off telling anyone of your disgrace.

2. The house next door catches fire in the middle of the night, and you need to get out fast! You grab your

a. best suit and your grandmother's quilt—and your robe, of course!

b. jewelry box and as much Chanel and Gucci as you can hold.

c. novel-in-progress, cell phone, and photo album.

3. At a party, you can't help but notice that a woman you don't recognize has been staring at you. It's so unnerving, you have to

a. approach her and introduce yourself.

b. move to the other side of the room.

c. confront her and ask what her problem is.

4. Your mom keeps sending you law school applications but you've always dreamed of opening a restaurant. You

a. thank your mother, tell her you're putting law school on hold to pursue your true dream, and ask for her peach cobbler recipe.

b. complain to your sister that it's high time Mom stopped trying to run your life, but take your time returning your mother's last phone call.

c. fill out the applications. Mother knows best!

5. Oh, lord! A chain letter arrives in the mail. You

a. write to the person who sent it to you and rip her a new one.

b. dutifully make ten copies and send them out as directed. Just in case.

c. laugh out loud, then toss it in the recycling bin. You make your own luck.

6. Your hairstylist goes a little scissor-happy. You

a. can barely look in the mirror till it grows out.

b. give it a chance. Short hair is so low-maintenance, and look, cheekbones!

c. make a scene in the salon, then never return—but be sure to bad-mouth that butcher shop to everyone you know.

7. Your sister-in-law calls on Monday to request your babysitting services for next Saturday night. You

a. tell her you have to check your calendar and will let her know in a few days. You have nothing lined up for next Saturday yet, but it's too early to pin you down.

b. say of course—you've got nothing better to do and you love those kids.

c. give her a flat-out "Sorry, I'm busy" (even if you're not). It's just ridiculous the way she tries to take advantage.

8. You've had a particularly trying week. To feel better you

a. add a massage to your regular mani-pedi appointment.

b. go out, get drunk, sleep in.

c. hole up at home with a chick flick and a bucket of extra-crispy.

9. The lamp you bought at a yard sale keeps flickering on and off. You

a. can't bear to throw it out, even though it was only seven dollars.

b. ring the doorbell of the house that had the yard sale and demand your seven bucks back.

c. break out your tool kit and home-improvement book and see if you can fix it yourself.

10. Whoo! This year-end bonus is a nice surprise! You decide to spend it on

a. boosting your down-payment (or stop-blowing-your-money-on-rent) fund.

b. the after-Christmas sales—as a head start on next year's presents.

c. a New Year's Eve party your rivals will be talking about till 2025.

THE SCORE
Give yourself points as follows:

1. a = 1, b = 3, c = 2   6. a = 2, b = 3, c = 1
2. a = 2, b = 1, c = 3   7. a = 3, b = 2, c = 1
3. a = 3, b = 2, c = 1   8. a = 3, b = 1, c = 2
4. a = 3, b = 1, c = 2   9. a = 2, b = 1, c = 3
5. a = 1, b = 2, c = 3   10. a = 3, b = 2, c = 1

HERE'S THE DEAL

Getting Yours the Hard Way (10 to 16 points) I pity the fool who tries to come between you and your goals. Generally speaking, you get what you want—but everything is such a battle, you reap little joy from the doing and not much more from the results. And when life does give you lemons, you turn sour. Chances are you've always had to present a take-no-mess attitude—it could've been the only way to be heard in your family, or survive on your block. I applaud your strength, but encourage you to channel it more positively. Instead of snap judgments that put you in smack-down mode, lighten up! A woman at a party might be checking you out because she admires your style. Telling off an officemate just because you're mad won't serve you down the road—when she lands in an influential position and could help you. Try tapping into your sweet side; volunteering with youth in your community is a great way to do that. Remember, kindness isn't weakness!

Getting Yours the Easy Way (17 to 23 points) You have a life and consider yourself fairly content, but you could have so much more! A kind, generous, soulful woman like you really ought to be running things; instead you hold yourself back. Sensitive but too tentative, you've feathered a small, insular comfort zone for yourself that you're afraid to step out of. Plus, you're a perpetual people-pleaser who'd rather not make waves. Perhaps you avoid aiming high and taking risks because the disappointment of failure seems like too much to deal with. Well, here's a little secret: Winning isn't everything—trying is! So unless you want to wind up moaning "woulda, coulda, shoulda," start being a bit more assertive. Politely insist that your stylist fix a bad haircut; just say no when someone asks an inconvenient favor. I bet you'll find this addictive! Oh, and that bonus in your paycheck? Do something good for the best person you know: you.

Getting Yours the Cool Way (24 to 30 points) You may not be reveling in everything this world has to offer yet, but you're definitely on your way. The main reason? You believe you deserve the best. That's clear, by the way you stand up for yourself without putting others down. Plus, you know how to put a positive spin on a bad situation—and kick a good thing to the next level. You welcome challenges, are up for new experiences. Whether a matter of good home training, positive role models, or simply an inherently honest and open mind-set (maybe all three in collabo!), your healthy approach is already paying off. But as life gets more complicated (bigger job, wider social circle, more people relying on you), you'll need to be vigilant about priorities—putting yourself first while attending to the many demands that are placed on you. Set reasonable goals and take time to relax upon accomplishing them.

START **TODAY**, GIRLFRIEND!

On the night of September 10, 2001, I hosted a party to celebrate an issue of *Honey* featuring Mary J. Blige on the cover. DJ Beverly Bond was spinning, the crowd was cool, and I spent most of the evening hanging out with Mary and dancing with a glass of champagne in my hand. I left the event around 12:30 AM, climbed into a taxi, and headed across the Brooklyn Bridge toward my home. As the lower Manhattan skyline became visible I got a warm, happy feeling, and I remember thinking, as I often did while crossing the bridge, *I will never, ever get tired of this view. I love this city.*

The next morning terrorists attacked the financial district, leaving a smoke-spewing, debris-filled crater where the World Trade Center towers used to be. Thousands of people lost their lives and the vibrant New York I knew and loved became instantly unrecognizable. The city felt, literally and figuratively, like a tomb. It took months before normal life could even begin to return. Going out, having fun, and celebrating in any way, seemed terribly inappropriate.

As that year came to a close and we all rebuilt our lives, the usual New Year's resolutions (lose five pounds, stop cursing, save more money . . .) felt meaningless. Instead, I vowed to be more tolerant, thoughtful, and patient. I decided to get to know my neighbors, join some community organizations, and become a better-informed world citizen. But most important, I resolved again to live like every single day is the most important day of my life. I reminded myself that life doesn't start when you get the promotion or the man or the car or the house. I vowed that, whatever I might be going through, I would never be a passive participant in my own life.

Want yours? Strive to make every day meaningful, and, for the most part, you'll have it. Stop waiting for that one big event, thing, or person that will bring you joy, because guess what? Time won't stop while you wait to achieve your goals. *Live every day now.* If you keep putting your life on hold and ignoring the incredible experiences you are having in the present, you'll look back at some point and think about everything you haven't done as opposed to what you have accomplished. Appreciate the positive things already in your life and recognize that the challenges are as much a part of a full life as the lovely moments. Regardless of what kind of day you're having as you read this, recognize that this is *your* life. No one can live it for you. Now, what are you going to do to make today count?

Today . . .

- **Celebrate right now.** Remember that today is a brand-new day—a new opportunity to create something wonderful.
- **Get organized.** Spontaneity is cool, but trying to be productive in a chaotic environment will stall you. To put your life in order, start with something small: a drawer, a desktop, or your purse. Or you could register for online bill paying, throw out everything you don't use in your bathroom cabinet, or log on to The Container Store's Web site and order an inexpensive file folder and some storage boxes.
- **Make better choices.** Avoid snap judgments and think things through, but also trust your gut. Again, start small: Choose a healthier lunch, put down the bag you can't afford, don't cancel movie night with your girls for a date with a random guy.
- **Be your best.** Believe that you are meant for excellence and start doing everything—at home, at work, at play—to the absolute best of your abilities.
- **Stop comparing yourself to others.** What she's got, that's nice for

her. But you, girlfriend, are *unparalleled*. Your life and your path are your own. Learn from others' successes and failures, but do *you*.

- **Define success.** Think about it on your own terms, what it means to you. And think big picture, a concept of success not restricted to finances or romances but complete, well-rounded happiness in life. At the end of the day, your definition of success should be whatever brings you joy—not what you think would impress your family, friends, neighbors, and man. Success is achieving goals that only you can set for yourself.

- **Picture the life you want.** If you can see it, than you can make it yours. So, dream big. Don't assume any limitations. Just sit down, close your eyes, and see yourself happy. Then figure out how to make it so.

- **Think positively.** Invent an affirmation (basically, a positive state-ment about yourself) and repeat it daily until it sinks in that you are beautiful and smart and deserving. It may seem corny, but affirma-tions work best if you say them aloud. Think about an aspect of your life that needs work, then write down, in present tense, how you'd like to feel (for example: I am a sexy, interesting woman and I deserve a loving, generous man in my life). Repeat it every morn-ing and night—and during the day when you have a few quiet minutes. Trust me, your subconscious will get the message and move you in the right direction.

- **Banish negativity.** Yes, that's the flip side. Don't think "Nothing good ever happens to me." Or you know what? It won't.

MAKE **THIS YEAR** COUNT

My son, Max, is almost six months old as I write this. He is strong, happy, healthy, funny, and beautiful. He is also huge (his daddy is six feet four inches) and he still gets hungry every few hours—which means I won't sleep through the night till he does. This morning, after feeding my baby, I had a choice: go to the gym, or to get back into my bed for another forty-five minutes. Even though my bed looked comfy and warm, I forced myself to get up. Walking up the stairs to my gym's lobby felt like climbing Mount Kilimanjaro, and I was definitely dragging for the first ten minutes. Then I started to get into moving my body. By the time I left an hour later, I felt awake, rejuvenated, and, most of all, proud that I found the will to do something good for myself. That positive feeling has lasted all day.

But until a month ago, I was making a different morning choice: to stay in bed as long as possible. Now, don't get me wrong, girlfriend—I'm not saying that new mothers should haul their poor, exhausted butts out of bed until absolutely necessary. Letting your body recover is essential after having a baby. I felt more than justified resting as much as I could. But after a few months, the thirty-five pounds I still carried from my pregnancy (I actually gained fifty pounds, but fifteen were baby and fluids) were weighing on me—literally and figuratively.

Aches and pains were the name of my game. I developed bursitis in one of my feet. I would try to go for long walks with my son and manage only half an hour because my body felt so weak and sore. Picking him up hurt my lower back, and I had trouble carrying him in a sling because the added weight hurt my shoulders. Plus, despite going back to bed, I wasn't getting real rest. I know you're supposed to nap when the baby naps, but I'd be too restless for sleep and would just read gossip magazines or surf the Net. The short-term pleasure of chilling in my pajamas would wear off, and I'd be bone-tired and listless for the rest of the day.

One night, after realizing that the Advils I was popping hadn't made even a dent in my back pain, I decided that enough was enough. That night I found some gym clothes that fit in the back of my closet (no easy task!) and laid them out along with my socks and sneakers. The next morning, faced with the sight of my workout gear, I couldn't come up with a good enough excuse to bail. Sighing deeply, I got dressed and went to the gym. Granted, I lifted only a couple of ultra-light weights, then walked slowly on the treadmill, but I did *something*.

As I began to feel better, I made my workout time more productive. I'd always been intrigued by yoga, so I found a class that I could do with my son. Yoga is perfect because it focuses the strength, balance, and flexibility that my body is regaining in a whole new way. I'm learning a new skill and slowly losing the baby weight—plus it's another way to bond with my son. I'm a happier mom as a result.

If you are a new mom, please don't beat yourself up for not losing the baby weight quickly. You need to give yourself a break—you just created a life! The reason I'm relating this story is to make the point that real, deep happiness is not about immediate pleasure, it's about long-term gratification. Reading a gossip magazine was fun while I did it, but learning something new and prioritizing my well-being makes me feel better about myself—and brings me that much more happiness. In other words, the choice that will make you happiest in the long run is not usually as enjoyable as those quick-fix seconds of instant pleasure. Vegging in front of the TV, for example, might be easier fun than practicing the piano, reading a book, or going to a photography class, but will it help you improve yourself or your quality of life? Probably not.

This year, go for the deep, lasting joy of fulfillment and gratification. Decide to round out who you are by making yourself a more interesting, skilled person. It might mean some short-term sacrifice, but you will feel like a better woman for it—which makes all the difference in the world.

This Year . . .

- **Start a journal.** Write down not only what's going on with you but memories from your childhood, dreams and goals, conversations you want to remember, places you want to visit, things you wish you could tell your boss or ex-boyfriend. It will help you better understand where you came from, where you want to go, and who you really are.
- **Embrace your true self.** Becoming comfortable enough to just relax by yourself is fundamental. So this year, get real: Think about who you really are (not who you want to be or who others want you to be). Maybe you're generous, but a little jealous. Or you have a gorgeous butt, but slightly narrow shoulders. Or you can do math problems in your head, but read at a snail's pace. Whatever. Just recognize that you are who you are, and that no one will love you like you should love yourself.
- **Celebrate your birthday.** Whatever number you've reached, revel in it. Don't think of what you haven't achieved yet, or, on the flip side, tell yourself you've got "plenty of time." Just be that age, and remind

yourself that this is your year. Spend the day only with people who truly love and appreciate you—whether that's a whole big bash, just a few friends, or (no, really) by yourself.

- **Create goals and make a plan of action.** Think of it as your plan of action, not a debilitating to-do list. And keep it short—no more than three things you really want to accomplish this year (and one thing is fine!). Then outline how you're going to go about it. For example, if the goal is to get a job in a different field, the outline would include (1) redo your résumé, (2) make new contacts, (3) sign up for a course in that area. If the goal is to find true love, outline points could be to (1) try online dating, (2) date the polar opposite of your ex, (3) be the first one to smile and say hi.

- **Organize your house.** Clutter is a dream killer, girlfriend. You cannot think clearly when you live in a tornado of stuff. Devote an entire Saturday to cleaning out your closet, resolving not to stop till you've filled two large shopping bags for donation. Give junk mail, magazines, and catalogs an expiration date—toss them within a week or two. Invest in a few items that will make staying organized easier—shoe racks, CD binders, shelving, drawer dividers.

- **Learn how to say no.** It's not a dirty word—there are only two letters, not four! One of the best ways to start is to remind yourself how valuable your time is. Think of the hours in your day as currency. Then focus on a person who tends to take advantage—he or she is about due for a turndown! Simply say "No!" Don't make excuses—as in "No, I can't drive you there because I have an appointment on the other side of town," or "No, I can't babysit because I have to have my appendix out." If a simple no is too hard at first, try "I'm sorry, but I can't help out this time."

GET YOURS **FOREVER**

My first year of high school marked my truly awkward phase. I had just spent three years in a school that required all students to wear green plaid uniforms—to say that my closet did not reflect my interest in fashion would be a massive understatement. My skin was, well, bad. And during that preceding summer, I decided one dull afternoon to cut my own hair. The result was a weird fuzzy 'fro, short on top and long in the back. To add insult to injury, I had an overbite and a huge gap between my two front teeth, so I was rocking a spiffy set of braces. My junior high school years were spent dodging a clique of the most vicious mean girls ever, and I worried I might encounter an even worse set in high school. Instead, I found a couple of girls I got along with instantly. We became great friends, spent all our time together, shared secrets . . . you know, teen-girl stuff. I was particularly close to one girl who became my BFF. Or so I thought.

The summer between our freshman and sophomore years, I left New York City to spend time with my dad in Boston. By the time I returned everything had changed. My girls had spent the summer hanging out and getting closer; I felt like an outsider whenever I called. Everything would be fine, I reassured myself, when we got back to school. Besides, my braces

"Life is what *you* make it and no one can live it for you."

were off, my hair had grown, and I had a new wardrobe. I was dying to show off my new look and figured they'd all be impressed, especially my best friend.

I ran up to her that first morning back at school and threw out my arms for a hug. She coolly looked me up and down, kissed my cheek, and said only, "Nice hair," before she turned away. As I watched her walk down the hall, I realized that somehow over the summer she had written me off and moved on. While I still considered her to be my BFF, I didn't figure in her life anymore. It brought back all the hurt from junior high and I retreated into my shell of insecurity.

After a few weeks of tears and moping, I finally told my mom what had happened. She sat me down and gave me a piece of advice that would take me years to understand, but turned out to be life-changing when it finally did sink in. "You have more control over how people respond to you than you think," she told me. "It's all about the message you send out. Act happy and people will assume you have confidence and purpose, and that you're fun. Even if you don't feel it, fake it at first. I promise the feeling will eventually become real."

At fourteen, most of that flew over my head, but I did catch the phrase "Act happy." So the next Monday I walked into school with a big smile on my face, waved hi to everyone, and behaved as if I'd had a blast all weekend long. While my former BFF did little but raise her eyebrows and look confused at my sudden obvious change of temperament, I saw a distinct shift in the way everyone else treated me. Walking around with my head up and a smile on my face made people notice me more, and smile back. If you say hi to someone, they're going to respond—and I found myself having conversations with people I'd never talked to before. While my friendship with my former friend never returned to its former glory, after a while I didn't mind. I made new friends and found cool new activities. And years later, I am still walking through the world with a smile, making friends and having adventures.

This is a life lesson, girlfriend. Energy matters and perception is reality. *The universe will give you back exactly what you put out.* What my mom really meant was: Act fun, smart, fearless, and beautiful and you will be all of those things because that's how you'll be treated. So, act happy and I promise you will be happy.

Always . . . ~ᵉᵉ℧

- **Be nice.** Treat everyone well: neighbors, coworkers, your grocer, the cabdriver, your ex's new girlfriend. Even if you simply don't care for someone, be the better person and behave pleasantly. This will draw good things to you. Besides, you don't want to be known as a mean, petty gossip.
- **Make time for you.** Wake up a little early, take a half hour at night, go for a walk at lunch. Just spend some time every day with the greatest woman you know (you!).
- **Enjoy simple pleasures.** You know, the whole stop-and-smell-the-flowers routine. A child's smile, a puppy's playfulness, your favorite jam coming on the radio, the color of the sky and the quality of the light—take a moment to appreciate these things. And, okay, sure, a great pair of shoes at 50 percent off! Just appreciate the small good things that exist around you all the time, even on the most challenging rainy day.
- **Pat yourself on the back.** Too often, we move on from a job well done to the next thing we have to tackle without taking time to

recognize our worth or acknowledge our achievements. For little things, like cleaning the bathroom, and big things, like finishing a degree. Sure, praise from others is nice, but reminding yourself how smart, kind, strong, accomplished, etc., you are is like gold for the soul.

- **Have integrity.** Check your ethics. If you have to question whether an action or decision is right or wrong, it's probably wrong. Pilfering a few notepads and pens may not bring the company to ruin, but that doesn't mean your home stationery items should come from the office supply closet. Deceit is not a place to sit down! Put yourself on the receiving end as a litmus test—you wouldn't want anyone to lie to, cheat on, or steal from you. So strive to do the right thing all the time.

- **Don't be a slave to others' opinions.** I'm not saying shut yourself off from what folks have to say. Some people give good advice, and your loved ones do have your best interests at heart. Just remember that you are the ultimate arbiter of what's right for you.

5 WAYS TO FIND BALANCE

Not enough hours in the day? Feeling pulled in a dozen different directions? Try these tips for centering yourself.

1. **Get your "me" time.** Devote ten minutes in the morning, before your day gets off the ground. Meditate or say a prayer, go over what you have to do that day, repeat your affirmation, and smile at yourself in the mirror.

2. **Prioritize.** Figure out what takes precedence in your daily life. What should fall to the bottom of the list? Spending hours solving everyone else's problems.

3. **Give yourself enough time.** In fact, give yourself more time than it will probably take to accomplish a task, even if you have to push a few things till tomorrow. You won't be late, you'll do a thorough job, and you'll be less stressed overall.

4. **Be as productive as possible.** If you're a morning person, plan to do

your biggest projects before noon. If you come alive at night, try to squeeze in some tasks after dinner.

5. **Get a coach.** You could simply find a mentor—someone you respect and trust—whom you could bounce ideas off and seek advice from. Or you could get a professional coach who would help you focus on your dreams, then strategize and plan to achieve them. I've partnered with the Handel Group, an extraordinary collection of gifted coaches, to offer both individual and group Get Yours coaching programs. Check out my Web site, www.amyduboisbarnett.com, for more information.

GABRIELLE UNION ON HAPPINESS

You've seen Gabrielle in films like the indie hit Running with Scissors, *such comedies as* Bring It On *and* Deliver Us from Eva, *tension-packed action flicks like* Bad Boys II, *and on television in her own series,* Night Stalker. *She's also known for being one of Hollywood's nicest, coolest leading ladies. I first met Gabrielle right before* Deliver Us from Eva *hit theaters. I was doing a* Honey *cover with her and LL Cool J—we bonded during the shoot and we've been cool ever since. Our friendship started on the set because we would run off and hide together whenever LL tried to get, ahem, extra-friendly. Plus Gabrielle got tons of cool points for being game for anything, including doing the shoot outside in the winter, wearing only a tiny skin-tight dress. Her teeth were chattering as she posed in the freezing cold. The clincher is that Gabrielle is one of the funniest women I've ever met. She had me cracking up all day, riffing on marriage (we both have ex-husbands now), Hollywood, and life. I caught up with the well-rounded star to talk about how she brings happiness into her world every day.*

Amy: *What is happiness to you?*
Gabrielle: Working out with [actress/trainer] A. J. Johnson. When you sign up with her, you're not just signing up to work out your body. It's a whole lifestyle change. The first day of the workout, she gives you emotional homework. She will say, "Write down ten things that make you happy." I started realizing that I am thirty-three years old, and as my life keeps changing, who I am and what makes me happy changes.

I find that each year it means something different to me. Every year I'm going to need to redefine what makes me happy—and try to eliminate from my life what doesn't make me happy.

AB: *Too many of us don't know how to get away from the things that are bad for us.*
GU: Or the things that you keep in your life because you're just used to them. Like a family member or a friend that you have had forever . . . but they are completely toxic. As we get older our free time is so limited, so we need to fill it with people and things that truly make us happy. We have to do an inventory check of the things in our life that may be past their due date and are spoiled and rotten.

AB: *I also feel like some people don't appreciate that life is the full range of emotions we have. You won't appreciate ups if you don't have downs.*
GU: That's why I appreciate my happiness so much more. When I'm feeling at my lowest, I ask: What is the light at the end of my tunnel? I say to the young girls that I talk to, "Bad stuff happens to people every day. It's how you choose to deal with it—whether you opt for church or going to see a silly movie with your girlfriends. You can have streamers and balloons at your pity party or just not show up!"

AB: *How do you create something positive from the negative? Part of living a really full life is knowing that every time a door closes, or every time something bad happens, a new or different opportunity arises.*
GU: Every time I go through adversity, I write it down, make a list of the life lessons and the negative things, make a note of what isn't [healthy]. Drinking to the point of oblivion isn't good for me. Being around really catty actresses is not good for me. When I get home after, let's say, an audition with a bunch of people cutting their eyes at each other and just being completely rotten, I feel bad for taking part in that, succumbing to some pressure, talking [bad] about somebody— because I've put all this negative energy out in the world. I write down how I feel about what I just did or experienced, so I can learn and grow and not repeat silly mistakes over and over and over again. When you actually look at a problem in print, it solidifies it and makes it real, and it's not something that you can push aside. I have to really think

about it. Why did this make me feel bad? And what am I going to do with this information?

AB: *That's really great advice. Take stock of what you've done and hold yourself accountable.*

GU: That's a big thing—accountability and responsibility for your own life. I've made the mistake of waiting for [a guy] to magically lift me out of a bad mood or a bad situation. The person that I needed to be most reliant on was myself. And I didn't give myself enough credit to be smart enough, savvy enough, or resourceful enough to know how to learn to solve my own problems and deal with my own issues.

AB: *It must be especially hard for someone in Hollywood. How do you deal with the pressure and the competition in your world?*

GU: When I was younger, I was like, "Bitch, bring it on and I'll slap the crap back on you." I'd be in a room and if someone walked in I'd give them a dirty look, or turn to my little actress friend and giggle. Now that I'm the old fart in the room, when I see that happening, I think it's so sad and pathetic. I don't know if it comes with age or having it happen to you or whatever. I just don't do it anymore.

I had to stop going on Web sites that celebrate negativity. I had to stop listening to radio shows that celebrate negativity. I had to realize that I am not in competition with anyone else. I can only be in competition with myself. If Tuesday's audition was bad, Wednesday's better be better. But I can't put that on some other actress.

AB: *So the idea is to make friends, not waste time making enemies.*

GU: I've realized more than anything that we keep each other working, people of color. I rely on my friends in the industry to keep me working. So don't bite the hand that feeds you. The best and brightest of our field is Halle Berry, and I've never heard of her talking about anybody. People who are truly successful don't need to be negative because they are already at the top of their game.

AB: *When I turned thirty, it was a momentous time for me. I fell in love with who I was at the core and even the flaws. It's a waste of time to hate yourself. Have you ever had to deal with self-image issues?*

GU: There are certain things that you have control over—your aspirations, ambitions, assertiveness. Then there are things [you cannot control]—how you look [without] plastic surgery, the amount of melanin you have, the grade of your hair. You have to get to a place where you think, "This is me," and be really comfortable with that. There were times certainly when I first started in the business that I would be the darkest person and each girl that walked in would be lighter with curlier hair and light eyes, and I would literally feel like I was shrinking. These girls could have been in Mensa, they could have just come from feeding the homeless. None of that mattered. All that mattered was, they were light, and I was dark. They were better, I was bad. They were pretty, I was ugly. Regardless of how I felt when I left the house, all of a sudden, magically, I just felt less than.

Then over time I began to think, "They can be pretty and so can I. Their hair can be considered beautiful, but so can mine." There doesn't have to be one standard of beauty, there doesn't have to be one standard of excellence, there doesn't have to be one standard of intelligence. We can all be different and celebrate it. Once I wrapped my brain around that, I've been working steadily. I've done okay in this business being exactly who I am.

AB: *Done okay? Your career has taken off! So let's talk about what success is to you.*
GU: Ooh, it keeps changing. In my twenties it was, "How much money can I make?" It wasn't just about the job; it was, "How much is this job paying me?" Then it changed. I feel successful if I can look at myself in the mirror and be happy with the person I am looking at. Not being able to live crazy lavish, but to live well. To be able to go to Whole Foods and get organic meat. To be able to have good credit, or to be able to help my parents or my family members. To be able to travel and not have to worry how the hell I'm going to get home. That's success and comfort.

AB: *Do you feel your life is balanced?*
GU: It's becoming more balanced. I used to not take time to eat, or sleep, or visit with friends or family. Then you see relationships disintegrate. There was a point where I looked up and I hadn't talked to my

mother in three months. That's crazy. I had to learn to make sure that I have enough time for my loved ones, health and fitness, and sleep. Sometimes that involves sacrifice. Bloomingdale's doesn't get as much of my time as it used to.

AB: *Any books you look to for inspiration?*
GU: The book that I really hold very close to me is *The Autobiography of Malcolm X*. Here is this person we all historically put in a box. But when you read the story of his life, he was an ever-changing and accepting and tolerant family man. Each year, I relate to something different. I look to that book to help me through change and to give me the courage to step out of the box that I get put in or put myself in. I feel a little bit freer to grow and embrace a more global view—to have a perspective that is not always that popular and be okay with that.

AB: *Is there anyone who has influenced you in a really positive way?*
GU: Well, my mom. As I have gotten older, and gone through a marriage, I learned what it is to sacrifice. It's not always about winning every battle but still winning the war, which is life—and having a good life and feeling okay with myself. I realized my mom was one of the strongest, most amazing role models; it's just how you choose to look at it. As an adult I see her strengths, and I see her sacrifice, and I see what a great and happy person she is.

PROMISE PAGE

My dreams and goals for my happiness are:

I promise that today I will:

This year I promise to:

I will always:

2

GET OUT THERE

A few years ago, a good friend of mine who owns a downtown New York nightclub asked me to guest DJ for a night. Because I'm a sucker for anything my girlfriends ask, I quickly agreed—then immediately got nervous. I'd done some bragging about my collegiate DJ skills (I worked Wednesday nights at a tiny club in Providence, Rhode Island—hardly Saturdays at Studio 54) and now someone was calling my bluff. To make matters worse, I told a few friends I was spinning and word started to spread. People from my office made plans to come. Then folks I knew in the music industry caught wind, sent me their artists' music to play, and told me they would be there. Don't get me wrong—I was grateful for the love and support, but I had been expecting only a small group of close friends. Instead, this was turning into an *event*.

True to form, I overprepared; I had twice as many CDs as I needed and a long playlist so nothing would be left to chance. I still felt a lot of pressure, though. Since I'd worked only with vinyl, never CDs, the club's regular DJ was supposed to walk me through the equipment before I started. But the previous show ran long, so I had to learn on the fly. By the time I was about to go on, I was freaking out! I kept glancing out at the growing crowd, thinking about what they were expecting and worrying that I wouldn't be able to deliver. Then an old friend came up to the DJ booth to wish me luck and gave me a piece of advice that saved my night. "Play for yourself," he told me. "All these people are here to hear what you think is hot, so spin whatever you want and you'll be fine."

It was exactly what I needed to hear. After putting on my planned first song (Biggie's "Hypnotize"), I abandoned my carefully constructed playlist and had some fun. Sure, there were some embarrassing moments, like when one record mysteriously cut off before I had the next one cued up and the whole club stopped dancing to watch me fumble through my CDs (okay, that really sucked!). But halfway through my set, you couldn't find an inch of space on that dance floor.

That evening reminded me of the resolution I'd made to honor my opinion of myself above all others. I used to spend a lot of time worrying about what other people thought of me. Growing up, I always did what was expected of me. I was afraid of disappointing others by veering left or right, afraid of disappointing myself if I set high goals and didn't succeed. For years, fear held me back: I was too afraid to be professionally ambitious, to reveal myself in relationships—even to fall deeply in love.

For someone who'd lived on three different continents and who had an adventurer for a mother, it was weird how timid I felt. It was only when I began to reflect on the things my mom had tried to teach me that I finally realized that insecurity is a hu-mongous waste of time—and that fear can be productive if you embrace it. Even though she died too young at forty-nine, Mom lived a full life and did more with her time on this earth than most people accomplish in twice that long. It occurred to me that the crucial difference be-tween how she viewed her life and how I'd been living up until that point was our distinct reac-tions to feeling scared. I avoided fear at all costs

> "Life is the greatest ongoing exploration of all time."

while she treated it like a sign that she was stretching and growing and becoming more evolved. Acknowledging this, I decided to become more of a risk taker, more of a doer—like my mom.

Over the years, as I became more confident and self-reliant, I cared less and less about external expectations, because I knew no one would demand more of me than me. And the less I worried about others' opinions, the more fun I had. Spinning at my friend's club initially scared me because it meant performing in front of my colleagues in a setting where the threat of public humiliation felt very real. But the moment I was reminded of this resolve, I got into it and had a blast!

Because women of color don't get a lot of reinforcement in our daily lives, we can often be paralyzed by self-doubt. Also, many of us don't have a wide breadth of exposure to different countries, cultures, and lifestyles. As a result, we tend to be conservative and apprehensive when it comes to new experiences, pretending, of course, that "we don't care about that stuff anyway." But really, our comfort zone is simply too narrow, and we're often too insecure to push ourselves outside of it.

So, I'm going to push you to push yourself! Life is the greatest ongoing exploration of all time, and the only way you can be sure you're getting yours is to know what's out there. Test your boundaries. Try new things. Jump into the deep end without first giving it a toe-dip. Scary? Damn right! But think of it this way: Confronting your fears proves that you're living your life to its fullest potential—and that you're becoming everything you're meant to be. Remember, as a kid, being afraid of climbing the ladder on the playground? Then you finally reached for a rung, and then the next, and then the next . . . until you got to the top of the slide. Then you slid down and had so much fun, you wouldn't stop until your braids had come loose and your mom was yelling that it was dinnertime. Life is a huge playground, and all you need to do is take a deep breath and reach for the next rung to make the most of it. This is an attitude shift that will allow you to take risks, set your professional goals higher, open up to people, and have great adventures every single day.

This day will never happen again, so what are you going to do to make it count?

Quiz: Ain't No Stoppin' You Now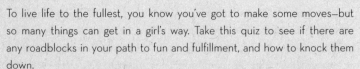

To live life to the fullest, you know you've got to make some moves—but so many things can get in a girl's way. Take this quiz to see if there are any roadblocks in your path to fun and fulfillment, and how to knock them down.

1. You and your girlfriends usually vacation in the Caribbean. When someone suggests Thailand for your next trip, you get

a. excited. You've heard the beaches are gorgeous, and hotels there are so inexpensive.

b. nervous. Isn't the food really suspect, and won't you need all kinds of shots, and talk about a loooong flight…

c. annoyed. The "someone" who suggested it was you—and they all shot down your idea!

2. You majored in business in college, and now you are

a. an administrative assistant.

b. getting your MBA at night.

c. working in a totally unrelated field.

3. You walk into a party a coworker is throwing and guess what? Not a brown face in the room! You

a. wait for your jam to come on and ask someone to dance. Let's get this party started, right?!

b. beeline for your work friends and chat with them until you can jump into a conversation with some new people.

c. sip a cocktail while circling the room, then beat a hasty retreat.

4. They now have a Brazilian Capoeira class at your gym. Intrigued, you

a. watch a session to see what it's like.

b. grab a spot front and center, directly opposite the instructor.

c. talk your gym buddy into trying it with you.

5. On line at a hot new club, you hear that if you "flash" the bouncer you get instant access. You

a. wish you had the nerve.

b. flash the bouncer, of course. They're just ta-tas, and you don't do waiting.

c. thinks that's demeaning and would really rather go elsewhere.

6. You're partnered with a man for an exercise during a business seminar. At the end of the seminar, he asks you out. He's smart and cool, but not really your type, so you say

a. you're busy, but ask for his card. You might as well keep in touch, even if no sparks were flying.

b. "no, thank you" on principle. It was inappropriate for him to try getting personal in a professional setting.

c. sure, why not. He's buying, and in more laid-back surroundings he may start looking better to you.

7. Your boss asks if you'd like to work on a project that is far afield of anything in your professional background. You tell her

a. you've never done anything like it before, but would be willing to try with direction.

b. sure thing, and wing it. Hey, you're a quick study.

c. that it's really not your area.

8. A new man suggests an Indian restaurant for your next date. You

a. tell him you're much more a steak-and-salad girl (even though you've never tried Indian food).

b. say, "Hmm, sounds interesting," but do some online research on this cuisine before you commit.

c. explain that you've been-there-ate-that, but there's this new Ethiopian place you've been dying to try.

9. You get an amazing job offer . . . in Chicago. You've never been to Chicago. You

a. ask the company to fly you in for a few days so you can get a feel for the place.

b. are so there. The blues! The beef! The Bulls!

c. couldn't possibly accept. Your family, your friends—your whole life—are here.

10. You're asked to sing in a charity talent show. You can blow like Beyoncé, but you don't have her body—and the costume leaves little to the imagination. You

a. suck in your gut, steel your nerves, and do your thang.

b. decline—unless they agree to some modest costume changes.

c. go for it. If the world can't handle some supersize bootyliciousness, that's the world's problem.

THE SCORE

Give yourself points as follows:

1. a = 2, b = 3, c = 1   **6.** a = 2, b = 3, c = 1
2. a = 3, b = 2, c = 1   **7.** a = 2, b = 1, c = 3
3. a = 1, b = 2, c = 3   **8.** a = 3, b = 2, c = 1
4. a = 3, b = 1, c = 2   **9.** a = 2, b = 1, c = 3
5. a = 2, b = 1, c = 3   **10.** a = 2, b = 3, c = 1

HERE'S THE DEAL

Too Fast, Too Curious (10 to 16 points) Nope, ain't no stopping you—sometimes, not even good sense! You're a risk taker who knows no boundaries, and while in theory that's an admirable attitude, in practice it can get you in trouble. All I'm suggesting is a little looking before leaping. Yes, be proud of your proportions and wear the short skirt in the talent show. Yes, ask a stranger to dance. But before you pull up your shirt in public, you may want to consider who's around. A dangerous gossip? A possible future employer? And you might want to do a smidgen of research prior to pulling up stakes and moving to a new city. There's a difference between blind bravado and true bravery—between calculated risks that get you somewhere and the kind of abandon that could potentially bring you down. Get it?

All Systems Go (17 to 23 points) Nothing excites you like a challenge, but you believe in weighing the win-lose factors before you take it up. That's smart. You're aware of your own strengths and weaknesses, and you're honest with yourself and others about what you *know* you can do, *think* you can do, and would only attempt in a parallel universe. You bring this approach toward obvious risks, like the prospect of exotic travel, and, perhaps more important, to your career and relationships. When you find yourself at a crossroads, though, you tend to play it safe, and may want to tap into your inner adventuress a bit more. For instance, do you really need your girl at your side to take a new class at the gym? And why spoil the surprise of trying a new cuisine? If it turns out you're not crazy about it, take your date to your favorite dessert place after dinner and have an extra scoop on top.

Staid in Your Lane (24 to 30 points) First and foremost, you are a lady—but don't let your conservative side keep you from fully experiencing life. And whose life is it anyway? Your parents'? Your pastor's? The neighbors'? No, it's yours. And the way you're living it, your Hollywood biopic would be called *2Safe, 2Sorry*. I'm not saying compromise your values, but be real: You have declined when deep inside you were intrigued—and may even feel a tinge of regret that your knee-jerk reaction was to just say no. You don't have to bungee-jump in a string bikini; try baby-step risks. Spread your wings and take a vacation somewhere you've never been. Have faith in your charm and wit, and strike up a conversation with a stranger at a party. Be willing to amp your skill set at work—there may just be a promotion in it. She who hesitates too much is lost!

START **TODAY**, GIRLFRIEND!

A friend of mine stayed in a serious rut for years. As long as I'd known her, she'd lived in the same apartment with the same furniture (including a futon from her college dorm), and had the same job (no promotion—just cost-of-living raises), the same haircut and color (at least it was a cute shoulder-length layered shag, but I don't think I'd ever seen her do anything with it other than the occasional ponytail), and the same personal style (jeans and a halter top for nights out, pantsuits for the office, skirts and heels for dates). I'd never seen her order fish or spicy food, wear bright colors, take a vacation out of the country, or splurge on a purchase that she couldn't find an immediate need for. She'd even been dating the same type of guys: workaholic control freaks with commitment issues.

On the surface, she seemed content in her routine, but after a while she began to complain of boredom. Her conversation topics turned from mutual friends and guy issues to more philosophical debates about the meaning of life and what our purpose was here on earth. Yeah, girlfriend, she was *definitely* in a funk. When her birthday approached, I had an idea for a present that would either succeed in shaking her out of her rut or be met with resistance and possible anger: a total makeover. I decided it was worth the risk and persuaded a few of my friends in the fashion and beauty business to consult with her for free. I got her a gift certificate at a cool department store as the final element to her daylong transformation.

At first, as I predicted, she refused to go along with my grand plan (at least she didn't get mad!). I had to cajole, explain, and finally beg her just to *try* it. When she saw I wasn't giving up, she reluctantly agreed. First stop? My hair salon. My stylist, a sweet but blunt woman who believes in style over length, grabbed the bottom three inches off my terrified friend's hair and said it had to go. After she stopped freaking out, my girlfriend took a deep breath and agreed. Frankly, I couldn't believe it, but out came the scissors before she could change her mind. When we left the salon a couple of hours later, my girl had a reddish-brown chin-length bob with beautiful copper highlights. She kept touching the back of her neck and smiling at her reflection in shop windows, so I knew she was into it and already felt different.

By the end of the day, a friend at M.A.C. had reshaped her eyebrows and given her a whole new makeup palette, and, on the suggestion of a fashion stylist I knew, we spent her gift certificate on a sexy fuchsia dress and high-heeled sandals with straps that wound up her calf. That night she wore her new outfit to a rooftop party a mutual friend had planned. I got there before her and watched the crowd part as she walked in. That was literally the beginning of a whole new life for her. She met a man who was moving to Atlanta in six months; they fell in love and she eventually joined him in Georgia. Since she had to quit her job, she decided to start an online retail business. Her relationship with the man didn't last, but it turned out that she is a Southern girl at heart. She's loving her life in the ATL, dating, living in a gorgeous house, and expanding her company.

Ah, if only that could happen to you . . . Well, it could! You never know what minor change in your routine will be a mini-adventure and what will have some life-altering impact. Today, get out and do something—anything—different. No, girlfriend, I'm not suggesting you chop off three inches of hair. How about something small, like going to a new restaurant or wearing a bright red lipstick or attending a lecture at a local college? Or here's one of my all-time favorites: Take a road trip to the next town over and go exploring. Just try to shake yourself out of your rut. You never know what will come of it!

Today . . .

- **Affirm that you can do whatever.** Tell yourself that the world is yours and you are in charge of your destiny. Now believe it and go *do* something!
- **Wear something scandalous.** In every woman's closet lurks an item that's kinda short, a little tight, or maybe even really bright—something she has no idea why she bought and has certainly never worn. Today, put it on . . . and actually leave the house.
- **Just do it.** Figure out something new to do. Check out the weekend activity listings in the newspaper or your city's local magazine, or go online for ideas. If nothing strikes you, just try taking a different route to work.
- **Fly solo.** It's great to have your friends around, but they can unwit-

tingly hold you back. Their very presence creates a cocoon, so when you do things alone that you normally do with them—go shopping, head for a local beach, eat in a restaurant—the ordinary becomes extraordinary.

- **Talk to strangers.** Okay, stranger—singular. Introduce yourself to one new person. Admiring a girl's shoes on the train? Compliment her and ask where she got them. Notice someone reading an interesting book on a park bench? Say excuse me and ask if it's any good. Trying on dresses next to a woman in a clothing boutique? Tell her you like the black, but the red was hot!

- **Tap your inner adventurer.** Think of a fictional or historical character, or maybe someone in your life, who's got that adventuresome spirit. Why do you admire her? How can you relate to her? Develop a risk-taking alter ego—give her a name, imagine excursions and experiences for her. Now pretend to be her and go do something exciting!

MAKE **THIS YEAR** COUNT

The day I quit my job at Lord & Taylor, I emptied my desk drawers, threw the contents into two big shopping bags, and hauled them to a bar to meet a friend for a celebratory cocktail. While we were hanging out, toasting my decision to pursue my passion for writing, we met some guys who wound up joining us. One of them—let's call him Aidan—inquired about the overflowing bags I had tucked under my chair. When I told him I wanted to be a writer, he immediately started going on and on about Ireland and its amazing literary tradition. As it turned out, Aidan was headed for the Emerald Isle himself, to attend medical school.

We hit it off—so much so that I actually started to research writing programs at Irish universities. I had lived in India as a child and in France as a college student, so Ireland didn't seem too unlikely an option for me. After all, I had no job and no concrete plans other than to try to land freelance gigs while building up my writing portfolio for grad school. Why not move to Ireland? Okay, it was a *little* crazy, but the University College Dublin accepted me to take classes that fall and

I calculated that I could make a little extra money subleasing my Brooklyn apartment. Plus, I knew it wouldn't cost me that much to live there; I could easily tutor students or waitress to pay for groceries. It seemed that I'd met Aidan the day I quit my job for a reason, so I made the decision to pack up and head to Dublin.

Now, imagine the reaction of my girlfriends. They thought that I had lost my mind, that my mother's death had unhinged me enough to throw my New York life away to follow some random guy across the ocean. Of course, they weren't entirely wrong. I *was* running from my pain, I hadn't known this guy very long, and subleasing my apartment was a major project. But I'd be going to school and immersing myself in a whole new environment for creative inspiration. It just seemed worth the risk.

> "Confronting your fears proves you're living your life to its fullest potential."

And I was right! The Irish had never seen anyone quite like me and they were fascinated; I got attention ranging from stares to blunt questions about my ethnic identity. But I met some cool people at my local pub (trust me, an Irish pub is a blast—especially after a couple of pints of Guinness) and made a few friends. My best class at UCD was taught by a well-known Irish novelist who forced me to live up to my potential with every piece I turned in. And the country is not only beautiful, it's close enough to the rest of Europe so I could travel a bit. I took my adorable Labrador retriever puppy everywhere with me as I explored.

Aidan? Oh, of course, that fizzled after a couple of months. But that didn't matter one bit. I stayed in Ireland for nearly eight months, finished my writing portfolio, and successfully applied to graduate school. I had a great adventure there that ended up shaping my twenties and possibly my life.

This year, be open to great adventures and try to have one. I dare you! Leaving the country might be a little extreme for your lifestyle, but perhaps you could take a vacation to someplace you've never visited. If that's too expensive or hard to organize, take a road trip to a state you don't know that well. Go to surfing camp or a yoga retreat or a spa. Go rock climbing or white-water rafting or hiking. Don't laugh off "crazy" opportunities that come up. Think "why not?" instead of "why?" This life will never happen again. Get out there, girl.

This Year . . .

- **Hit a party by yourself.** Okay, you've already done a baby-step solo mission; now it's time to go all out. It could be an intimate get-together or a big bash, a soiree where you'll know some people or not a soul, a house party or a throwdown in a club. Just put on the outfit that you look great and feel most comfortable in. Tell yourself you have to stay only half an hour. I bet you'll stay longer!

- **Ask him out.** Yes, ladies, it is time. That man you've had your eye on for months . . . or minutes? Just get into a conversation (a simple "Hi" is enough of a starter), and when you find a common bond (kung-fu movies? basketball? come on, anything—Italian food?!) you will say, "Hey, I'm into that, too. You want to catch a flick watch a game grab some lasagna with me next week?" Whatever the answer, you will have accomplished something every woman wants to do. The worst he will say is some version of no, at which point you will give him a half-smile, a head-tilt, and a mysterious damn-you-missed-out shrug . . . and be out. The best response will be some version of yes—so have fun!

- **Commune with nature.** Okay, for some of you this will mean climbing a mountain or going horseback riding, for others it will mean taking a walk in the park or building a sand castle by the shore. The point is to play outside. Spending time in the great outdoors kindles your adventurous spirit and makes you feel like a kid (and you know how fearless children are).

- **Lose your inhibitions.** There's got to be something, sexually speaking, that you've wondered about. So why not try it? Do it with the lights blazing—or while blindfolded. Try *that* position—or *that* technique. No man in the picture? Pick up that battery-powered device that every other *Sex and the City* episode seemed to center on and indulge a fantasy. I bet you'll walk around with a smile you can't wipe off for days.

- **Ride the roller coaster.** No, I don't mean the up-and-down drama of your everyday life. I mean literally—go to an amusement park, buy a ticket, get on, and scream your head off. It will reintroduce you to the exhilaration of fear.

GET YOURS **FOREVER**

I was in Canada at a banquet honoring prominent black women in the music industry when I heard the devastating news. I'd left the dining room to get a drink from the bar and was taking a quiet moment to reflect on the solidarity I felt with the fabulous women I'd met that day. Suddenly, I heard someone yelling into a cell, people talking all at once, and then a sob. Clearly something terrible had happened. Finally, a clearly distraught woman told the gathering crowd that the singer Aaliyah had died in a plane crash earlier that evening.

We all rushed back into the dining room. As the news spread, the room grew hushed—soon all conversation and clinking drinks stopped. Spontaneously, we all joined hands for a moment of silence and prayer. Here was a gathering of the most powerful black women in music: smart, ambitious label executives, publicists, journalists, managers. It was the first time we had all come together and we couldn't believe that on this night of all nights we lost one of our greatest talents.

The next day, I was scheduled to board a plane back to New York— and I was petrified. I seriously considered rescheduling my flight to give myself some time to calm down. But I couldn't stop thinking about how I could, as the editor of *Honey,* memorialize Aaliyah. By the time she was twenty-two years old (the age when most of us are looking for our first low-paying, photocopy-making postcollege gig), she had already achieved international success as a musician, model, and actress. She was sexy, smart, and unafraid—an incredible role model for *Honey* readers.

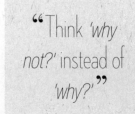

"Think 'why not?' instead of 'why?'"

I got a positive vibe from her the very first time we met, at an album release party that she held at a restaurant in Harlem. Not that we had that much time to hang out—she was busy joking around with her family, her Blackground records team, and her producer and partner-in-crime Timbaland. We talked a little about her album and the up-coming cover shoot I had scheduled for her, but really Aaliyah pre-ferred chilling with her crew. Watching her from afar, she seemed nothing like the typical spoiled celebrity and more like your superfly, funny girlfriend who loves fiercely, laughs deeply, and attracts the atten-tion of everyone in the room.

Aaliyah gave *Honey* her last-ever interview. Of course none of us knew it at the time. She was supposed to be on our cover the month after she died, and the notoriously press-shy star had granted us a brief Q&A as a precursor to a larger interview. We asked her: "Your parents gave you a name that means 'highest exalted one.' That's a lot to live up to. Do you ever feel pressure to achieve?" She replied: "I feel my name, being that it has such powerful meaning, is motivation in itself. I don't feel pressure to achieve. . . . It's my love for the art that drives me." Spoken like a true *Honey* woman.

The least I could do was get on that airplane and start working on the tribute issue I was already planning in my head. Also, I hated the idea that my fear could influence me enough to force a bad decision. So, I stepped onto the plane, strapped myself in, and closed my eyes. It wasn't until we had been flying safely at cruising altitude for half an hour that I could unclench my fingers and relax. I was afraid, but I didn't let it stop me.

I thought about many things during that flight: my family, my friends, my career—everything I was grateful for. I thought about the fullness of my life, how much I'd already experienced, and what I wanted to do next. And I thought a lot about Aaliyah and the lessons of her life. Clearly this was a woman who had shared the philosophy of making every day count. Aaliyah's painfully premature death just strengthened my resolve. I would continue to be adventurous, to try new things, and to take calculated risks. I would continue to *live*.

If you never have adventure, take chances, and strive to live up to your potential, you will rarely be afraid. But is that the life you want? Remember, this is your life, girlfriend, and no one can experience it for you. Think of embracing fear as a sign of personal growth and never let it slow you down.

Always . . .

- **Expect more from life.** It's simple—anticipate a life brimming with adventure and it will be more likely to unfold for you. Visualize yourself doing exciting things, whether it's speaking assertively to a rapt audience or skiing down a mountain.
- **Triumph over what terrifies you.** Compose a list of ten things that frighten you. Just being able to write them down will make them seem less scary. Then resolve to tackle at least half of the list during your lifetime.
- **Take reasonable risks—not foolish chances.** There's a huge difference. The concept of calculated risk means considering the consequences—what you stand to gain versus what you could possibly lose. A foolish chance is a blind leap, usually into something you already know is unwise, such as having unprotected sex.
- **Check out Outward Bound.** This organization is all about developing character through challenge and adventure—and helping regular people take the plunge. Go to www.outwardbound.org for more information.

5 WAYS TO TRAVEL ON A BUDGET

Don't say you can't afford to have adventures! Try these tips for inexpensive trips:

1. **Hit the right Web sites.** Travelocity, Priceline, Orbitz, and Expedia compete with one another to get you the lowest prices. Visit them all to book flights, hotels, and more. Or Google "budget travel" and check out all the sites that come up!
2. **Go in the off-season.** Sure, the Caribbean is costly in the winter and Europe is pricey in the summer. But do you really want to visit a foreign country when it's swarming with American tourists? Cut the bill and maximize the thrill by traveling when others don't.
3. **Be spontaneous.** Sometimes planning way in advance means paying through the nose (especially for plane tickets). But you can often find

great last-minute deals. Why not see where you can get away to this weekend?

4. **Chart new territory.** The most popular and the most exclusive places tend to be the priciest, but it's a great big world. Discover adventure off the beaten path. Lonely Planet (www.lonelyplanet.com) is great for travel advice, guidebooks, reviews, and more.

5. **Do a home swap.** Eliminate the cost of lodging altogether and swap homes with a fellow adventurer. If you live in a tiny town in the heart of the snowbelt, this might not be the best option. But if you have a cute apartment in a warm climate (California, Florida, Hawaii) or a big city like New York, you might be able to exchange spaces with someone who lives in Paris, Rome, Barcelona, etc. The three largest exchange clubs in the United States are www.HomeExchange.com, www.inter-vac.com, and www.homelink.org.

SANAA LATHAN ON ADVENTURE

The actress whose name means "work of art" in Swahili has clearly taken quite a few chances as well as taken advantage of many fabulous opportunities. She has a master's degree from Yale, starred opposite many of our most prominent leading men (Denzel Washington, Omar Epps, and Taye Diggs, to name a few) in everything from romantic comedies to action adventures, garnered a Tony nomination for her moving role in the Broadway play A Raisin in the Sun, *and even addressed the controversial issue of interracial love in her movie* Something New.

And she and I have had our share of adventures together. One night in L.A., she locked herself out of her Hollywood apartment. My ex was hanging with us and had to climb up the outside of her apartment building to pry open her window, squeeze through, and let her in. The next time we hung out was at one of Diddy's famous white parties in the Hamptons. Together, Sanaa and I dodged autograph seekers, random hoochies, and irate rappers' wives (looong story, but it involved a case of mistaken identity and a bottle of Veuve). All of this is to say Sanaa is mad cool, whip smart, and totally real. Any wonder I sought her out to talk about making life an exciting journey?

Amy: *How do you define a full life?*

Sanaa: A full life is a balanced life where you can be passionate about something you do, work toward something in your career, and have a partner . . . and great friends.

AB: *What does happiness mean to you?*

SL: It is a choice that you make every moment every day of your life. I have a discipline in terms of attempting to see the positive in things. I truly believe that when you think positively, your thoughts, words, and actions truly create positive things in your life.

AB: *Are there particular things that you are grateful for and make you feel happy?*

SL: We always think that when we attain certain things, we'll be happy—when I get this job I will be happy; when I win this award, I will be happy. Those moments give you satisfaction, but it's fleeting. What I'm really working on is just being in my life and appreciating the journey, and trying not to be dissatisfied with the in-between times. I try to have fun in my day-to-day life whether it is with my pops or my dog.

I met this director the other day from an area in Russia. He was saying that his people are nomads, and when you are a nomed you can't really keep things. Everything you have is on your back, because you are always traveling. So in their culture, the jewels of life are between two people, the emotions and connections that you have when you talk to a person, whether it is a family member or a friend or even just a stranger in the street. That is the pleasure in life for them. It was a moment of insight for me. Today is my life; not the day I win the Oscar, but today. I think that if you are truly present in the moment, you can't be unhappy.

AB: *I think a lot of people make the mistake of waiting for life to start. To me, it is an ongoing adventure.*

SL: As an actress and being a "celebrity" you get invited to so many things. I had this reclusive mentality—I am only going to hang out with my three girlfriends, I am not going to go out. [But] this year I went to Miami for New Year's and had a great time. When it came up,

I was like, "Why not?" In the past, I would be like, "No, I'm just going to stay here." It's really about saying yes to the opportunities that present themselves. I am trying to be more open and not judge things off the surface. I have met new people who are going to be friends now.

AB: *I think sometimes women of color can be very conservative and not open to opportunity.*

SL: Yes! When I am seventy-five, I want to look back and say that I lived. It is not always going to be about the jobs you did. I want to say, "Remember New Year's 2006, I partied and I was wild. Your grandmommy was wild!"

AB: *Did you feel that you were taking a risk, pursuing acting? So many of us go into law or medicine because we're afraid of "wasting" our opportunities.*

SL: Both of my parents are in the business, and my dad still did not want me to go into it. He knows how rough it can be. As soon as he saw my commitment, passion, and that I was really studying, he was behind me a hundred percent. Everyone is going to have challenges. You can look at someone and say, "Oh, they have it so easy." That's another thing that I am trying to do—you have to focus on your road, and not compare yourself to others. You can never know what is going on inside someone's world; all you can do is focus on yourself.

AB: *It is such a waste of time to be envious of other people. Also, I think we carry a lot of fear of the unknown that holds us back.*

SL: I feel that we have some insecurity at some times, but then there are times that we are stronger. So much emphasis is put on the external, a certain type of physical beauty, youth, attainment of some ideal that does not necessarily give you happiness. I think all women are going to have insecurities in a society that doesn't honor the true beauty of us as women.

AB: *You're right, black women are very strong and we have been the rocks in our households. Yet I know so many women of color who don't want to leave the country, or don't even want to try different types of food.*

SL: In my movie *Something New*, that is what we were trying to say.

It's not about saying, "You should go date a white boy." It was just saying be a little bit open, say yes to more things, step outside of that comfort zone. We all have these boxes that we put ourselves in and the lines get more solid as we get older. Maybe take one bite of that cuisine, or travel someplace that you would have never thought of, or go on that blind date with that Asian man. Just say yes to more things, that is how you grow. You never know what life has in store for you.

AB: *How do you triumph over fear?*

SL: It's okay to have that fear, but you still have to put one foot in front of the other. I have a mentor who says fear is an acronym for false evidence appearing real. It is really just an illusion of a huge, terrifying monster, but as soon as you step through it, it dissolves. That is why they say face your fear and it will die. If you have a fear of public speaking, do it and it will go away.

AB: *Did fear ever hold you back?*

SL: I was terrified of public speaking, even though I had been onstage a lot. Then a friend of mine who runs this charity organization that I am part of called. He said, "I want you to speak to one thousand sixth-graders about the work they are doing, why it is important, what it means for the world." I took that seriously and I did it. And it was so great. I was really nervous but I did it, and it was a success. And now I say yes to more opportunities like that, and I have no problem speaking in front of groups.

AB: *Do you think you are more confident now, or just okay with fear?*

SL: I know that now when I have fear, it does not have any power over me. I am definitely more adventurous now, saying yes to more things, trying out more things. I feel like I have a richer and fuller life.

AB: *I always ask people, "What are you going to do today? How are you going to make it more meaningful?" Is there anything that really opened you up?*

SL: This doesn't sound adventurous, but for me it was. I was invited to a Women in Hollywood event honoring all these fabulous women, very prestigious—but they only gave me one ticket. My publicist said,

"You should go; this is the company that you want to be in." I really didn't want to go by myself. I thought I wasn't going to know anyone. It was so amazing because I had such a great time. There was so much interesting conversation. It was an example of: Step out, and the universe will support you in that decision. Go out to dinner by yourself. See how that feels. Don't be afraid to do things alone. *The Artist's Way* by Julia Cameron talks about how if you are an artist, to cultivate the artist in you, you need to nurture that person in yourself. So go to the beach, go to a museum, do something like that. It is fun and fulfilling.

AB: *Who or what has influenced you in your life?*
SL: I think everyone should have a spiritual leader—the head of their church, or a therapist, counselor, or coach to talk to and get a perspective on their lives. I have a spiritual mentor and I can talk to her about anything in my life. I don't know what I would have done without her. Your family cannot see you clearly because they are so emotionally invested in you; the same with your friends. They may want the best for you, but they are not objective.

AB: *What has your most important life lesson been?*
SL: That we are in control of the quality of our lives. You can be happy washing the dishes, or you can be miserable washing the dishes, and it is in your power and it is your perspective. Be careful what you think and say because [words] create what you get in your life. If you want the quality of love, think loving thoughts. You can even be more specific and say, "One day I want to buy a house." Start imagining that for yourself. You have to see it before it can happen. The more real that you can make that, the closer you will get to it.

AB: *What is the best piece of advice you have ever gotten?*
SL: Your life is now—make the most of it!

PROMISE PAGE

My dreams and goals to live a life of adventure are:

_____

_____

_____

_____

_____

_____

I promise that today I will:

_____

_____

_____

_____

_____

This year I promise to:

_____

_____

_____

_____

_____

I will always:

_____

_____

_____

_____

_____

_____

3

GET HEALTHY

A few years ago, I ran into a woman I worked with briefly back in 1993. We were at a club, and I was wearing low-slung jeans and a tank top. "Look how skinny you are!" she yelled, grabbing my shoulders and spinning me around. "You used to be *so* much bigger!" How true: Since she'd last seen me, I'd lost about twenty-five pounds and was three sizes smaller. What she didn't know was that I had gained all that weight during the emotionally wrenching year before I'd met her.

Some of you may think twenty-five pounds is a lot, while I know others are like: "That ain't nothing!" For me, though, it was a big deal. I ran track in high school and have always been athletic. I was never su-perskinny, but I always managed to exercise enough to keep my weight within shouting range of in shape. During that deeply unhappy period after my mom passed, however, I didn't feel like brushing my teeth, much less going to a gym. I just wanted to eat egg rolls every night while I watched the tube—alone.

I couldn't see it then, but I was compounding my unhappiness by damaging my health, since I felt tired and sluggish all the time. But it did ultimately dawn on me that my mom had died at age forty-nine. Would I suffer the same fate? The thought terrified me. When I finally got my mind together, and realized I had a lot to live for, the next thing to take care of was my body.

I cut back on Snickers bars and introduced myself to the wonder-ful world of yogurt. But since I hate to diet (seriously, what a cold, cruel world it would be without pasta), I decided exercise was my way out and found some terrific dance classes near my neighborhood. Because I was doing an activity I actually loved, I went to class religiously sev-eral days a week. Next thing you knew, I could button my skirts again, men were acting stupid around me, and I felt energetic enough to pur-sue the goals I set for myself. Obviously, no one should have to lose someone they love in order to lose weight, but I've kept the exercise and nutrition habits I developed back then.

I love that, for the most part, women of color are not afraid to be ourselves, whether we're a size 8 or not. (The positive feedback we get from our men doesn't hurt!) But the reality is that, according to the Centers for Disease Control, approximately 78 percent of black women are overweight and 51 percent are obese, and the numbers for Latina women are almost as bad. Those percentages are much higher than for other ethnic groups in the country—and it's just not healthy. In fact, there is a direct association between body weight and deaths from all causes for women aged thirty to fifty-five.

Too often we damage our physical health by eating poorly, avoiding exercise, and ignoring symptoms of the illnesses that we disproportionately contract (such as diabetes, fibroids, and high blood pressure). We aren't traditionally into health food, vitamins, and drinking eight glasses of water a day. Plus, many women of color come from a culture of heavy, greasy fare; we grew up with fried chicken, sausage, butter-covered grits, Kool-Aid with extra sugar, and sweet potato pie—and as adults we love our fast food (just look at the number of fast-food-chain commercials targeted right at us!).

Don't get me wrong: I'm not telling you to starve yourself to minuscule model proportions, an equally unhealthy idea. I'm just talking about getting in shape. Next time you have a checkup, ask your doctor to help you figure out a healthy weight range. And believe me, I know it's not easy to squeeze fitness into your schedule when you have so many responsibilities and so little time. But if we don't treat ourselves well, who else will? Plus, how can you pull a ten-hour workday, hit a networking event, and meet a guy for late-night drinks (then get up the next morning to do it all again) if you're not in serious shape?

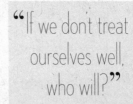

"If we don't treat ourselves well, who will?"

It's not as hard as you might think: Hit the gym a few times a week, cut back on (not necessarily eliminate) burgers and brownies, eat some veggies, and try not to drink more cocktails than your body can safely handle. If you're looking to lose a few pounds, check out Dr. Ian Smith's book *The Fat Smash Diet* for a realistic program that regular women like us can actually follow. I work hard and party hard and pig out and go to the gym and take my vitamins. It's that simple.

I had my personal health revelation during a time when I was truly scared of dying young. Even though I would never wish that terrible year on anyone, I know that being healthy has helped me to live better and take full advantage of my time on this planet. The added bonus is that I feel pretty good about how I look from the back in a pair of low-slung jeans. These days, I feel more alive than ever and refuse even to entertain the purely negative energy that is the fear of dying at the same age my mother did. Keep your body strong, your mind focused, and think positively about your life. You'll feel fabulous and the miniskirt will look that much better!

Quiz: Are You Taking Care of Number One?

To be on top of your game, you've got to feel your best (and know how to deal when you don't). This quiz will help you figure out if you've got a good handle on your physical and mental health.

1. You've been averaging three headaches a week for a month now. You

a. buy another bottle of aspirin.

b. make a doctor's appointment to find out what's up.

c. resolve to stress less—that's what must be causing the pain.

2. A man you don't know remarks "Big sexy!" when you walk by. You assume

a. you've got a glow about you.

b. you carry your weight well.

c. you ought to drop a few pounds.

3. Your date wants you to pick the restaurant tonight. You choose a

a. soul-food buffet—you've been jonesing for fried chicken.

b. seafood place—you need more omega-3s in your diet.

c. steakhouse with a good salad bar.

4. Your fitness routine is

a. varied and fun—so you'll stick with it.

b. not too challenging, but you try to walk when you can.

c. nonexistent—you really don't have time to work out.

5. Nothing's really wrong, but lately you've been feeling sad and hopeless. You

a. know it will pass—everyone gets the blues sometimes.

b. try not to dwell on it and don't mention it to anyone.

c. wonder if it might be depression and go online to read up on it.

6. You know high blood pressure is a problem for a lot of black women, but you don't have to worry because

a. your blood pressure tested normal at your last annual physical.

b. you feel fine.

c. your mom didn't start to show symptoms till she was in her forties.

7. None of your jeans fit! Exasperated, you

a. cut out carbs and sweets till you can zip them again.

b. join a gym and just say no to seconds.

c. buy some new jeans.

8. Sure, you'd love to sleep in on Saturday, but you wouldn't dream of missing

a. your hair appointment.

b. your yoga class.

c. the breakfast special down at the IHOP.

9. Strawberry shortcake is brought in to celebrate a coworker's birthday. You

a. have a piece, and skip dessert later.

b. partake, even though you don't really *like* strawberry shortcake all that much.

c. be the one to cut the cake, so you can have the size slice you want.

10. You swore you'd never let it happen, but it happened—you had unprotected sex. You

a. call the guy for assurance that he doesn't "have" anything.

b. go to your doctor immediately to be tested for sexually transmitted diseases.

c. pray you're all right.

THE SCORE

Give yourself points as follows:

1. a = 1, b = 3, c = 2	**6.** a = 3, b = 1, c = 2
2. a = 3, b = 1, c = 2	**7.** a = 2, b = 3, c = 1
3. a = 1, b = 3, c = 2	**8.** a = 2, b = 3, c = 1
4. a = 3, b = 2, c = 1	**9.** a = 3, b = 1, c = 2
5. a = 2, b = 1, c = 3	**10.** a = 2, b = 3, c = 1

HERE'S THE DEAL

Hardly a Healthy Attitude (10 to 16 points) While you may be a take-charge person when it comes to career and social activities, you seem to think your health amounts to your lot in life—something you have to accept. Untrue! You have the power to be positive and proactive about your mental and physical well-being. And you owe it to yourself—not to mention the people who love you—to take charge. Enough with the excuses (like "Gyms are too expensive" or "I don't have time to go to the doctor") and be real. Schedule an appointment for a physical, a gynecological exam, and a dental checkup, calling your doctors' attention to anything that's been bothering you. Resolve to live healthier in increments—you can start by just saying "No!" when the girl behind the counter asks, "Supersize that?"

Half-hearted Healthy Attitude (17 to 23 points) Living healthfully is a full-time thing. It's not about depriving yourself of food so you can fit into your jeans or taking a walk occasionally and calling it a fitness regime. Sometimes you can be blinded by your own optimism, telling yourself "Everything's all right" or that a problem will go away if you ignore it. There's no need to get neurotic and start running to the doctor for every hangnail, but getting regular checkups, keeping your weight on point, and learning what ailments your family is prone to so you'll know a red flag when you see it—this is all common sense. Put a little more effort into gaining and maintaining good health now, and you'll possibly spare yourself pain and suffering in the future.

Hale and Hearty Attitude (24 to 30 points) You do an amazing job of taking care of yourself, mostly because you don't look at staying healthy as a chore. Your workouts are enjoyable, not grueling; your diet is about balance, not denial. Plus, you know how to listen to your body and be realistic about what it's saying. You investigate symptoms and deal with them quickly, rather than pray they'll disappear and possibly have them grow worse. In order to live life to the fullest, you have to feel great. Good health enables you to achieve professionally and soar socially—and it's the secret to shiny hair, clear skin, and that aura of attractiveness and confidence you radiate. Not a bad bonus, huh?

START **TODAY**, GIRLFRIEND!

One night I went to dinner with a group of girls to celebrate one of our friends' recent promotion to vice president at her company. We had a great time, laughing, toasting her good fortune (and hard work!), gossiping . . . and eating. Everyone was in a great mood—relaxed and happy—until our waiter dropped dessert menus in front of us. I was busily reviewing my options, deciding between chocolate mousse and pecan pie, when I noticed the thick silence. Looking around the table, I realized the atmosphere had gotten almost tense. Everyone was trying hard not to look at the tempting list, while stealing glances at the rest of the women to gauge if anyone else was going to order. It was clear that no one wanted to be the first to speak up. The only thing that could silence my smart, creative, fun girlfriends was the specter of cheesecake?

"Well, I'm thinking of the pecan pie," I said, hoping everyone else would follow suit.

Instead, one after the other, they all declined, saying they didn't want to be "bad." Incredulous, I told them that there was no such thing as bad food, just bad eating habits, and they looked at me like I was crazy. "That's easy for you to say," one of my girls piped up. "You don't have to work to be thin."

I couldn't argue since it really doesn't feel like work to me—mostly because I never deprive myself. I believe that while there's definitely good food, there's no such thing as bad food. And if you think you're being "bad" every time you have a bit of cake or a spoonful of ice cream, you give dessert the sexy sheen of the forbidden. Trust me, everything is fine in moderation. If you take out a teacup and fill it with ice cream after dinner, you've had a reasonable dessert, but you haven't unnecessarily gorged. That's so much better than thinking the

> "Being healthy has helped me take full advantage of my time on this planet."

ice cream is "bad," going to bed unsatisfied, then polishing off the entire pint at two AM.

You have to satisfy yourself, otherwise you'll always feel deprived. That's why I ordered dessert that night with my friends—the way I always do. It was huge, so I ate until I was full and happy, then passed it around the table for my friends to taste. Sometimes I finish all my dessert, sometimes I split it—but if I want it, I order it. Sure, I do try to save room so that I'm not stuffed when I'm eating it (the best tip I give people who want to lose weight is to eat what you want, but stop when you're full). And I'll make an effort to hit the gym the next day. But I refuse to live a brownieless life.

I'm not going to ask you to lift weights or call your doctor for an appointment or read a book on nutrition. Girlfriend, all I want you to do is eat your dessert. That's right, treat yourself. You want it, you deserve it, so eat it—and then move on. Indulge in moderation. Translation: Savor the treat—no one's going to snatch it away from you—and stop eating when you're full (not stuffed, full). Go to bed happy tonight with the knowledge that being healthy does not mean sacrificing the delicious things in life.

Today . . .

- **Schedule medical checkups.** It's not enough to "feel fine"; you need to *know*. Make an appointment for a general physical, an ob-gyn exam, an eye exam with an ophthalmologist (not an optometrist), and a visit to the dentist. Go to the doctor armed with questions and knowledge of your family health history. Be honest—about your diet, habits, sleep patterns, stress level, or any old ache and pain. Do not let her rush you out of the office until you feel that you have answers to all of your questions and a follow-up plan and referrals, if necessary.

- **Lose your bad body image.** The percentage of the population that is physically perfect is very small. I know this because I've worked with tons of models, actresses, and musicians who earn their living by their looks, and very few of *them* are perfect in person. What's more, even the perfect ones obsess about their flaws! So stop trippin' on your too big this or too small that. Today, put on the outfit that flatters your form the most. Flaunt your assets (you know you've got them!) and forget the rest.

- **Start eating better.** It's much easier than you think. Start your day with a quick fruit smoothie (throw a banana, some berries, and a little yogurt or skim milk together in a blender; add whey protein for a long-lasting energy burst). Sneak some broccoli and carrots into a salad at lunch, and watch out for dressing overload. Cook some black beans with green and red peppers as a tasty side dish for dinner. Cut back painlessly—sugar-free gum and diet sodas go a long way, and low-fat frozen yogurt is fabulous!

- **Examine your breasts.** If you're having your period, wait a week, but get into the habit of giving yourself monthly self-exams. Don't know how? Go to www.breastcancer.org.

- **Drink water.** Health experts recommend eight to ten eight-ounce glasses per day. Need more convincing? Drinking this amount of water will help you feel more full—and less inclined to overeat. Plus, every makeup artist I ever met insists that keeping hydrated is the key to clear skin and even healthy hair.

- **Don't overdo it at the gym.** Know what will happen if you run on the treadmill for an hour, then take three exercises classes back-to-back? You'll be in agony for days after, and won't even want to drive or walk down the street of your gym ever again! Challenge yourself, but start slowly. Since a well-rounded workout includes aerobics, weight training, and stretching, try to do a bit of all three each week, but not on the same day.

- **Avoid skipping meals.** Not a breakfast person? Become one! You'll be less likely to pig out at other meals if you start your day with something healthy (come on, you know that a muffin is just cake without the icing!). Plus, the more you skip meals, the slower your metabolism gets as it tries to compensate for the calories your body is not receiving when it needs them. Want a snack? Have a snack. Consider making it an apple—it just may satisfy you. By sticking to your three squares a day, you won't be tempted to gorge on sweets. One more hint: Make lunch or even breakfast your biggest meal of the day. That way your body will have more time to burn the calories before you go to sleep.

MAKE **THIS YEAR** COUNT

I have a close friend who, despite my many attempts to convince her otherwise, has always felt heavy and unattractive—and insecure as a result. A naturally curvy woman, she developed a lifelong unhealthy relationship with food. She refused to eat in public and stuffed herself late at night when no one was watching. She had never been athletic, and felt too embarrassed to go to the gym.

As my girl approached her thirtieth birthday, she began to panic. She wanted to enter her thirties feeling strong and fabulous, so she decided to take charge. First, she started eating regular meals, beginning with a decent breakfast of some protein and some carbohydrates. Then she joined a gym. Now, this is a girl who had never done sports and is actually a bit accident-prone. (One time, on the way to a party, she fell on an uneven stretch of sidewalk. We missed the whole event because she had to go to the emergency room, and she ended up needing crutches!) But she resolved to hit the gym five days a week—she chose an aerobics class and got a trainer.

> "Keep your body strong, your mind focused, and think positively about your life."

In the beginning it was really rough for her. She had trouble keeping up in her aerobics class, her muscles ached all the time, and she felt like the biggest girl in the gym. Around then, my schedule got crazy, so when I saw my girl next, a month or two later, I literally could not believe my eyes. She was wearing slim-cut jeans, a great blazer, a cute little silky top, and high heels. Men's heads swiveled as she sashayed by. She told me she still hadn't achieved all of her fitness goals, but felt stronger and sexier than ever.

When her big 3-0 arrived, she wore a fabulous little black dress and gold heels—and danced on the tables until dawn!

Inspiring? You bet it is! Make this year count by promising yourself that you will create an exercise plan. I know it's hard—especially if you're not used to pushing your body at all. But even if working out is no fun at first, the combination of looking great, feeling strong, and sticking to a plan will make you happy in the long run. Watching my girl dance and flirt on her thirtieth birthday reminded me that sometimes happiness isn't just about fun—sometimes it's the gratification of having achieved a goal. Yes, my friend looked gorgeous, but she was also happier than I'd ever seen her—and that's more important than anything.

This Year . . .

- **Establish realistic health/weight goals.** It starts with those doctors' visits that you'll be making once a year. If you have or are heading for certain conditions (like hypertension or diabetes), your primary goal is to control or stave off these ailments. If your family history makes you prone to a disorder, do all you can to stay healthy. Also, figure out what is the right weight range for your frame, height, and age, and get there.
- **Find the right fitness program.** Tae Bo or yoga or belly dancing may be the fitness rage at the gym near you, but to stick with a work-out regimen, you've got to find activities you really enjoy. So try a bunch of different things. Some women love the camaraderie of a class; others prefer to go the solo route. Also, consider teaming up with an exercise buddy. It's so much easier to stick to a program when you've got someone to work out with.
- **Fight fatigue.** Between full-time jobs and family/home responsibilities, it's no wonder women are tired a lot of the time. You might not be able to do less, but you can get better rest. Begin by establishing a prebed ritual—reading, taking a bath, having a cup of caffeine-free tea, whatever helps you wind down. Do this every night, and it will give your body cues that it's time to sleep. Make your bedroom as restful (cool, quiet, and dark) as possible. Wake up at the same time each day (believe it or not, sleeping in on the weekends can make you more tired!). And finally, schedule only

what you can realistically accomplish every day so that you're not constantly running to get that last task done.

• **Get screened for STDs.** If you're a grown woman, chances are you've had a sexual encounter that didn't involve a condom (excuse me, but intercourse is not the only sexual encounter there is). Therefore, you should be screened for STDs (sexually transmitted diseases). Yes, girlfriend, that includes HIV/AIDS. Getting that clean bill of health will make you feel so relieved, and prompt you to always protect yourself in the future.

GET YOURS FOREVER

Before I had my health revelation, I wasn't simply out of shape and eating poorly, I also never scheduled medical checkups and ignored most of my illnesses. I would "power through" all kinds of aches and pains without it even occurring to me to see a doctor. I just didn't truly care enough about my body to take care of it. I would limp until knee pain subsided, deal with severe headaches, and sleep away extreme colds. It seemed that I was always a little sick, but never actually being treated. I prided myself on being tough and resilient—and I mistakenly thought that denying sickness was an example of that.

At one point, I got a terrible cold that landed me in bed for a couple of weeks. When I got well enough to leave my apartment, it was with a wracking cough that would stop me in my tracks while I doubled over and hacked away. Still, I went out, assuming the cough would eventually go away. After three weeks, I began to cough up blood and gasp for breath. I could ignore it no longer and scheduled an appointment with a doctor I found in the yellow pages. It turned out that I had walking pneumonia, and if I hadn't made that appointment I might have wound up in the hospital.

While treating my pneumonia, the doctor decided to perform a few tests to check on the state of my overall health. It turned out that I was anemic, slightly hypoglycemic (low blood sugar), and developing arthritis in my neck. Of course, I was completely freaked out, but after a month of adjusting my diet and visiting a physical therapist, I felt great. It was around that time that I decided to get fit. By my next doctor's appointment, I was no longer anemic or hypoglycemic, and my arthritis was at least being treated so I wasn't in constant pain.

Taking care of yourself is not an act of weakness—it's an act of self-love and respect. I will never disregard and disrespect myself again.

Please love and take of yourself, girlfriend. You are the only one who can.

Always . . .

- **Be flexible about fitness.** Vary your exercise routine so it feels like play. Keep your eyes open for new activities, and never be afraid to try something that sounds interesting—a team sport, in-line skating, martial arts, whatever. Listen to your body—it will tell you when it needs to run, stretch, dance, build strength, and, yes, rest.
- **Eat in front of men.** Men don't like women who just eat leaves with lemon juice. I swear. Showing a healthy appetite indicates an enthusiasm for life. Picking at your appetizer salad while he downs a steak just makes him nervous and you look like a drag. Sure, good table manners count, but remember: Eating is sexy!
- **Be strong.** Whatever fitness routine you choose, it should include some element of strength training. This can mean lifting free weights, working out with machines, or using the resistance of your own body weight (as in yoga). Building muscle not only makes you feel strong and look toned now, it helps stave off osteoporosis later in life.
- **Have safe sex.** There will always be that moment of truth in the dark when passion is at its peak and it would be so much easier to just do it. That, however, is a risk you must be *unwilling* to take, no matter how hot you feel or how much he begs. If you are not in a monogamous relationship, where you and your partner have both been tested and found to be free of STDs, you must always use a condom. Yes, I know you learned this in health class, but until you live by the "no glove, no love" rule, there will always be people like me around to repeat the message.
- **Slather on sunblock.** No one is immune to skin cancer. Not even black folks. Or wrinkles. The cause of both? Unprotected skin exposure. Fortunately, most good moisturizers and many foundations

on the market today have sunblock built in. Use one on your face daily. When at the beach, apply an SPF of 15 or more to all exposed areas.

• **Consider alternative remedies.** While I encourage everyone to visit a medical doctor, I also believe that Western medicine is not the be-all and end-all. Holistic health approaches, Ayurvedic medicine, herbs, acupuncture—all these practices have their own merit, and sometimes taking a pill or having a surgery is not the only answer to treating a condition. Keep an open mind when it comes to your body!

INSTANT HEALTH MAKEOVERS

1. **Eat breakfast.** Can't say it enough: Do not skip meals. Start the day with some eggs, fruit, yogurt, or oatmeal, and your health, mood, and appearance will improve dramatically.

2. **Take vitamins.** After breakfast, pop a women's multivitamin (make sure it contains your daily recommended dosage of iron), 1,200 mgs of calcium, and omega-3. Add vitamin B_6 just before your period to improve your mood. Of course, nothing can replace a balanced diet, but this will ensure that you get the essential nutrients on those days that you have a Big Mac attack.

3. **Banish neck and backache.** Take a break every hour and do some easy exercises. Lift your shoulders to your ears then drop them in a shrugging motion. Repeat several times. Then rotate your neck slowly in both directions. Try to press each ear to your shoulder. Make sure your office chair has lumbar (lower back) support and save your sky-high heels for after work. Doing these simple things will prevent knotted muscles from cramping your style.

4. **Eliminate computer-related eyestrain.** Position your screen at a right angle from the window to minimize glare, at least an arm's length away, and tilt it slightly downward. Blink and look away often.

5. **Minimize menstrual cramps.** Visit the ladies' room as soon as you feel the need. A full bladder will press against your uterus and make your cramps even worse.

6. **Drink water.** You've read this a million times, but dehydration has so many negative effects on your body—most common are fatigue and severe headaches. By the time you feel thirsty, you're already dehydrated. Keep a bottle of water (that you refill with tap water) next to you all day.

7. **Get some sleep.** I know, another thing you're tired of hearing. Here are two great reasons to try for eight hours a night: Sleep deprivation can make you stupid and fat (yes, there's medical evidence that it slows your brain function and metabolism). Got it?

10 BAD HABITS TO KICK

Do yourself a favor and quit

1. **Smoking.** That's number one for a reason, girlfriend. If you do nothing else, do this. Please.

2. **Saying "Sure!" to supersizing.** You really don't need a gallon of soda or a tub of popcorn you could bathe a small child in.

3. **Postponing vacations.** Your mind and body need to rest. A change of scene, even if only for a long weekend, can work wonders. And that doesn't have to mean jetting to Saint-Tropez. Taking the train to visit an old friend will do the trick.

4. **Adding extra sugar to your Kool-Aid.** And please, don't get kids in the habit either.

5. **Skipping the floss step.** Brushing your teeth is half the job; you've got to get in there and floss. Not only does it help prevent cavities and gum disease, studies show that flossing also may help prevent diabetes and heart disease.

6. **Letting in sneaky calories.** You think you're having a healthy meal with that salad, then you drown it in blue cheese dressing. You order only the small fries, but you douse them with ketchup (ditto for the small popcorn that's virtually glowing with fake butter product).

7. **Oversprinkling the salt.** Salt may not have calories, but it can cause you to retain water and look/feel bloated. It's also a concern if high blood pressure is an issue. Season your food with herbs and spices instead.

8. **Thinking therapy is for crazy people.** Recognizing that you need help (with depression or anxiety, or to cope with a loss) and going for it is one of the greatest acts of self-love there is. And that's not crazy. It's true.

9. **Counting French fries as vegetables.** Eat something green every single day (a few times a day would be ideal). Add something orange or yellow for health-boosting extra credit.

10. **Comparing yourself to others.** Especially that bony chick on the cover of *Vogue*.

VENUS WILLIAMS ON A HEALTHY LIFE

World tennis champion Venus Williams has won many major tournaments, from the French Open to the U.S. Open to the prestigious Wimbledon. In 2002, she became the first African American woman to reach the number-one ranking on the WTA tour. And as the CEO of her own interior design firm, V Starr Interiors, she's also a successful businesswoman. I had never met Venus before our interview, but after once spending an entire day with her sister Serena, I do feel as if I have a real sense of the Williams sisters and their special bond.

On the day of the Boris Kodjoe cover shoot for Honey, *Serena showed up to keep him company. He is a great tennis player and, apparently, the two bonded over the sport and were great friends. All I know is that one minute I was trying to talk Boris into some leather pants (can you blame me?) and the next Serena (and her tiny dog) was on set, wearing a miniskirt that showed off her impossibly strong thighs and giving opinions about what her friend did and did not look good in. At first, I was a little nervous about having another huge star appear out of the blue, but Serena was really sweet. She obviously cared about Boris, but she also spent a good portion of the day talking about her family, specifically Venus. The rivalry was clear, as was the deep and unconditional love. Just by listening to the affection and respect in Serena's voice, you could tell how close the two are and how much influence they have over each other.*

Clearly Venus is one of the world's best athletes, but I felt that her approach to fitness for the rest of us mortals would be real and reasonable. She and I got together to chat about the importance of health for a full life.

Amy: *How do you get the most out of your life?*

Venus: Being able to play tennis and spend time with my family gives me a lot of happiness. Working hard, reaching goals, and feeling accomplished is a strong source of contentment for me.

AB: *Do you feel that your life is balanced?*

VW: I used to take on too much. But I've gotten a lot more balanced in the last year. It takes time just to realize who you are, what you are about, your good habits, and your bad habits. I hit twenty-five and realized I was an overachiever. Not that that's bad, but sometimes it's not a healthy attitude—you try to do everything, and be good at everything. So, I am trying to balance work and life off the court.

AB: *Let's talk about the rest of us mortals. Do you think it is important for women to be strong?*

VW: I think that when you are physically strong, and you give your body some work to do, it stimulates a sense of well-being. It brings about happiness in terms of how you feel about your appearance, and just doing something good for yourself.

AB: *What role do you think discipline and mental stamina play in staying fit? I personally believe that so much of being physically fit is mental: getting your head in a place where it's not just about being skinny, but where you prioritize your body and what your body can do for you.*

VW: I think you have to be mentally strong in this world; if you are not, there is a chance that you might not survive. But I've been working out my whole life. It's just normal for me.

AB: *How do you motivate yourself when you don't want to work out? I know it's your profession, but there have got to be days when you just don't want to do it.*

VW: Sometimes I feel like it and sometimes I don't. But [working out] has to get done some way and only I can do it for myself. I like being fit. I should not be carrying any extra weight for performance purposes, but I like looking strong. I like looking in the mirror and seeing my muscles.

AB: *Have you ever felt any pressure to be thin? How do you handle that?*

VW: I never really felt pressure to be thin from anyone or myself.

AB: *I think that might be a function of being black. Women of color appreciate curves more than white women. What do you feel about the new diets on the market?*

VW: I think diets don't work. Deprivation—you can't have this, you can't have that—that's not normal, because once you get off the diet, you go back to your habits. I believe in having a balanced lifestyle—eating the right things, and having some fun things, too.

AB: *What's the best thing the average woman can do to maintain her health? Do you have any insider tips as a professional athlete?*

VW: I think the best thing you can do to maintain your health is to have self-confidence, because not everyone is going to look like the people in the films and the magazines. I think it is important to have a sense of self-worth, and base what you think about yourself on what you have inside, not on the outside.

Be aware of how you treat your body and what you put in it. Even drinking and partying, if it is to the point that you are getting wrinkles, you are partying too much. With work, if it's too stressful, it might mean that it's time to move on to something else.

AB: *Do you think the confidence that a woman who works out gets from knowing she's doing something for herself, and that she looks her best, will help her to achieve other goals?*

VW: I definitely think so. Because, unfortunately, in this world, people judge you on your looks. I am not saying that you should look good for the rest of the world, but you can present yourself better if you feel good about yourself and what you are doing for yourself.

AB: *Has anybody ever given you advice that helped you to achieve your highest level of performance?*

VW: Yes. Definitely. I was playing Wimbledon, and it was a really tough match—I was pretty much losing for almost three hours. Serena said, "If you take the opportunities, more will come." It's the things that your parents say, your sisters say, and it helps you to stay motivated. Not that I wasn't motivated, but I found that extra energy and power. [Also] my dad always says, "Success comes to successful people," another way of saying you have to take your opportunities.

AB: *What is your most important life lesson?*

VW: The most important life lesson that I've learned in the last year or so is not to be judgmental. It is so easy to judge. Like this girl should get rid of this guy, he's no good. . . . You really never know what it is like in the next person's shoes, although it may not be the right decision for you, or maybe you are smart enough and wise enough and strong enough to do something different, the next person might not be in that situation. So a lot of times you need to be a listener and give someone a listening ear and sometimes that is enough. You learn to never judge anyone.

AB: *What lesson would you like to share?*

VW: Watch out for yourself, because no one else will. Serena and I say that all the time because if we get injured or hurt, the next player will move in. You have to be able to take care of yourself, because no one is going to come to your front door and say, "I heard that you are not feeling well, let me take care of you." It does not work like that. Watch your back!

AB: *Do you have any final words for women of color on happiness and success?*

VW: You have to work harder as an African American, but that's fine because it builds character. Not everything is set up in the world for you, but that doesn't matter, because you can make [life] yours.

PROMISE PAGE

My dreams and goals for my health are:

_____
_____
_____
_____
_____
_____

I promise that today I will:

_____
_____
_____
_____
_____

This year I promise to:

_____
_____
_____
_____
_____

I will always:

_____
_____
_____
_____
_____
_____

4

GET GREAT GIRLFRIENDS

A few years ago, when I was still single, I attended a work conference in Miami and decided to spend a couple of extra days in South Beach on my own. While there, I ran into a group of people I knew from New York. Needless to say, it was nice to find a familiar crew. I ran over, hugged everyone, and said how great it was to see them. The guys seemed happy to see me, too, and pulled up a chair so I could join them for drinks. But the women looked me up and down and literally refused to speak to me. If they could have wiggled their noses like Samantha from *Bewitched,* they would have deleted me from the face of the planet.

During the course of the evening, I kept trying to figure out what was up: There were more than ten people in their group, so I wasn't interrupting a romantic rendezvous; I'd spent time with all of them in New York without incident, so there was no obvious bad blood; and I wasn't interested in—or flirting with—any of the men. I was just pleased to have cocktails with friends. But the women kept whispering to one another behind their hands while completely ignoring me. Well, it's just no fun to be around people who clearly don't want you in their mix. When the icy stares became too much, I put down some money for our last round, claimed I had an early morning, and said my good-byes.

The incident left me feeling hurt and confused. I had genuinely thought I was cool with those women—they weren't my nearest and dearest, but before that night I would have called them casual friends. On the plane coming home I ruminated on how women, especially women of color, can hate on each other like that. What does all that negativity accomplish? It does nothing but show a lack of confidence!

Soon after the trip, a girlfriend invited me to an event that she periodically hosts for women of color in the New York area. About thirty of us gathered that Saturday afternoon for the sole purpose of meeting other smart, caring sisters. We went around the room and introduced ourselves, and after we said our name, one or two other women who knew us were supposed to chime in and describe the kind of person we were. Most of us got teary as our friends talked about how we were reliable, fun, nurturing, loyal, great mothers, hard workers, etc. I've rarely experienced so much love and support at one time. It restored my faith in women and renewed my resolve to bring as many of us to-gether as possible.

When it was my turn, a good friend spoke up and said I was a real girl's girl. She said a woman could trust me with her deepest secrets, that I'd do all I could to protect a friend from harm. It was one of the best compliments I have ever received—and it soothed the sting from my Miami experience. Yet it did not erase the fact that traditionally black women do have a tremendous amount of "drama" surrounding our friendships. We often mistrust one another, steal one another's men, and fail to treat one another with respect. Imagine how powerful women of color would be if we all decided to take care of ourselves and look out for one an-other at the same time?

> "Prioritize your relationships with girls who give as much as they receive."

Since I moved around so much as a child, for years my friendships suffered. I let users and generally untrustworthy people into my life, gave too much to people who didn't deserve my attention, and had no core group of girls I could count on when things got rough. Having lived through that, I gained enormous appreciation for the true friendships I developed as an adult. I now have a small but solid circle—women (and men) who have proven to be dependable and loving—and I value these relationships above almost everything. My good friends are like family.

I never did get to the bottom of the chilly reception I received from those women in Miami, but I still believe strongly in sisterhood—and my close girlfriends reinforce that belief on a daily basis. We support our projects, applaud our successes, and help one another deal with personal and professional challenges. And that is what I want for you: a tight-knit crew you can count on, and a loving attitude toward all your sisters. I want us to treat one another with kindness and respect, and I think we can. We just need to work together to remember that we women have a unique bond that transcends everything!

Quiz: Are You Getting Enough from Your Girls?

No one has your back like a true, trusted friend, and you need to be there for your girls, too. But somehow it's easy to lose sight of how important female bonding really is. This quiz will help you check how you stand with your sister circle.

1. At the end of a particularly long, trying week, you
a. get together with a huge group of friends and party like you just don't care.
b. have dinner with one or two close friends who will help you sort things out.
c. go into self-imposed lockdown with a stack of magazines and DVDs.

2. At a party, you notice your friend and your boyfriend talking together in a corner. Naturally you assume she's
a. counseling him on what to get you for your birthday.
b. trying to steal him from you.
c. trying to get the hookup for something—a date with his friend, an interview at his company, etc.

3. The girls are convening at your place before going out, and one of them shows up looking like she just stepped out of Nelly's "Tip Drill" video. You
a. don't say a word. If she wants to dress like a fool, that's her affair.
b. pull her into your bedroom, tell her gently that the navel-scraping neckline is not working for her, and ask her if she wants to borrow a jacket.
c. tell her she looks fabulous, then roll your eyes at the other girls while she basks in your praise.

4. You want to befriend the new girl at work because
a. she dresses great, and you heard her mention she's in good with the bartender at your favorite place (can you say "free margaritas"?).

b. she's in the department you want to make a move to, and she's got some clout.

c. she seems nice but a little shy, and you want to ease her new-girl jitters (you were the new girl once, too!).

5. Your man has not been living up to his potential, and this frustrates you. You

a. call your best friend and confess your concerns, asking her to give you some straight-up advice.

b. write an angry rant about him in your journal to vent, but otherwise keep this private matter private.

c. get annoyed when a friend asks how he's doing (what does she mean by that?!) and make a snide remark about her own no-good lazy-ass boyfriend.

6. You love your best friend because she

a. always has great fashion tips and a tampon when you need one.

b. keeps your secrets and has your best interests at heart.

c. respects you and doesn't butt into your business.

7. Which statement best describes your social circle?

a. You have a lot of acquaintances but very few close friends.

b. They're a diverse group—friends from grammar school to the new girl in your building.

c. They're fun and fly, and when the bunch of you hit the dance floor— watch out!

8. When a good friend suddenly loses her job, you

a. are not surprised—she was always slacking off.

b. offer to proofread her résumé when she's ready to look for a new gig.

c. ask her if she needs a loan—she can pay you back when she's on her feet again.

9. You catch your friend's guy getting up close and personal with another woman. You

a. cannot wait to share this juicy bit of gossip.

b. call the guy, tell him what you saw, and inform him that if he doesn't speak to your friend about what he's up to, you will.

c. suck your teeth about what a loser she is when it comes to men.

10. Your friend comes out of the salon with hair that is so not hot. When she asks you to be honest, you tell her

a. you preferred her previous look, but what's important is that she likes it, and wears it with attitude.

b. she looks cute—no one really wants honesty when they say to be honest.

c. she should sue the stylist—hey, she said to be honest!

THE SCORE

Give yourself points as follows:

1. a = 1, b = 2, c = 3	**6.** a = 1, b = 2, c = 3
2. a = 2, b = 3, c = 1	**7.** a = 3, b = 2, c = 1
3. a = 3, b = 2, c = 1	**8.** a = 3, b = 1, c = 2
4. a = 1, b = 3, c = 2	**9.** a = 1, b = 2, c = 3
5. a = 2, b = 3, c = 1	**10.** a = 2, b = 1, c = 3

HERE'S THE DEAL

Fly-by-Night Friend (10 to 16 points) To you, friends are for hanging out, going shopping, hitting the clubs—and you've got a ton of them. Sure, you and your girls should wanna have fun, but you sell yourself (and them) short with such shallow relationships. Right now, your sister circle is not tight—not cutthroat, perhaps, but gossipy and fair-weather. Maybe you've never known what it's like to have a great friend, so you never learned to be one. Start choosing your friends less on surface value (the clothes they wear, the status they have) and more on deeper, richer qualities (they care about you, they have time for you, you feel comfortable around them). Once you have a few solid friendships, you will understand their value and reciprocate with your as-yet-untapped loyalty and empathy.

Solid as a Rock (17 to 23 points) Hey, girl—wanna have coffee sometime? You're the kind of friend no one can have too many of: trusting and trustworthy, compassionate and generous, honest without being brutal. You know what friendship really means—you value it, rely on it, and return it. While you may not have a hundred random chicks on speed dial, the girls you've got—from your kindergarten double Dutch pal to the new coworker you made feel welcome—would do anything for you. Or so I'd like to hope. I'm not saying take a refresher course in suspicion; just don't sleep when it comes to character judgments. Not everyone is as nice, sweet, and loyal as you:

Sometimes another girl *is* out to get your man—know what I'm saying? I just don't want you to get hurt!

Diva of Distrust (24 to 30 points) Trust much? Um, how about at all? I doubt it. While generally speaking you're not a mean girl yourself—you don't go out of your way to belittle people, and you respect their space—you sure don't bend over backward to be, well, nice. Maybe some junior-high chick stole your crush or embarrassed you in front of the whole school and you're still licking your wounds, but you've got to get over this. One way to find good friends is to start with shared interests—at least you'll have things in common to discuss, because you won't be baring your soul right away. So if you're a new mom, join a mother's group; if you want to get in shape, take an intriguing exercise class. I urge you to seek out at least one female friend you can really relate to and rely on—the relationship will enrich your life so much!

START **TODAY**, GIRLFRIEND!

My best friend from college and I were as close as two friends could ever be. We lived together our junior and senior years and became like sisters. Anything I did or thought about doing, she was the first to get the call. I cried on her shoulder when I learned my boyfriend cheated on me. When my mother passed away, she was the one who went with me to pack up Mom's house.

Once we graduated, she moved to a small town to pursue a graduate degree and I returned to New York City. We still spoke regularly, but with our diverging schedules it became more difficult. Then my girl moved to another small town, got married, and had a baby, while I was moving up the corporate ladder in New York, traveling, hanging out in clubs. I still loved her like a sister, but we didn't speak as much. After a while, it became almost impossible to reconcile our vastly different lifestyles. I still loved talking to her, but I never wanted to disturb her late at night when I got a moment to call; likewise, she didn't want to wake me up at the crack of dawn. We missed each other, but became caught up in our totally different worlds.

The truth is, I was far more to blame for us growing apart. I was gaining recognition in the realms of fashion and entertainment, and with that came the hangers-on who just wanted in on the action. While I had a sense they weren't really my girls, they were available to party, so I ignored my better instincts and spent most of my time with my new crew.

At some point, I confided in a few of them some details of an office crisis I was dealing with. I'll spare you the gory details, but it involved a well-known female rapper and a cover article for *Honey*. The incident itself was pretty ridiculous. Picture the rapper—who shall remain nameless—dressed head to toe in a fuchsia fur jumpsuit, screaming at me in the middle of a club that she "didn't say that BS you printed in your @#$%* magazine!" Fortunately, I had the interview tape to prove what we ran was a verbatim quote, but there were a few things about the whole affair I was still trying to keep quiet. A short time later, a couple of my new fake friends were at a party with the head of the rapper's record label and, in an attempt to gain favor with an even more powerful ally, told him my secrets. He and I were cool and our issues were resolved over a lunch, but I learned a valuable lesson. *Of course* folks will want to be your friend when you have access and money. But you're better off surrounding yourself with people who love you for who you are rather than what you have. I decided that I would never again confuse physical proximity with emotional closeness.

> "Surround yourself with people who love you for who you are rather than what you have."

Over the next couple of months, I focused on reestablishing tight relationships with my old friends—especially my college sister. Now she and I are closer than ever. We still don't have time to talk the way we used to, but I feel so good knowing she's just a phone call away. Today, why don't you reach out to a friend you really care about whom you may have lost touch with? Give her a call, shoot her an e-mail, or send her a card. The people who know you and your faults and still love you are more important than anything—and they will always be there for you.

Today . . .

- **Evaluate your friendships.** Do you respect and admire your friends? Or do they make you sigh and shake your head? Friends should inspire you to be a better person.
- **Tell them you love them.** Friendships are the purest relationships you've got because you choose them—you're not bound by blood like you are to your family or drawn to them physically like you are to a man. If you take them for granted, they might just walk, so treat them like gold and tell them how much they mean to you.
- **Listen to them.** When a friend wants to talk, especially if she's struggling with something, be there for her. Hear her out; ask caring questions—help her get to the root, and the solution, of her problem. Even if you don't agree with what she's doing, don't judge her.
- **Befriend yourself.** One way to become a better friend is to truly make friends with yourself. Praise yourself, treat yourself well, enjoy spending time solo, and trust your instincts. This will make you the sort of person others will want to call a friend, and get you accustomed to treating people right.

MAKE **THIS YEAR** COUNT

When I first got into journalism, I went to as many industry parties as possible. At one networking event, I met a woman who, like me, wrote style articles for women's magazines. We clicked right away since we had so much in common: We were both young, single women of color trying to make a name for ourselves in the publishing world. We even lived in the same Brooklyn neighborhood. I was glad to find a new running buddy, and we had a blast for a few months. But I began to notice that she was always in the middle of a major crisis. Her car got impounded for unpaid parking tickets, her man turned out to be a drug dealer, her wallet was stolen from a bag she left on the table at a club . . .

In the beginning, I felt sorry for her and would try to help out, even lending her money once so she wouldn't lose her apartment. But after a while, hanging out with her became exhausting. And I couldn't help but feel that much of her drama was her own fault. (I mean, who leaves

an expensive purse on a table in a crowded club? How did she not notice her man's beeper, wads of cash, and weird absences?) Still, I wanted
to be a good friend, so I continued to be there for her as she dealt with
the ongoing soap opera she called her life. In the meantime, I had my
own issues—boyfriend problems, job hassles, family conundrums—but
we never seemed to talk about my life because her plight was always
more urgent. She would call me at all hours of the day and night, regardless of what was happening in my life, to strategize about how she
could get out of her latest disaster.

I finally realized that her bad energy was like a toxic cloud, and that
instead of adding to my life all she did was drain me. I had to slowly
and gently pull myself away from her. And when I did, I felt better,
more energized and happy to face the world. This year, think about
which of your friends make you feel good and who tires you out. I'm
not saying that you should drop friends who may be going through a
tough time. You need to be there for your girls. But a real relationship
is mutual, so your friends need to be there for you in the same way that
you help them. And if you have a particularly drama-prone friend who
calls you only when she needs you, then she's not really your girl.
Prioritize your relationships with people who give as much as they receive.

This Year . . .

- **Work through the drama.** If you have unresolved issues with a
  friend you've decided is worth keeping, settle the beef. When the
  two of you are relaxed and alone, tell her you want to talk about
  something and bring it up—then hash it out. When you get it
  sorted through, move on. Really put it behind you so the friendship can start fresh.
- **Plan her party.** Take it upon yourself to organize a bash to celebrate
  one of your closest friends—whether it's her baby shower, birthday
  party, or a girls' night out to fete her new job. The time and effort
  you put into it will mean more than any amount of money you
  might spend on a gift.
- **Make one new friend.** No one needs a million best friends, but by
  the same token there's no reason not to expand your circle. Think

about what's lacking in your life—is it someone who shares an interest of yours? Are most of your girls married now, and you'd like another single friend? Do you want someone who'll encourage you to have adventures? Then seek out people who will nurture you—join a book club, take a continuing education class, volunteer in your community, etc.

- **Have a girls' getaway.** Take a weekend away with several women or a longer vacation with a close friend. Once out of your regular stomping grounds you'll discover new things about one another, and bond big-time!

- **Assess her roommate compatibility.** She may be a great girl—that doesn't mean you should live with her. Before you move in with a friend, try to make sure that your attitudes match up when it comes to housekeeping, bill paying, partying, boyfriend hanging out on the sofa in his underwear, etc. You don't want your friendship to suffer.

- **Fix her up.** Know a cool guy who needs a great woman in his life? Introduce him to one of your friends. If it doesn't work out, at least you'll have tried to bring happiness to two people you care about. If it does, hopefully the bridesmaid's dress you'll have to wear won't be too hideous!

- **Find a guy friend.** Male friends are invaluable. They tend to be fun and easygoing, and they can supply the guys' perspective on everything from relationships to what looks hot on you. Of course, there are challenges. The current man in your life may be justifiably uncomfortable about your new friend, so you'll have to deal with that. And the guy himself may like you "that way"—you have to be careful that there are no mixed signals being passed in either direction.

GET YOURS FOREVER

Somewhere toward the end of last year's holiday season, I had a major panic attack when I looked at my crazy calendar and realized I had exactly one free day to get most of my shopping done (and no clue what to get anyone on my list!). Since I needed some serious help and support, I called one of my girlfriends and we made a date to meet up on the morning of my free day to get an early start. I got to the first stop on our shopping tour just as they were pulling up the gate, and proceeded to wait for my friend. After forty-five frustrating minutes, I called her cell. Homegirl was still getting ready, but promised to hurry and meet me in half an hour. Two hours later, as I was taking a lunch break, she rolled up to the table, sat down, and ordered coffee like it was all good. "Sorry," she finally said, noticing the frosty expression on my face. "I got on a roll shopping online."

I wanted to yell at her about all the times she's screwed up our plans over the years and how flaky and selfish she is. I wanted to storm out and leave her with the bill. Instead, I

> "Good friends are like family."

thought about the loud, dramatic fights I've had with friends, men, and family. The unfair accusations and unreasonable demands. The hateful language you can never take back. And I decided to take a different approach. "I'm really annoyed with you," I told her calmly, "but let's discuss it later when we're not in a crowded restaurant." And I kept it moving.

The next day, I called her to explain how I felt. I told her in an even tone that although I care about her, I was no longer interested in our friendship unless she could be more reliable and respectful. Then I told her not to respond, but to call me back after she had a chance to absorb what I'd told her. I hung up the phone feeling great! I had avoided a public scene and given myself a chance to figure out what I needed to say to her. I hadn't yelled or said stupid, unkind things that had nothing to do with the issue at hand. I just requested that she be a decent friend or we could no longer hang out.

I have nothing against well-deserved dramatic scenes (for example, if you catch your man on a date with another woman, you have every right to dump a drink over his head!). But being a drama queen rarely accomplishes what you want. If you make a huge deal out of small things—i.e., everything—people won't know when you're really upset. And screaming at someone in the heat of the moment always makes the situation worse. When was the last time you were able to work through a problem at the top of your lungs? Don't get me wrong— controlling your emotions doesn't mean acting like a doormat. If someone is treating you badly, you need to let her know what is and is not acceptable. Then tell her to act right or be cut.

My flaky friend took a couple of days to think, then called to apologize and say she didn't want to lose me. Calmly expressing how I really felt saved our friendship. Now, I'm not going to tell you that she became a paragon of dependability overnight, but she has been trying, and I appreciate that. One of the best things you can do to nurture healthy relationships with your girls forever is to cool off and get your thoughts together before you tell it like it is. So, speak up, girlfriend—just count to ten (at least!) first.

Always . . .

- **Understand the difference between true friends and acquaintances.** Relationships with acquaintances tend to be transient. These people come into (and go out of) your life due to proximity or business or whatever. True friends, on the other hand, are there for you through thick and thin . . . and they will be, forever.
- **Be choosy.** See above, and remember that not everyone who's nice to you has your best interests at heart. Be selective about who you let into your inner circle. Give friendships a chance to develop so you can see what someone's really made of. Your time and attention are valuable, so don't be compelled to insta-bond with anyone.
- **Avoid competition.** For smart, ambitious people, competition may come naturally—but try not to be competitive with friends. If you know your girl is interested in a man, don't flirt with him. If she's saving for a purse that you can afford, don't go out and buy it. If you work in the same field, you may need to go for a job that she may also want, but just be open with her before sending your résumé.
- **Remember how sensitive she is.** It's a biological fact that, as females, our feelings get bruised easily. Tease her and she may remember those mean girls from middle school. Forget her birthday and she'll be righteously upset. Be brutally honest about what she's wearing or something she did and she'll want to hole up in her apartment for weeks. Just like you! So be kind.
- **Swear an oath to your girl.** Be trustworthy—do not blab her secrets. Do not gossip about her—no matter how juicy the situation may be. Be loyal—when she needs you, come running!

- **Respect her boundaries.** You just want to help, but sometimes your friend has to work things out on her own. Avoid giving unsolicited advice. Don't meddle in her romantic affairs, tell her why her look is outdated, or explain why she'll never get ahead at work. If she wanted your opinion, she'd ask.

DETOX YOUR FRIENDSHIPS

Let a poisonous person into your life and it can be hard to shake her loose. Try these tips for curbing, or at least controlling, toxic types—and be firm!

If she's . . .
a flake who takes advantage of your time
Tell her . . .
"I will meet you at seven-thirty, and if you're not there by seven-forty-five I'm going in without you."

If she's . . .
a troublemaker looking to lead you astray
Tell her . . .
"I've made a resolution to steer clear of gossip and too many late nights out. But you have fun!"

If she's . . .
a vampire who drains your energy with her constant drama
Tell her . . .
"I'm sorry that you've got a problem, but I'm really busy right now. Why don't you call your mom for advice?"

If she's . . .
a bossy bitch who acts like she knows best
Tell her . . .
"I appreciate that you want the best for me, but I'm going to work this out on my own."

If she's . . .
a man-stealer with her sights set on yours
Tell her . . .
"If you call him, text him, or, God forbid, touch him, I will hurt you. Do I make myself clear?"

10 FUN THINGS TO DO WITH YOUR GIRLS

Friendships do take work—you've got to give them the time and attention they deserve—but sometimes girls just wanna have fun. A few ideas:

1. **Go shoe shopping.** Then give each other strength not to buy more than one pair!
2. **Get creative.** Take on a cool project you *both* can do, like writing a children's book or even a novel, making a scrapbook of your friendship, stenciling your respective kitchens in matching patterns, etc.
3. **Travel together.** Go to an island that's sunny by day and hot by night.
4. **Promote pampering.** Make a plan with your girl to spend a Saturday doing nothing but hooking up your hair, nails, and toes. Book a massage, too, if you feel like splurging.
5. **Challenge each other.** Go for a long hike and dare each other to feel the burn.
6. **Be silly.** Attend an event with a serious snooty factor (like a high-end designer's trunk show) and act as goofy as humanly possible.
7. **Play hooky.** Take a long lunch or leave work a little early to catch a chick flick.
8. **Have a movie marathon.** Rent a few of your favorite flicks (*Love and Basketball,* anyone?), make a vat of popcorn, and have a comfy, relaxed night in.
9. **Act like guys.** Go to a professional sports game and drink beer, eat junk, yell at the players, and otherwise get rowdy.
10. **Take a road trip.** Load a cooler into the car and take off for the country. Have a picnic in a field and take a walk in the woods. Just breathe some fresh air together.

KELLY ROWLAND ON FRIENDSHIP

Though a gifted solo artist in her own right (the follow-up to her debut CD Simply Deep *is due out in 2007) and an actress just beginning to spread her wings, Kelly Rowland is best known as Beyoncé's buddy. And a great friend she is! In all my years of knowing the Destiny's Child ladies, Kelly has always been fiercely loyal to her girl and the whole Knowles crew, never having anything but loving and generous things to say. Of course, we all know about the drama years ago with DC's third member, so it's not as if Kelly's entire experience with friendship has been sweetness and joy. But I can honestly say that after all the craziness, Beyoncé, Kelly, and Michelle seem really tight. At photo shoots they would pose as a team (with Miss B often insisting on being placed on the side instead of in the middle), then giggle among themselves in a corner until the next setup. They were all cool, but Kelly was the most daring—she was the one who'd put on the crazy outfit first then talk her girls into trying it, too! Beyoncé was clearly the (often unwilling) center of attention, but Kelly had the liveliest spirit and the most influence over her crew. Needless to say, the former Destiny's Child diva has a lot of insight about girl bonding.*

Amy: **Tell me a bit about your circle of friends. Who are you tight with?**
Kelly: Of course, Beyoncé and Michelle. Solange. And my best friend, Barbara, who I know from the eighth grade. She is the sweetest person. She just had a baby yesterday—I cried my eyeballs out because I could not be there. Serena Williams—I love Serena's spirit. La La Vasquez is another close friend of mine; I love her to death. I'm also very close to Beyoncé's mom, Tina, who I call Momma T. I just love talking to her—I can be totally real and honest with her.

AB: **So many of your friends are in the industry, so they understand the stresses of the industry. Is it a little harder with Barbara?**
KR: I don't know how, but she totally understands if you can't call her back right on time. She is so funny because she keeps it real with me. If I explain a situation to her, she will say, "*Honey,* you are wrong." That is the most important part of friendship—being honest. When you are honest with somebody, that [shows] true love for them, because you don't want to see them hurt.

AB: **You want someone who loves you enough to protect you from the outside world—and from yourself if they have to. That's really hard, especially because many women of color have trust issues. Have you noticed that?**
KR: Yes, totally. I think some of it stems from our own insecurities, so it is important to know who you are as a woman. [With Destiny's Child] all three of us are very secure within ourselves, we love each

other genuinely, and we will be there for each other no matter what the situation.

AB: *How do you avoid competing with your friends?*
KR: I think it important to know that nobody is perfect and you have room for growth. Not everyone is at the same level, so if Michelle or Beyoncé do something that I admire, I'm not going to hate on it.

AB: *Are you a good friend?*
KR: My grandmother used to say that with a special friend it is important to nurture the relationship and bring something to the table. I know it is important to give good advice. I know it is important for me to spiritually cover my friends in prayer whether they are traveling or making business decisions.

AB: *How do friends make you happy?*
KR: Their energy. I can't even put a finger on it. It is just something you know you have between friends. These women are strong and independent and extremely supportive; they are blessings.

AB: *And how have they helped you through difficult times?*
KR: When me and my ex-fiancé broke off our engagement, all they heard me say was "Hello," and they were like, "We are on our way." I remember them immediately coming to the door—Beyoncé, Michelle, and Momma T. They all covered me in a four-way hug, and I just cried. In that moment I felt so good.

AB: *A lot of women prioritize men over their friendships, which I think is a mistake. Have you ever done that?*
KR: Yeah, I had to learn that [lesson] the hard way. One time I didn't call the girls for weeks. They were like, "Okay, just because you have a boyfriend does not mean that we do not count." I will never do that again!

AB: *Have you ever had any conflict or been betrayed by a friend?*
KR: One time. But she is not [in my life] anymore. When someone betrays you, it is important to search your heart. What is this person

bringing to my life, what am I bringing to hers? Friendships are supposed to be equal. For me, with this specific young lady . . . she just wasn't right.

AB: *Yet every friendship has a minor conflict here or there. What is the healthiest way to resolve a minor conflict with a friend?*
KR: I think you apologize if you are wrong. "I'm sorry I did this, and it hurt you." You think about it together, as friends. Then you need to scoot that over to the side, because it is not that important.

AB: *What have been some of the most important things you've learned about friendships?*
KR: One of the greatest ones is "Do unto others as you would have them do unto you." Treat people the way you would like to be treated. Also, put your pride and ego aside. Always know who you are as a person, be secure within yourself as a human being, and let your light shine.

PROMISE PAGE

My dreams and goals for my friendships are:

I promise that today I will:

This year I promise to:

I will always:

5

GET YOUR FAMILY TOGETHER

My mother grew up in Lackawanna, New York—a depressed stepchild to Buffalo whose only claim to fame was the Bethlehem Steel factory, an industrial behemoth that employed most of Lackawanna's men, including my grandmother's husband. Like in a lot of small towns, people tended to live their entire lives right there. Not my mom. She shook the expectation that she would get just enough local education to teach elementary public school. Instead, she traveled, alone (pretty rare for a female black teenager in 1959), to attend Antioch College in Ohio, which at that time was a liberal hotbed of civil rights activism. There, she met my dad: a leather-jacketed, goatee-wearing, jazz-loving Jewish Marxist from New York City. They quickly fell in love and married during their junior year abroad—he at the London School of Economics and she at the University of Leeds.

Their romantic adventures took them around the world (a motorcycle trip across Europe, hitchhiking through Turkey, camping in Morocco). They landed in Chicago for graduate school, and my mom became the first black person to get a Ph.D. in political science from the University of Chicago. After that, they traveled to New Jersey, where they both became assistant professors at Princeton University.

I'm not sure when the drama started, but they separated by the time I was seven and divorced before I turned nine. My dad married my stepmother (a white woman who had been one of the graduate students in his department) very soon after the divorce was final. Yeah, it was a rough time. However, my mom tried her best to make sure that my relationship with my father stayed positive and that I always felt supported and loved.

My maternal grandmother's husband died just before I was born, so she lived with or very near us throughout my formative years. And my mother eventually remarried. The four of us (me, Mom, Grandma, and my stepfather) developed a rhythm and self-sufficiency so that even as we moved from town to town, we felt solid and insulated.

But Mom was the glue that held us all together, and when she died, everything fell to pieces. My grandmother couldn't handle the loss and insisted on returning to frigid Buffalo. I had barely gotten her into an apartment when she developed rapidly progressing Alzheimer's, and I then had to move her into a nursing home. I visited her for years, long after she stopped recognizing me. My stepfather also came apart and, in a move that I can only assume reflected his utter terror at being alone, tried to take a significant chunk of the money Mom left to me. For a long time, I mourned not just Mom, but the loss of my stable if unconventional family. I even questioned whether I'd *ever* had family that I could count on, and started to distance myself from the few relatives I had left.

A year or so after my mom's death, I received a beautifully written note from a former hairstylist I hadn't seen in years. Growing up, my family developed a ritual of going to the hair salon every Saturday. Every week, Grandma, Mom, and I, all wearing our respective Saturday morning wig, head scarf, and ponytail, would pile into the car, stop for doughnuts and juice on the way, then spend the day getting our hair washed and set. We would repeat this ritual wherever we lived—and when I went to college, it was one of the things I was most homesick for. This hairstylist who wrote to me was from St. Louis, where we lived for a while at the end of my high school years; she had only just heard about my mom passing away. In her card, she talked about how we were such a nice family and how she always loved to see our three generations come through her door, arm in arm, laughing and offering doughnuts to the entire room. She couldn't possibly have realized how much her words would mean to me: It made me understand how special my upbringing truly was.

> "Ultimately, you have the power to choose your family."

I challenge you to find more than a few families that fit into the white-picket-fence model of what American family units are supposed to look like. And even if they do on the outside, you know that behind closed doors every home has its own unique issues as well as its joys. Instead of constantly bemoaning everything I didn't have, I made peace with my dad, started calling my aunt and remaining grandparents more frequently, and began thinking about what kind of family I wanted to create for myself.

As my mother was, black women have traditionally been the rock of our households. Unfortunately, too many of us grow up without fathers, and watch our moms work overtime to put food on the table and buy us schoolbooks. And too often, we overcompensate by having babies at an early age or by accepting bad treatment from men—all to fill a void that we retain from our family situations. We also frequently end up following in our mothers' footsteps by shouldering the responsibility of making our households function, regardless of what that does to our personal happiness. Even if you don't recognize it in yourself, I know you've met a sister who has become defensive and emotionally "hard" as a result of some of this trauma.

One of the most difficult things we all have to learn is how to cope with family and the accompanying responsibility in a more healthy, fulfilling way. While I've never had an easy time with every member of my family, the dynamic of dealing with them has taught me invaluable lessons about myself. And maybe that's the trick: recognizing that no one's family is ideal and that the things we don't love about our relatives can make us take a more honest look at who we are, who we want to be—and who we want to share our lives with. Ultimately, you have the power to choose your closest family—whether that means your sister circle, a husband, even having or adopting a child. Never settle, girlfriend. But at the same time remember that human beings are, well, human; no one's perfect and we're all on this journey together. Realize that the people you love the most may be the most different from you—and understand that it's in accepting those differences that you'll grow as an individual.

Quiz: Are Your Family Affairs in Order?

Your family may seem totally separate from your social world and career sphere, but the truth is, how you feel about and deal with your parents, siblings, steps, etc., affects your success and satisfaction in other areas. This quiz will help you see what facets of family life you may need to confront.

1. Just like your mother, you

a. are always falling for the wrong man.

b. are the person who takes care of everything and everyone.

c. have good teeth, a pretty voice, and a mind of your own.

2. When it comes to your father you wish

a. there were more men out there like him.

b. he had been there for your mom more.

c. your relationship was better.

3. Around the holidays you are generally

a. exhausted—you do so much shopping and cooking and traveling.

b. depressed—all that forced merrymaking in close quarters.

c. amused—it's fun to catch up with everyone.

4. When the man you've been seeing asks about your family you

a. get uncomfortable and change the subject.

b. haul out the photo album and regale him for three hours.

c. tell him the basics and ask him about his people.

5. Your sister, who lives in another town, says she misses you. You

a. visit her for a weekend of shopping, partying, and talking, talking, talking!

b. assume she wants something and wish she would cut to the chase.

c. say you miss her, too, but don't suggest a plan for getting together.

6. The TV show that best depicts your family is

a. *The Jeffersons.*

b. *The Sopranos.*

c. *The Cosbys.*

7. Unlike your mom, you intend to

a. wait till your career is on track to have kids.

b. take time for yourself—and not feel guilty about it.

c. do *everything* differently.

8. When you bring your boyfriend home to meet the family, you hope

a. your parents will deem him good enough for you.

b. no one does or says anything to embarrass you.

c. he can roll with it when someone suggests charades.

9. You and your siblings

a. get along fine.

b. are supertight.

c. tend to deal with each other better than any of you deal with your parents.

10. When a cherished aunt passes, you

a. fight back your tears and do all you can to make things easier on your cousins.

b. don't go to the funeral—too much drama.

c. compose an inspiring, uplifting speech to say at the service.

THE SCORE

Give yourself points as follows:

1. a = 3, b = 1, c = 2   **6.** a = 1, b = 3, c = 2

2. a = 2, b = 1, c = 3   **7.** a = 2, b = 1, c = 3

3. a = 1, b = 3, c = 2   **8.** a = 1, b = 3, c = 2

4. a = 3, b = 2, c = 1   **9.** a = 1, b = 2; c = 3

5. a = 2, b = 1, c = 3   **10.** a = 1, b = 3, c = 2

HERE'S THE DEAL

Family Control Freak (10 to 16 points) Who are they gonna call when they need comfort, support, maybe a loan? Yes, you, the family caretaker. Chances are you acquired this role from your mom—she was responsible for everybody and never took time for herself—or you were raised in a rigidly do-the-right-thing household. It's great to be a giver, but believing everyone "wants something" from you can make you cynical, and even—ironically—distant and cold (you give and give, but you don't *feel* much). This will exacerbate when you start your own family. Do you really want to be the type of wife and mother everyone depends/dumps on? Put yourself on more equal footing with family members. Consider taking a real vacation during the holidays (they'll live without your pecan pies!). Tell your sister you're busy when she needs a last-minute babysitter; teach your dad how to use a computer so he can research his own insurance.

Remarkably Functional Relations (17 to 23 points) Okay, your family affairs are too perfect for anything but the Disney Channel! You get along great with your parents and siblings without feeling compelled to bend over backward to earn/keep their love. Clearly your folks nurtured independence and encouraged you to feel good about yourself without feeling like you "owe them something." Sure, you may still spat with your brother at times or roll your eyes at your mom's satellite dish of a church hat, but you were raised right in an environment of respect, trust, and understanding. This will serve you well when you start a family of your own: You won't feel guilty asking your husband to share the load of housework and child rearing, and you'll pass on the importance of developing a healthy sense of self to your kids.

Drama in Your DNA (24 to 30 points) You've got more family issues than Kleenex has tissues. Whether it was an absent/neglectful father, a demanding mother, so many siblings you couldn't hear yourself think, or some loaded combination of the above, your upbringing may have been a downright mess. And, like most women of color, you probably never uttered a peep of complaint, but just slapped on your game face and accepted your lot in life. Well, it's time to sort out your family drama—now!—before you continue the pattern and pass the problems on to your own kids. Telling yourself you're nothing like your mother or that you'd never get involved with a man like your dad isn't enough. To truly deal, you've got some serious confrontations ahead—both with family members and within yourself. The healing that happens once you are brave enough to do this work is well worth it. And you needn't go it alone; help is out there.

START **TODAY**, GIRLFRIEND!

The last time I saw Lisa "Left Eye" Lopes was at a party I threw for *Honey* magazine's annual spring fashion issue. Unlike all the other celebs in attendance, she wasn't rocking flashy designer gear, nor was she surrounded by an entourage or hulking bodyguards. Instead, in jeans and a T-shirt, she spent much of the evening sitting on a sofa, drinking water, and chatting with friends and fans. She seemed calm yet very intense. People were drawn to her, even as she attempted to have a low-key night out. There was no hint of the "crazy" third member of TLC, the wild child notorious for burning down her boyfriend's house. Lisa had really grown and seemed content. That's what I held on to when I heard about the car accident that took her life.

While TLC stood out as strong, smart, and sexy role models for a generation of young women of all colors, it was the unpublicized things Lisa did that impressed me the most: her adoption of a ten-year-old child, her involvement in the Make-a-Wish Foundation and the Lost Boys Foundation, her will to change the way she lived to have a more pure and healthy existence. Clearly, Lisa had become a deep and interesting person during the period before her untimely death. Unfortunately, as I worked on the "Left-Eye" tribute article *Honey* published after her passing, I spoke with many people close to Lisa who told me that, because she had changed so drastically, so quickly, they never got the opportunity to tell her how remarkable she was, what she meant to them, and how much they loved her.

That really made me stop and think: What if I lost a loved one tomorrow? Would he or she know the depth of my feelings? When I closed (industry lingo for *finished*) that issue of the magazine, I called everyone I loved and told them what they meant to me and why. It was a simple thing and it took only a couple of evenings. But it gave me the satisfaction of knowing that the people who meant the most to me *knew* it.

I urge you to start improving family relationships today by calling one relative and telling her what she means to you. If it's too hard or awkward to call, send a note or an e-card. And, girlfriend, I'm not saying you need to go into crazy detail—your message can be very simple and brief. Just step back, think about who means the most to you, and show her your appreciation.

Today . . .

- **Take a look—literally.** Pull out a family photo album you haven't perused in a while. Reminisce about what was going on when the pictures were taken. (Even if the memory isn't happy, deal with it, then move on.) Check out who you resemble. Think about whom you'd like to reconnect with.

- **Offer an update.** Call a family member and fill her in on what's been going on in your life. This will make her feel involved with you, no matter how far away she may be. Devote the rest of the conversation to what's happening with her.
- **Banish bad blood.** Think back to a petty disagreement you might have had with a relative and didn't resolve effectively. In your mind, forgive the person and also own up to your part in the misunderstanding. You needn't raise the issue the next time you see her; just putting it in the past and greeting her with love may be enough.

MAKE **THIS YEAR** COUNT

Since journalism was my third field after stints in finance and fashion, I was very eager to make up for lost time and establish a name for myself. When I say I was focused on my career, I mean I was *focused*. Late nights and weekends at work were par for the course. I'm not complaining, because I loved what I was doing, but it left me little time for anything else. When I had a spare hour, I sneaked in a dance class. If I had a spare afternoon, I'd try to catch up with a girlfriend. The rare evenings I wasn't in my office or out networking were devoted to dating. And when I met my husband, Jeff, all bets were off—I wanted to spend all my free time with him.

Despite the effort I'd made to reconnect with family members after mourning my mom, it suddenly felt too difficult to keep up the relationships. To rationalize my lack of contact I'd tell myself I was just temporarily overwhelmed—that things would calm down soon. But my schedule never seemed to free up.

Eventually, I went to a holiday family gathering and found out that my aunt and uncle were divorcing, my cousin was moving in with her boyfriend, and my sister was practically engaged! I couldn't believe I was so out of the loop. For years, I had felt sorry for myself for having a family that didn't stay in touch, but when I heard all the news I'd missed, I realized that I was the one at fault. I had prioritized everything other than family.

As Jeff and I became closer, I was inspired by his relationship with his family. Not only is he in close contact with his parents (he speaks with them just about every day), but he is also tight with his brother and sister, calling them at least once a week. He goes home to Ohio for holidays and to visit whenever he can, claiming that he gets strength from being around his people. Is everything hunky-dory all the time? Of course not. But he loves his family deeply and there's nothing he wouldn't do for them. As he and I were contemplating creating our own family, I was truly grateful for the example of his: the closeness of his parents who had been married for more than forty years, the warm way his siblings welcomed me into their fold, and the way they all rallied around one another whenever anything was amiss.

When Jeff and I moved into our apartment, one of the first things we did was to get a huge grill and lounge chairs for our deck so we could invite people to come and hang out. We figured it was the best way for us to see folks we love. Now we try to have family over as often as possible. The summer Max was born, we had our local family (my dad, stepmother, sister, aunt, and cousin, and Jeff's brother, his wife, and our niece) to our home at least once or twice a month. It was great because Max got comfortable with his extended family and we stayed connected—over hot dogs and ribs!

> "This year, plan at least one day to get together with family members."

This year, plan at least one day to get together with family members. Be the one to initiate this. If you don't have room to entertain everyone at home, go to a park or the beach for a picnic or barbecue, or choose a restaurant (it doesn't have to be fancy). If you don't live near family, visit some folks you haven't seen in a while (those cousins down South you keep meaning to call, for example). Pack the car and take a road trip, or find an inexpensive flight and head out their way. Just make an effort to reach out, then continue to keep in contact. We all get so busy that it becomes easy to take for granted the people who matter most.

This Year . . .

- **End the excuses.** Go through your calendar inputting the dates of family members' birthdays and anniversaries. Then make random notes reminding yourself to call various relatives for no reason.

- **Send a newsletter.** One great way to keep people abreast of what's going on in your world is to create a family newsletter that you send out once a year, or as often as quarterly. You can include photos and artwork, and have each member of your immediate family write his or her own contribution. Need help pulling one together? Plug "family newsletter" into your search engine and you'll find lots of Web sites dedicated to ideas.
- **Become independent.** If you're still living with family or are otherwise financially reliant on a relative, do your best to move out and establish your freedom. This will help put you on more even ground with those folks.
- **Pick a day a month.** Schedule family time once a month. This can be anything from a full-scale reunion to a one-on-one with your sister.
- **Make lasting peace.** If you've got a beef with a family member, try to resolve it. Do this during a calm moment by yourselves (not in the middle of Thanksgiving dinner), and listen to her side. If you can't clear things up in one session, tell her that it's important to you that you do, and keep at it until you come to terms.

GET YOURS FOREVER

A long time ago I mentored a really bright, sweet high school girl from an inner-city neighborhood. She was so smart that her school counselors had encouraged her to join a mentoring program so she could see alternatives beyond her troubled surroundings. Her school was in a violent area and the dropout rate was astronomical. Though she was earning straight As, studying at home was difficult. Neither of her parents went to college and they were struggling to get by. Worse, her father was a recovering drug addict and her mother had a violent temper. The stories she told me made me ashamed of obsessing over my problems, which seemed so trivial in comparison.

When I met her, her grades were beginning to drop and she was talking about quitting high school to start earning money to help her family. When I first tried to talk her out of it, she resisted, saying she just couldn't see the point of busting her butt in school when she was going to end up like everyone she knew: working day and night only to live paycheck to paycheck. Telling her how much potential she had and how it would be a shame to waste it did nothing to motivate her. The only examples she had were her unhappy family and her classmates, none of whom seemed to aspire to improve their situation.

Finally, in desperation, I took her to see a college friend of mine who was from a rough area in the Bronx. Growing up, my girl lived in the projects in a two-bedroom apartment with one parent and three brothers, one of whom is now in jail. She was the only one to attend college—and when she graduated she got a job as an assistant to an advertising executive, and rose through the ranks to become an account executive at a prestigious advertising agency.

While I had been soft-pedaling my advice to my mentee, nervous about being too confrontational, my friend had no such issues. She sat this girl down and told her that she'd better wake up to how the world really worked. Yes, her family was messed up and her school was a hellhole and she had no college fund sitting in a bank account. "So, you gonna decide to have a miserable life just because you don't have a silver spoon?" my friend challenged her. "And you think that everyone with a silver spoon just has to lay back and let their maids feed them grapes? No, girl. You've got to work for the life you want, and the harder you work the more you'll enjoy it when you get there."

My mentee was pretty silent on the subway back from visiting my friend and I worried that the tough love had been a little too harsh. But before we got back to her home, she turned to me and asked if there really were people who could pay for her college. I helped her do some research, and she ended up getting a scholarship to a state university, graduated with honors, and is now applying to law schools. She wants to be a public defender so she can represent her peers who weren't lucky or focused enough to break out of the cycle of poverty, crime, and drugs.

"Love your family, but live your life."

Recognize that as much as you love your family, you do not have to turn into them. Whatever your family situation, rich or poor or middle class, *you* control your destiny. Your future is in no way limited by your past. You don't have to fight with your man just because your par-

ents battled; you don't have to live in a ghetto or a suburb simply because that's where you're from; you don't have to be a conservative
Republican like your dad or a stay-at-home mom like your mother.
You can go to college or live in a foreign country or open a business
or become an artist. It is *your* choice, girlfriend. Love your family, but
live your life.

Always . . .

- **Maintain meaningful connections.** Make keeping up with family
  members a habit. Don't let too much time go by between calls,
  e-mails, or visits. But if you do, don't let that prevent you from getting back in touch. They're family!

- **Recognize toxic relatives.** Yes, you have obligations to blood, but if
  someone in your family simply is not healthy for you to hang out
  with, keep that person at bay. Just because you're related doesn't
  mean you have to endure unlimited exposure to her. Think small
  doses!

- **Face your family responsibility.** Don't act like a child when it
  comes to your relatives—that means no mooching. Go the extra
  mile and help out, especially with older folks and children. And if
  and when you have your own kids, put them above all others and
  be the best parent you can be.

- **Learn from your elders.** Invite the older generation to impart their
  wisdom and experience—they have so much to share. Whether you
  ask your grandmother for her cornbread recipe or listen to
  Granddad talk about the old days, you'll learn about yourself, understand your parents, and give the old folks the attention they deserve.

- **Accept unconventional family structures.** Your aunt's been married
  four times? Your sister is helping to raise her boyfriend's children?
  Your gay cousin wants you to be the maid of honor at his wedding?
  Your mom adopts her new husband's child? The "typical American
  family" is whatever yours happens to be. Accept it, support it, and
  love it; it's the only one you've got.

DON'T LET DADDY DRAMA RUIN YOUR RELATIONSHIP

If your pops wasn't exactly Cliff Huxtable, deal with it now, once and for all.

1. **Allow for the pain.** Nothing hurts quite like an absent father, and it doesn't just go away when you become an adult. Let yourself feel that pain, and, if necessary, seek counseling to help ease it.
2. **Keep on forgiving.** Even if you don't get a chance to hash things out with your dad, forgive him his human failings.
3. **Find some male friends.** Get to know men as people. Find out that they're not all like your dad.
4. **Don't let history repeat itself.** Avoid getting into relationships with men that mirror what your mom went through with your dad. Address conflicts in your own romantic relationships—don't scream and rant, or pretend they don't exist. Stop looking for a father replacement in the men you date. Often, these patterns aren't conscious, so if you find yourself making these mistakes, consider seeing a therapist to help you break the cycle.
5. **Let Mr. Right see your vulnerable side.** You may have built up walls when it comes to men, and perhaps this defense has worked for you. But when you meet the right guy, remember you don't have to be tough all the time. He will love you for your softness as much as your strength.

5 WAYS TO APPRECIATE WHERE YOU CAME FROM

1. **Chart your family tree.** Plug "family tree" into a search engine for research ideas.
2. **Spend a day with your mom, doing whatever she wants to do.** And thank her on your birthday. Trust me, she'll appreciate it more than you can imagine.

3. **Organize a family reunion.** Yes, it's a huge project, but someone's got to do it. Besides, it will all be worthwhile when you get to do the electric slide with your Virginia cousins!

4. **Visit where your grandparents were raised.** Sure, you may be living the cosmopolitan life, but remember the sacrifices your elders likely made so you could drop ten dollars on a cocktail.

5. **Guard the images.** Take those old crinkled black-and-white photos of your family out of the drawer and place them in a photo album with acid-free paper (to protect photos long-term). Or frame them in a collage format and hang it on your wall so you get opportunities to talk about your family whenever people visit you.

MO'NIQUE ON FAMILY

Though best known for her public life as an outspoken comedienne, actress, and author, Mo'Nique is a wife and mother—most recently of twin boys. I wanted to sit down and get real with her about family matters since I knew she'd have a refreshing take. But what I didn't anticipate was how warm and loving she'd be. Mo'Nique's public persona is somewhat brash and feisty, but get her in private and a whole other side comes out. I spoke with Mo'Nique on the phone while she was hanging out with her twin sons and enjoying some down time. Sure she was funny and outspoken, but I could also feel the deep love she had for her family right through the phone. Her voice would even change when she was talking to her young boys, getting softer and more intimate. We had a really special conversation, both for what was said and for what was left unsaid as she interacted with her crew.

Amy: *How do you define success?*

Mo'Nique: Success is simple: It's happiness. If I am happy, I'm successful. When I first came to Hollywood and got *The Parkers,* money started coming in. I got the house and cars and trips, but I wasn't happy, so I couldn't appreciate it. Now that I'm married to my best friend of twenty-five years [Mo'Nique and Sidney Hicks got married in 2005] and I have two more beautiful children, when I come home I can just totally unwind and be free. My babies are healthy, my husband is healthy, and I am healthy.

AB: *Tell me how your life has changed now that your family has grown.*
M: It seems like my career got much busier since I had the twins. I'm on the road every weekend. But because I am best friends with my husband, he totally understands my life. He understands what I do. If you balance it out, you do not have to give up anything. You can have it all.

AB: *There is so much pressure to be supermom, but it can be hard to do it all.*
M: Some people would look at me and say that I'm a supermom; some would say that I'm a horrible mom. It depends on their definition of a great mom. I have been gone every weekend since my babies were three months old, but I make sure everything is taken care of. I know that the work I'm putting in right now is so their lives can be easier than mine.

AB: *Were you nervous about getting married for the third time?*
M: I was so excited, because I knew what I was getting. I know what I have in my husband. I have known him since I was fourteen. You know how women say, "I want to marry my best friend." I literally married my best friend.

AB: *Was that friendship missing in your previous marriages? Is it about trust at the end of the day?*
M: Definitely. The other guys I married were not bad guys. We just didn't *know* each other. You get over the "Oh, he is cute, she is cute," and when you really get to know them it is like, "Oh, I don't like that, it doesn't make me feel good."

AB: *So, clearly before you marry someone, you want to really get to know him. What do you think about living with people before marriage?*
M: I think it's great. We get so stuck on the piece of paper, but you have girlfriends and boyfriends who act like married people. They pay bills together, they raise kids together. So what's the difference other than the law saying, "This is your wife."

AB: *So your definition of family is not about being married, but being committed to each other?*

M: Yeah. It is about that total trust, honesty, and open communication where there is nothing too crazy, too insane, nothing you can't say.

AB: *Many of us grew up with family drama. Did you learn any lessons from your childhood that you used to create a happy family of your own?*

M: What I learned from my family is never play favoritism with my children. I would never have one child feel different than the other. I want them to all grow up with the feeling of, "Wow, we had a wonderful time, we were treated good, we were treated fairly."

AB: *I'm sure like all married people, you and your husband don't see eye to eye on everything. Do you make an effort for your kids not to see you argue?*

M: I saw my parents argue, I saw them not be lovey-dovey all the time, but I think that was very healthy. I don't think a kid should see a mom and dad fight, but it is okay to disagree. And when that child sees you come back together even after you disagree, they understand, "This ain't nothing that will make us walk away from each other; we just disagree."

AB: *Have you ever had a conflict with a family member that was difficult to resolve?*

M: My sister, but she was sick at the time—she was a junkie. She's been clean for ten years, thank you, God. It was very hard and painful, and I don't think we every really resolved it, I think we just moved on.

AB: *Do you think that is the key? Letting go and realizing that family is family, and they have their flaws? Or should you try to talk it out?*

M: I think it is extremely important to talk it out, even when it's painful, because it allows you to grow as a family.

AB: *Your family must rely on you a lot. Do you find yourself figuring out how to say no to people?*

M: Yup, but I have become great at it. I've practiced it in different languages! Family has a sense of entitlement. They feel, "If you live like that, we should live like that. If you drive that, we should drive that." It took me a long time, but once I got to a comfortable space, I was like, "You know what? I've done enough!" And that is part of my success, too. I stopped feeling bad, like, "Oh, God, they are going to be mad with me." Now I don't give a damn. When I got to a point that was like, "I'm not going to do that," it was not because I didn't have it [to give], I just wanted to tell you no because you need to stand on your own. Every time I tell you yes, it makes you weaker.

AB: *Sometimes it's so difficult to say no, even the twentieth time your mom asks you to contribute to the church bake sale, or your cousin is asking you* **again** *to babysit on a Saturday night. How can we resolve that in our hearts—say no and still feel good about ourselves?*
M: You can't have it both ways. If you say yes to something you don't want to do, you get mad. And if you say no, you are bothered because you think you are being selfish and inconsiderate and only thinking of you. Say yes if it will make you happy, because if you are unhappy, you can make everyone else around you feel bad.

AB: *Tell me some of the important lessons you have gotten from your family.*
M: My dad taught me to be a lion, and get what I want. If there's something you want, find a way to get it. I have heard people in Hollywood say, "Oh, no, we are not going to go with *fat*." I had to figure out another way to make it happen, because I really believed in me.

My sister taught me what not to do. She lived on the fast track. I watched her go from a beauty queen to a dope fiend. I could not understand how this beautiful woman could allow something like that to overtake her. I watched her go through that disease and I said, "Never will I do that."

AB: *What about your mom?*
M: My mom taught me how to be a mom. My mom was a typical mother. She cooked dinner at six o'clock. She checked our homework and combed our hair before she put us to bed. She believed that this is what a woman should do, even though she worked.

AB: *Do you think that a man and a woman having certain roles is the key to a happy family?*

M: Not at all. I believe that people should stop getting caught up in the way they think it should be and do what works for them. Like when a man and woman get married and think: "She is supposed to cook and clean, and he is supposed to bring in the money." Well, it may not work that way for those people. He may be able to clean a house until it's sparkling and she might have a big job, so let's not play roles here. Let's all do what we need to do to make it work.

AB: *Have you learned any lessons from yourself—from being a mom to having a third marriage?*

M: See, in this marriage, this is the first time I have been married to a "man." Now, I don't want to say this to put the other two down, but I've always been the "man" in my relationships. I've always been the dominant one. I've always made the decisions. In this relationship, I'm very clear that I am a woman and Sidney is the man.

AB: *So even though you think roles are outdated, you still think that it is important for a woman to be a woman and for a man to be a man?*

M: Yes. At nighttime when I go to bed, I always make sure I have on sexy lingerie and always make sure I smell good. Because when my man lies next to me, I want him to know he is lying next to his woman. I always make sure that I'm presentable, even on my bad days. I don't go back and forth with my husband, because I trust his word. And he has never given me a reason not to.

AB: *So if you don't agree, what happens?*

M: If we don't agree, we will discuss it. We agree to disagree. As black women, we've been taught to fight, fight, fight, and sometimes that is needed. But with my husband, if we have a disagreement, and he says, "I understand what you are saying, but I think that it is best that we try it this way," I say okay, because I trust what my man tells me. But I'm married to such a man that if he is wrong, he will say, "You know what, baby, my bad—I'm wrong." Once we talk it through again, he will say, "You know what, you are right, baby."

AB: *Do you have any final thoughts for women on family and being what you want to be versus what your family expects you to be?*

M: Remember that this is your life. Not your mother's, not your father's, not your husband's, not your children's, not your friend's. It is only yours.

PROMISE PAGE

My dreams and goals for my family
relationships are:

_____
_____
_____
_____
_____

I promise that today I will:

_____
_____
_____
_____

This year I promise to:

_____
_____
_____
_____

I will always:

_____
_____
_____
_____

6

GET THAT GIG

During my first few months of working at *Teen People,* I gave a speech at a Delta Sigma Theta function. My sorority—so you know I was thrilled! Afterward, one of my sorors asked me how I got to be editor of *Honey,* and then *Teen People.* I rattled off the obligatory "Well, I went to school and I studied real hard, then I got a job and I worked real hard, blah blah blah." Of course, this was all true, but, upon further reflection, not the real deal. What I should have said was that I got these cool jobs by pushing myself to do things I had no idea I could do, by following my passion, and, most important, by accepting risk and, therefore, fear.

As a liberal arts major graduating from a liberal arts college, I quickly realized I was qualified for basically nothing in the actual job market. Still, I did have a diploma and that let me land a gig—and on paper, an excellent one—at a prestigious Wall Street bank. So I bought a briefcase and some sensible pumps and prepared to get my corporate career on. I was the envy of all my friends, but I secretly hated it. It's not that I wasn't good at it. In fact, it was easy. Too easy. I crunched numbers all day, every day, and felt like I was sleepwalking. Still, the thought of resigning was terrifying. Like so many of us, I'd been taught that job prestige and financial stability were the primary goals.

Well, I threw those life lessons right out the window when I decided to leave Wall Street and go into the fashion industry, an obsession of mine since I rocked my first pair of Sergio Valente jeans in fifth grade. I went to Parsons School of Design to study fashion merchandising, but when I realized that my subsequent position as an assistant buyer at Lord & Taylor consisted mostly of sitting in a dingy cubicle in a windowless back office, calculating markdowns on polyester knit dresses, I wasn't too sure I'd made the right decision. Fashion seemed a glamorous alternative to finance, but I wanted to *love* my career; I wanted to wake up each morning excited about the day in front of me. I took another deep breath and quit to become a writer.

While writing had always been my biggest love (yes, bigger than the Sergio Valente jeans!), I had no idea how to earn a real living doing it. And I didn't at first. Because no one would pay me to write, I contributed articles to Web sites—for free. Those "clips" (writing samples, in journo-speak) helped me get longer features, and after my first year of grad school, I landed a writing job at a start-up Web site.

Eventually I became the fashion and beauty features editor at *Essence,* moving up soon after to head their lifestyle department. There

"Be happy and success will come."

I fell in love with journalism as the ultimate profession for a curious person who likes to speak her mind. And it was the desire to have a voice—and to ultimately give voice to my peers—that led me to *Honey.* But it was my risk tolerance and acceptance of uncertainty that got me the job as editor-in-chief.

I'll never forget the day I ran into Keith Clinkscales, the founder of Vanguarde Media, the publishing company that owned *Honey.* I'd been working on my own business plan for a lifestyle magazine directed at young urban women, one that would address our unique questions and concerns and represent our distinct aesthetic. So when I recognized Keith (from a business magazine profile) sitting in the *Essence* lobby one day, calmly reading a newspaper, I ignored my nervousness, marched over, and stuck out my hand. "Hi, I'm Amy Barnett and I have some ideas for a magazine that I'd like to share with you." He looked a bit startled but gave me his e-mail address, and thus began our discussion about publishing for the urban demographic and our negotiation for my ultimate role at *Honey.*

During the several months it took Keith to realize that I was right for the job, I summoned every ounce of courage and confidence I ever had. I swallowed any self-doubt about my ability to do the job and convinced him that I had what it took to make that magazine successful. Still, when he called to offer the position, I had trouble believing what I was hearing. I'd achieved a major goal by the age of thirty!

Of course, I was petrified, but I pushed through it, believed in myself, and just knew I'd figure it out as I went along. And I did. As the editor of *Honey,* I doubled its circulation and brought national attention to the magazine. Best of all, I was finally able to combine my love for fashion, writing, and business into one dream job. I couldn't wait to get to the office every day!

As much as I loved *Honey,* I felt I should continue to push myself. I knew I was too young to have already reached the pinnacle of my career. As well, I felt I had another calling: to edit a major mainstream magazine. People of color, particularly African Americans, are sorely underrepresented in senior positions at nonethnic magazines. At the time, there was only one black editor-in-chief of a major mainstream magazine in the country (Mark Whitaker at *Newsweek*), and there had never been a black female head of a mainstream consumer publication. Looking around the landscape of journalists, I realized this was *my* door to break down. I believed I could be even more of a role model—for women of color and for a mainstream audience—if I could achieve that history-making goal.

So I set another huge and seemingly impossible target for myself—and began working toward it. I networked and developed relationships, joined professional organizations, built my reputation as a journalist, and targeted specific companies and publications. I entered and lost a couple of battles for editor-in-chief positions, until the top spot at *Teen People* came up.

Time Inc. had never appointed a black person to run any of its key consumer titles, and *Teen People* was a huge one. A sister publication to *People,* the world's most widely read magazine, at its peak *Teen People* was a 1.45 million circulation magazine with a monthly readership of 14 million—the largest readership of any teen title in the market. Again, I was afraid that the job was too big, that the corporate heads of Time Inc. wouldn't accept me into their ranks. But I swallowed my fear, and worked on convincing them that I was the right person for the job. Urban culture drives pop culture, I argued, and teens are clearly influenced by pop culture more than any other demographic. I'd been working in the urban market for three years and was, therefore, an expert in what teens cared about.

> "You are smart and resourceful and creative enough to do anything you want."

Ultimately, they agreed—and offered me the job!

If I had followed the professional advice I received when I graduated from college, I would still be slogging away in finance or law—in a position I'd hate, probably doing a mediocre job because I would be desperate to "punch out" every evening. Most of us are steered toward highly regarded professions (lawyer, doctor, engineer, etc.) where money is "guaranteed" and success is respected. It's so difficult to go against convention—especially as a person of color with opportunities—because God forbid you "squander" your advantages. Instead, I decided to honor my passions and believe in my dreams. Conventional wisdom says stay the course, even if you hate your job. I say be happy and success will come.

Pushing yourself means attempting things you're not entirely sure you can do and setting goals that are beyond what is easily achievable. It means trying different things until you find the field you love, even if the salary isn't great at first (trust me—if you have passion for a profession, the money will follow). This is scary, but it's the only way I know to be truly successful and live a full life. Each time I quit one of those early "great" jobs I had, I was afraid, yes, but also very excited. I'm not saying to start working on your letter of resignation because you've always dreamed of taming tigers for Ringling Bros. But life, after all, is possibility. Think about what you absolutely love, prepare yourself, then do whatever you have to so that you're doing it every single day.

Quiz: Are You the Head Honey in Charge?

To feel fulfilled in your career, you've got to build more than your bank account. Take this quiz to find out if you've got your eyes on the *real* prize.

1. You just awoke from a horrible nightmare. In it, you were
a. standing—stark naked!—in front of a large group of laughing, jeering people.
b. stuck in a deep, dark hole and could barely breathe.
c. trying to get from point A to point B, but all kinds of crazy obstacles impeded you.

2. You had a job interview today, and are confident you aced it because

a. your look was tight.

b. your résumé is impeccable.

c. you asked a lot of probing questions.

3. Maybe you don't love everyone at your current job, but for the most part your work friends are

a. cool people who share your passion for life.

b. fun to party and gripe with.

c. intelligent and motivated to succeed.

4. You have a T-shirt with your personal career motto printed on it. The T-shirt reads

a. "The early bird catches the worm."

b. "Money isn't everything."

c. "Work is a four-letter word."

5. You've been at your current job for six months and can't keep pretending anymore—you hate it! You

a. come in late, split early, and basically stop applying yourself. If they lay you off, you can collect unemployment while looking for another gig.

b. grin and bear it for another six months before thinking about a move—to quit any sooner would look awful on your résumé.

c. explain to your boss why this isn't a good fit. If you two can't figure out a solution more suited to your talents, resign with plenty of notice—so she can find a replacement and you can search for something better.

6. Your boss asks for your help preparing a huge presentation. You say you'll do it, but are a bit resentful of the extra hours because

a. it will interfere with your continuing education class in Web design.

b. promotions in your department were just recently made, so there's no chance working on this will result in immediate career gratification.

c. you intended to spend the time planning your best friend's bridal shower.

7. One of your coworkers hasn't been pulling her weight lately. You

a. tell her you're sick of her slacking off and if she doesn't step up you'll complain to the boss.

b. ask her if anything's wrong and what you can do to help.

c. make sure the powers that be see you shine against her lackluster performance.

8. When you come down with a terrible head cold, you

a. call in sick. You're worthless when you're stuffed up, and you don't want to infect the whole place.

b. take an extra day to really get your strength back. Never underestimate the healing powers of a mani-pedi.

c. take massive doses of OTC meds and drag your butt in to work, where you belong.

9. Your boss wants some last-minute changes on a project you've practically completed. You

a. call your girl to complain for ten curse-filled minutes, then make the changes, whether you agree with them or not.

b. tell your boss the changes are a great idea (even if you don't really think so) and make them with a smile.

c. consider the changes thoughtfully. If you don't believe they'll improve the outcome, express your reasons to your boss. If she convinces you they make sense, you keep it moving and make the changes.

10. Your boyfriend gets a huge promotion and raise. You are

a. happy for him but a little jealous—men have it so much easier in the business world.

b. inspired by his achievements to pursue your own dreams as diligently as he does.

c. ecstatic—he's got to pop the question now, he's just got to!

THE SCORE

Give yourself points as follows:

1. a = 3, b = 1, c = 2		**6.** a = 2, b = 3, c = 1
2. a = 1, b = 3, c = 2		**7.** a = 1, b = 2, c = 3
3. a = 2, b = 1, c = 3		**8.** a = 2, b = 1, c = 3
4. a = 3, b = 2, c = 1		**9.** a = 1, b = 3, c = 2
5. a = 1, b = 3, c = 2		**10.** a = 3, b = 2, c = 1

HERE'S THE DEAL

No Pleasure in Business (10 to 17 points) Work is that irritating necessity between sleep and your social life. You do your job, and you're good at it, but it brings you no joy. Possibly you took the first thing that came along, or entered a "safe" field because parents or teachers pushed you toward it. Now, despite how much you earn, how lofty your title, or how "successful" you are on paper, you dread getting up and facing the same old grind. This negative attitude can spill over into other areas—it may even cause you to slip into depression. Plus, you may feel that someone (a husband?) or something (a lottery ticket?) can save you from this drudgery, but that'll just win the grand prize in a kidding-yourself contest. First, believe that a career can be satisfying and (gasp!) fun. Second, putting aside your skill set for a minute, list all your interests, then think of gigs that go with them. You love organizing a friend's bridal shower? Maybe a career in party planning is for you!

Living to Love What You Do (18 to 23 points) You may not have your dream job yet, but you will! In fact, you may have several before you retire. Your ambition is balanced by an understanding that your career should nurture your mind, heart, and soul. In your book, a fat salary doesn't necessarily mean success—you wouldn't stay in a job you hated no matter how much it paid. Plus, you seek out people who are passionate and inspiring, surrounding yourself with possibility. Of course, the underside to all your goals and desires can be anxiety and doubt—no one, not even a confident, talented woman such as yourself, *likes* the prospect of failure. Some tips to avoid it: Stay out of debt and invest wisely (so you can live off your savings for a while if you have to); make connections before you need them (it's not brown-nosing, it's networking); and finally, it's better to plan than act on impetuous impulse. Having a pencil blueprint of what you want and how you'll get there really helps.

Get Rich or Die Tryin' (24 to 30 points) With your skills, education, drive, and ability, it's clear you're on top of your game. You're doing your parents proud and living up to those "most likely to succeed" notations in your yearbook—and have the home, the ride, and the wardrobe to prove it. Just one question: Are you happy? If your honest response is "Not as happy as I thought I'd be by now," you need to stop and breathe for a minute. I recommend taking a real vacation, before you crash and burn. Once you're truly relaxed, let your mind meander to some of those issues blind ambition has kept you from seeing. Think about how you define success, whether your career satisfies your personal interests, and what calculated risks you might take to change things. Seek advice from people you respect, not so much for their position but for their positive outlook. If you decide to go back to school, say, to pursue an unearthed passion, it will take strength. There's a chance that your loved ones won't understand or agree, but this is your life. Make it count.

START **TODAY**, GIRLFRIEND!

As my first year of grad school drew to a close, I visited Columbia University's student employment office. The listing I found seemed too good to be true: a new style Web site called Fashion Planet was looking for a writer. Since I'd studied fashion merchandising at Parsons School of Design and worked as an assistant buyer at Lord & Taylor before applying to Columbia, this job seemed tailor-made for me. After my interview, they hired me on the spot, and I started working there right after my classes ended.

It was perfect. I interviewed fashion designers and beauty entrepreneurs; I covered industry events and gossip; I even got to attend fashion shows and exclusive store openings. But the site was a severely understaffed start-up, and when they figured out how fast I could turn around a well-crafted story, they began to give me more responsibility, assigning me longer profiles and feature stories. When I took a look at someone else's copy and made a few solid revisions, they began to let me edit as well as write. The company was too small to hire a wordsmith to craft their press releases and marketing materials, so that often fell on my shoulders, too. My days stretched longer and longer as I struggled to finish the mountains of work that piled up on my desk.

Even as I toiled around the clock, I never complained once. In fact, I did the opposite: I always asked what else I could do to help. And I met every deadline, even if I had to stay late to get it done. One afternoon, the Web site founder hustled over to my cubicle in a panic. With no small amount of hysteria, he told me that there had been some kind of large computer malfunction, and that we had lost all of the new material that was supposed to go up on the site the next day. "Please," he begged me, "what can you do?"

Interviews, product reviews, profiles, and event coverage—gone! Virtually all of our content—kaput! (Remember, this was the mid-1990s and computers were not quite as user-friendly as they are now.) I had my notes for the pieces I'd worked on, but how did they expect me to come up with content to fill the entire site?! I spent the next sixteen hours (working through the night and early morning) writing from notes, researching new material, and road-testing extra products sitting around the office that beauty companies had sent us for review. When I left the next morning at 7:00 AM, I had single-handedly cranked out an entire week's worth of content.

When school started in September, the Web site founder gave me a raise and convinced me to stay on and work part-time. Later, he gave me the title of managing editor, and basically let me run the site. After some time had passed, he informed me that his company would be starting a magazine called *Fashion Almanac,* and that he'd like to make me a senior editor of that new venture. That became my first job in the magazine world. Because of my willingness to consistently go above and beyond, I was able to bypass the years of coffee fetching and photocopy making most young journalists have to endure, and I began to write and edit major pieces, direct editorial focus, and think about design and layout. The experience was invaluable.

> **"Make others feel your purpose and passion."**

Bottom line? It's not enough just to do your job—even if you do it well. The job market is so incredibly competitive, you need to find a way to stand out. Of course, you first have to master your job skills. Become brilliant at what you were hired to do. When you feel confident that you've got your job under control, volunteer to help on extra projects, ask for more responsibility, make it clear that you will get the job done no matter what. There is always another candidate for your job, and your boss does not have to promote you (she doesn't even have to *keep* you). Try to prove how invaluable you are every single day, starting today. Finish your work, then go above and beyond by asking to do more. Your boss will remember your enthusiasm when it's promotion time.

Today . . .

- **Consider starting over.** So you have a decent job that you're good at. If it doesn't fulfill you, it's not enough. Allow yourself to at least entertain the possibility of leaving it to try something new. Yes, even if that means taking less money or going back to school.

- **Uncover opportunities.** Okay, you posted your résumé on mon-ster.com—great. But that's just the beginning. Explore all possible fields on employment Web sites; you may find fascinating careers you didn't even know existed. Look for job leads everywhere—in the paper, through talking to people you know (and don't know), by joining professional organizations and community groups.

- **Dress for the job you want, not the job you have.** You don't have to look like a clone, but dark colors (particularly navy blue) and for-mal touches like a crisp white shirt and a tailored blazer convey a sense of ability and authority. In general, avoid wearing anything to the office that you might rock at the club (yes, that includes your short dress, your tight, low-cut shirt, and even your sky-high stilet-tos). Tone down your accessories, too—replace huge earrings, lay-ered necklaces, loud eyewear, and anything with a large logo for more sedate, classic pieces. And remember that casual Friday is not an excuse to wear your frayed jeans and stained sweatshirt to work.

- **Do an attitude check.** Be as pleasant as possible and leave all nega-tive vibes at the revolving door. This is incredibly difficult when you're going through a hard time personally, but look upon work as the place where you can escape all that. Resist the temptation to tell a work friend your private business unless you're absolutely sure it won't be spread around. And if you do snap at someone, apologize immediately.

- **Stop waiting to be noticed.** Write a memo to your boss updating her on your progress on all the projects you're working on. Ask to get on her calendar so that you can talk about your future. If there's an assignment you want, ask to be considered for it. Don't just fan-tasize about making a career move—talk about it so people know that you're eager for new challenges. Continually sharpen your skills in preparation for surprise opportunities . . . and go for it!

- **Ask questions.** Don't be afraid of "looking stupid." Number one, if you don't understand a request from your boss, get more direction—it's much better than making a mistake. Also, ask coworkers how they do certain tasks (perhaps this will enhance your own skill set or improve your efficiency). In meetings, inquire about the objective of a project. Paraphrase to eliminate any ambiguity (for example: "So, to be absolutely clear, the research department will begin to put together the project, then sales and marketing will follow up in two weeks to complete the presentation, which should be with you for review in a month?") And remember, one of the most important questions you can ask is "May I help with that?"

• **Stop putting your work ahead of your personal life.** Whoa—bet you didn't expect that. But I mean it. A successful person is fulfilled in all areas, not just on the job. Work hard, play hard, get a massage, repeat!

MAKE **THIS YEAR** COUNT

When I took over *Honey,* it was a little-known, little-respected start-up in the crowded field of women's magazines. During my tenure, it gained national recognition as a major player in fashion, beauty, and entertainment publishing. We had cover subjects ranging from Destiny's Child to Sanaa Lathan to Mary J. Blige. We gave Alicia Keys her first-ever magazine cover and published the last interview Aaliyah ever gave during her short life. We also broke the story that Erykah Badu's dreds were fake (well, they were!), were the first to give T-Boz and Chilli a cover after Left Eye died, and signed on Wendy Williams for her first-ever magazine column. Various television shows called regularly, asking me to comment on air about style, pop culture, and urban women's issues. I began to get recognized wherever I went across the country (nice in general, but slightly embarrassing on a no-makeup Sunday morning grocery run).

None of these things happened automatically. No, girlfriend, redefining *Honey*—from its design to its content—and making possible its success took months of hard work and strategy. I realized that the only way the entertainment and style industries would fully appreciate the message and mission of *Honey* was if I personally explained it. I needed to build relationships with all the key players so that they knew me and, by extension, the magazine. So, I embarked on a crusade to meet all the decision makers I could, from Russell Simmons to L.A. Reid to Clive Davis. I didn't just focus on the top dogs—I also hung out with their public relations managers, a.k.a. the folks who either entertain your request or throw it in the trash the moment you get off the phone. Plus, I was friendly with everyone's assistant—because they are the screens for the powers-that-be.

For several months, I devoted my spare time to lunches and dinners with, literally, everyone I wanted to know. Some I really bonded with and others wound up being influential business acquaintances. After a while, I had a list of people I could call for help, and vice versa. They would ask me for coverage when they had a new client in need of a break, and I would hit them up when I wanted a story on someone major. One time, I was in competition with another magazine for a cover story on a major female artist (who shall remain nameless to protect her public relations manager, who is still my girl to this day!). Based on the numbers, the other magazine should have easily gotten its cover first—it was bigger, more established, better known. But I had the ace in the hole: I'd been wining and dining the artist's PR rep regularly. I called her up and had an "off-the-record" conversation. I told her I needed a solid and that I would eventually repay her effort. Well, not only did she get me my cover (to the surprise of everyone, including my boss), but that issue was one of our best sellers ever.

The point? Make relationships *before* you need them. By the time you really need someone, it's a bit too late to start cultivating that person as an ally. This year, identify the players in your industry and reach out to them. Try to set up a lunch or coffee date. Some may be too busy, so try to get fifteen minutes on their calendar to meet in their office. At least get an e-mail address so you can shoot them a message. Making sure that these key people know your name is crucial. Ditto for their assistants. Being a snob is a bad mistake I've seen ruin the careers of talented people. Assistants will take you down if they don't like you! And if the major players won't make time for you, take their assistants to lunch. By the end of this year, you should have a new list of contacts who may be able to help you sometime in the future.

This Year . . . ~eeℚ)

- **Schedule a performance review.** Most big companies do this as a matter of course. If yours doesn't, request one. And prepare for it. Before leaving the boss's office you should understand exactly what she thinks of you, where you need to improve as well as where you excel, and where you stand in terms of advancement.

- **Set your eyes on the next prize.** Whether you enjoy your current career or have determined that it's not for you, start looking for the next opportunity now. It may seem like I just up and quit two jobs impetuously, but in fact I had laid the groundwork. I'd already been accepted at Parsons School of Design *before* I left my finance job. Leaving my Lord & Taylor gig was, admittedly, more of a shot in the dark, but I had researched freelance writing outlets and graduate schools, and then decided to take that calculated risk. It is much more difficult to find a job when you're unemployed.

- **Self-promote like a pro.** Be your own publicist. Talk up your achievements, reminding busy bosses of projects you've done or are doing and informing people in other departments who might not know your work. Just don't be obnoxious about it or put down others in the process.

- **Learn to love networking.** Go to every career-related function you're invited to. Introduce yourself to people in your field and related fields—it's a lot easier than walking up to a random stranger at a regular party, since that's what networking events are all about. Collect and exchange business cards (if your employer doesn't furnish you with one, print up your own). Keep your contacts up to date in your PDA. When an associate gets promoted or takes a new job, drop a line of congratulations.

- **Expand your skills.** Think of your career as chocolate cake—your appetite for it should be endless! Take a continuing education class in your field or a related field (your company may pay for it; if not, you should be able to write it off on your taxes). Attend seminars offered by your employer (even if they don't sound fascinating). Go to trade shows. Find books on your field and study them as if there'll be a test on them tomorrow (because, after all, there will be!). And remember, one of the best ways to learn is to ask your boss or coworker to bring you onto a new project.

- **Make over your résumé.** Even if you're not looking for a job right now, give your résumé a tweak every six months. Add the new responsibilities and projects you've taken on. List any freelance work, volunteer work, new computer skills acquired, additional education, awards, or honors. This way, your résumé will be good to go when opportunity knocks.
- **Find a professional mentor or a coach.** If you cannot afford to pay a coach for career guidance, try to identify a mentor through your company or while networking, or look to more senior members of your professional organization. Give this person a reason to mentor you (maybe help her out with some grunt work) and take notes when you meet with her so she'll know how seriously you value her wisdom.
- **Maximize your job perks.** It's not just a job, it's a gold mine! Contribute all you can to your 401(k) plan. Look into continuing education and gym membership reimbursement. Take advantage of flexible spending accounts and child care.
- **Ask for what you want.** Just as you can't rely on your man to read your mind, you should not expect your employer to do so either. Let your boss know what your goals are, whether you want to make more money, explore work in a different department, even take time off. You're not demanding, you're simply politely inquiring—and you never know what the answer will be unless you ask.

GET YOURS **FOREVER**

I still remember my first day as the editor of *Honey.* I had come from *Essence,* where I had been in charge of the magazine's largest department, so at least I'd had some recent experience managing a staff. I had also completed a freelance assignment where I had to create a large guidebook to New York City, so I knew how to direct a project from start to finish. But none of that, or my other journalism gigs, had truly prepared me for helming a magazine. To get the job, I generated great ideas, talked a good game, and convinced the CEO of Vanguarde Media to hire me on the strength of my conviction. My first day on the job, I realized I was unsure where to even start. The September issue was almost done, but my predecessor had assigned no material for any further issues. I walked into my boss's office and asked "casually" if there was anything he wanted me to be working on. He stared at me and said, "Uh, the October issue," then looked back at his computer.

Riiiiiiight. October.

I went back into my office, shut the door, and allowed myself ten minutes of pure and utter panic. Then I got myself together and met with *Honey*'s minimal and shell-shocked editorial staff to come up with a table of contents for the next issue. Then I pulled out my Rolodex (I'm dating myself here, but I did still have a Rolodex!) and started calling freelance writers I had worked with in the past to execute our ideas. Most major magazines work on three issues at once: You read the proofs of the issue that's about to be published, edit the text of the next issue, and conceptualize and assign for the following issue. But *Honey* had fallen so far behind in the months before I arrived that I had literally two weeks to pull the entire issue together—a Herculean task for even the most experienced editor.

Not only did I get it done, I got Jada Pinkett Smith to agree to a cover interview. I even managed to take real strides toward changing the look of the magazine. My first issue, executed under extreme pressure with a skeletal crew and on a shoestring budget, generated enough positive response that publicists began to call my office to ask what they needed to do to get their clients in the magazine. My boss summoned me into his office, shut the door, and thanked me for making such a huge difference in just one month.

The message of this story: Always believe in yourself. You are smart and resourceful and creative enough to do anything you want. Convince yourself and the person in charge of giving you the opportunity by believing this. Then, when you find yourself with new responsibilities that may scare you, know that the fear you are experiencing is a sign of your professional and personal growth. Allow it to pass through you and remember that you are the perfect person for the job. Get to work!

Always . . .

- **Be *that* girl!** Make others feel your purpose and passion. Be your own cheerleader. Always be positive about your projects and sell people on your ideas by expressing yourself with enthusiasm.

- **Be clear.** No matter what your field, communication is key and perception is reality. You never want to be misunderstood. Express yourself well—the right tone, the right words, the right volume for small meetings and in front of large groups. And speak! Too often women are the last ones to talk in professional settings. In meetings, try to be one of the first to offer an idea or a comment. Join an organization like Toastmasters to help you learn how to present yourself to the absolute best of your abilities.

- **Master negotiation.** There are often many ways to get what you want. Learn to compromise and cooperate. Be flexible, and listen to all sides. Remember that your salary, benefits, and extras are not necessarily carved in stone. Negotiate them so that you can create not only the job you want but also the employment package.

- **Keep a record.** Every time you go above and beyond the call of duty, make sure to write it down. Your boss may or may not notice the extra project and extra hours you're working, but being clear about your accomplishments and being able to back them up with specific examples will be very helpful when asking to be considered for new opportunities.

- **Manage upward and sideways.** You have a boss, sure, but in a way you "manage" your relationship with her. Boss management entails respect, but not blind obedience. Ask the right questions, don't waste her time, know your boundaries. You should develop and maintain a rapport with her so that your conversations about new projects, promotions, raises, etc., will go that much more smoothly. You also want to "manage" your relationship with your peers. They, in large part, will determine your reputation at your company. Do not make the mistake of ignoring their influence on your success. Be considerate, helpful, and fair—and don't succumb to office gossip or the temptation to be mean or condescending. It will bite you in the butt eventually!

- **Refuse poor treatment.** As a woman of color, you may have to battle bias and/or sexual harassment in the workplace. Begin by firmly telling the person who dares try to mistreat you that you will not tolerate it. If it continues, go through the proper channels to make sure you make your complaints by the book. Keep records of every instance of unfairness so that you have evidence. Don't be afraid of being fired. Justice is on your side, and most employers these days recognize that women of color do not make claims of sexual harassment or bias casually.

- **Don't let e-mail run your day.** Those dings in your inbox can drive you to distraction! So turn off those message alerts and concentrate on the tasks at hand. Schedule specific times every day to read and return e-mails (the frequency depends on the industry you're in).
- **Do you still love it?** You may be the sort of person who finds her calling early or, like me, goes on a quest. Either way, you should evaluate your professional happiness regularly to see if you need to make a change.
- **Know when to quit.** Okay, even an optimist like me knows that not everything is going to go your way. I have fought for jobs/assignments/promotions and seen them go to someone else. I have tried to get people on my side who just wouldn't budge. And sometimes you just get bored silly. Your gut will tell you when it's time to walk away like a lady and move your sights to the next opportunity.

MOVIN' ON UP

Plenty of people slog away at their jobs, content with the annual cost-of-living raise. If you want more—not just more money but more responsibility and a better title—try these five tips:

1. **Target your position.** If you're an assistant now, set your sights on the associate's spot. Research the job description; if skills are required that you don't have, get them. At your next performance review, tell your boss what position you'd like to see yourself in next.
2. **Talk to your mentor.** Ask your mentor for counsel on how she rose up the ladder. See how you can adapt her strategies to your situation.
3. **Get connected.** There are other bigwigs in your company besides your boss, and they all fraternize. Make an impression on those people, even if it's simply by saying hello in the elevator. Get to know and make yourself useful to the person whose position you ultimately want. When she moves on, she can recommend you.

4. **Work out of the box.** If you're not content to wait till the person directly above you moves on, convince management to create a new position or title for you. Do so by showing how you could make a difference—by increasing profits and productivity, easing someone's workload, improving company morale, etc.

5. **Just ask!** Hey, it can't hurt. Even if you get turned down the first time, the boss will see you have ambition. If she doesn't want to lose you, she'll find a way to move you up.

GAYLE KING ON CAREER

Though best known as Oprah Winfrey's right-hand woman, Gayle King has had a lengthy and impressive career in broadcast journalism, at one point even launching her own syndicated talk show, The Gayle King Show. *She is currently the editor-at-large of* O, The Oprah Magazine *and a cohost of* Oprah & Friends *on XM satellite radio. She is also the very devoted mother of two children (when I interviewed her in her Hearst office, the room was filled with beautiful shots of her kids). I first met Gayle at an event for the National Association of Black Journalists. Even with a swarm of people constantly around her, Gayle remained warm and inviting. When she and I spoke that evening, she told me that she admired my work and my career. She was kind, authoritative, calm, and generous—all at the same time. I thought Gayle would be a great person to talk to about getting it right professionally.*

Amy: *What is success to you?*
Gayle: For me it means doing something you enjoy doing and getting paid for it, but it is more than just professional success. I think you need to be pleased with what is going on at home and feel good about the job that you do. If you can get both of those at the same time, that's heaven. Sometimes you have one without the other, and it is just a matter of working to bring them in line with each other. [Also] success always changes.

AB: *To what would you attribute your success?*
GW: It is very difficult for me to take no for an answer. If it is some-

thing that I really want, I will figure out another way to get it. In addition to that, you have to be prepared. When opportunity comes, you need to grab it, you have to have faith in yourself. I don't believe in taking foolish risks, but I do think it is okay to take a risk if you feel good and strong about yourself.

AB: *Tell us how you got started.*

GK: I went to the University of Maryland and graduated with a degree in psychology, never intending to be in journalism. I was working part-time in a camera store located near channel nine, the CBS station in Washington. One of the people who came in was a top executive of channel nine. I did not know what he did, but I was always outgoing and friendly. One day he asked me if I ever thought about television. He said, "We have an entry-level position. Would you be interested?" I walked into that newsroom, and I was hooked. I'm a news junkie until this day.

AB: *Was there a moment when you realized that you'd "made it"?*

GK: I don't recall ever feeling that I "made it." My first job as an actual reporter was in Kansas City, Missouri, at age twenty-three, and I felt very proud of myself. Then it went from one thing, to one thing, to one thing, to here.

AB: *What would you say your top skills are?*

GK: When I was fifteen years old, I worked at a hamburger stand, and I always thought, How can I be the most efficient? I would get my lettuce and tomatoes together in little piles to make the best use of my time. I am a very solution-oriented person. I have always been very resourceful.

AB: *What is one thing you learned that some people tend to overlook?*

GK: I discovered very early the beauty of the boss's administrative assistant. I made a point of making contact with the person, and addressing her like a human being. I didn't want to be just another résumé tape that goes into an office with tons of people. Even though a position may be filled, you never know if the station is planning on making changes. I would call the assistant to the news director who I'd want to see that tape and say, "I know you guys get tons of tapes, and I don't have a lot of money to keep sending tapes. Can you level with me about the possibility of employment there?" They were almost always very honest. You can get so much by being nice to people on the telephone.

AB: *I think it is helpful for people to hear stories when people did not succeed. Do you have any?*

GK: The first time I applied for a reporter-training program, I didn't get it. I remember being so devastated. I just saw myself as perfect and knew I was going to get it, so I was very disappointed when I didn't. I remember asking the news director, "Why didn't I get it? That just seems so unfair." He said, "Gayle, life is just not fair." I did not have a response to that. I was expecting, "Well, there were other candidates that were better, blah-blah-blah." Sometimes there isn't a good reason why you didn't get it. There isn't an explanation and you have to keep going without letting that throw you or derail you or make you think you are not good enough.

AB: *Have you made any sacrifices for your career?*

GK: I made sacrifices once I had kids. Once I was offered a really great job, but it would have meant leaving Connecticut and my babies' daddy, and I decided that his being involved in their life was very important to me. It didn't work out as a marriage, I didn't think much of him as a husband, but I did think of him as a father. It would have been a great career move, but the price for [my kids] wasn't fair. I've never regretted that.

AB: *That is a great point that speaks to the idea of balance. Do you ever worry your professional life will take over your personal life?*

GK: I wanted to be married, and I wanted to have children, since the seventh grade. If that hadn't happened for me, I would be very unhappy. As a working mother, can you go to every game and play? No, you cannot. But I felt like I was there for all of the important things. People lay this guilt thing on you, like, "You weren't there when they took their first steps." They took their first steps at three PM and I got home at six-thirty. So when I saw it, it was still the first steps for me.

AB: *Do you think it is better to follow your dreams rather than following the money?*

GK: It is more important to find something that you love to do, and figure out a way to get paid very well to do it. I would be very unhappy making a ton of money but being miserable in my job. It is easy to say, though, from someone who has money, can support themselves, and is living well. But even when I was living paycheck to paycheck, and making minimum payments on the bills, I still was happy because I was doing what I wanted to do.

AB: *How important is it to find a mentor?*

GK: I never really had a mentor. [But] whenever you are in a company you will find that some people are more willing to help than others, and I would try to glom on to those people. I have never forgotten who helped me and I always make a point of trying to help people, if they really express that they are interested.

AB: *Any pitfalls that women should avoid in the office?*

GK: I never got caught up in the "he said, she said, they said" office politics. I just always refused to play that game. Don't get sidetracked by the drama of office cliques that inevitably form in every office. I refuse to get sucked into that. Once you start playing that game, you can't get out. It is a dangerous place to be.

AB: *Do you feel a lot of extra pressure given your visibility and given the opportunities you have to affect people's lives?*

GK: No, I don't. I hope someone looks at my life and thinks, "I would like to do that," or, "I wonder how she did it." I feel very honored by my success but I don't feel pressured by it. I know that I'm human like everybody else and I will make some mistakes.

AB: *What is the best piece of advice you can offer up?*

GK: Nothing beats the experience of doing. Find an entry-level position in the place that you would ultimately like to work. Everybody starts in an entry-level position. Don't be afraid and always go above and beyond the call of duty. That will take you far. That thing about cream rises to the top is not a cliché. It is very true.

AB: *Do you ever stop learning?*

GK: I believe in surrounding yourself with people who are as smart and smarter than you. Even at this stage in my life, at fifty-one years old, I always feel that there is a way to learn something, to do better and be better. There is more that I can do, more that I can learn.

PROMISE PAGE

My dreams and goals for my career are:

_____
_____
_____
_____
_____

I promise that today I will:

_____
_____
_____
_____
_____

This year I promise to:

_____
_____
_____
_____
_____

I will always:

_____
_____
_____
_____
_____

PHOTO ALBUM

Here are a few of my favorite pictures of my closest family members. Plus, I've met many truly interesting people over the years. I thought I'd share some of those shots, too, and my impressions.

This photo was taken in
India when I was around
four years old. I love how
much I look like my mom
in this shot.
Personal Collection

With my mom and dad.
Not sure what we were
toasting, but I hope I'm
drinking apple juice!
Personal Collection

This is how I looked at age thirteen. Check out my crazy haircut and the glasses I'm self-consciously holding. My awkward stage lasted years.
Personal Collection

My husband, Jeff, and I at an American Music Awards after party. He remains the most handsome man I've ever seen.
Personal Collection

With my husband and beautiful son, Max, on a family vacation. Max is perfecting his "Whatchoo talkin' 'bout, Willis?" look. *Personal Collection*

This is Max at his first birthday party. The preschool girls better watch out for my little ladies' man! *Personal Collection*

This shot was taken at a party for my redesign of *Honey*. Ananda Lewis was our cover girl, and Lisa "Left Eye" Lopes was one of our guests of honor. That was the last time I saw Lisa alive. *Johnny Nunez*

I'm pictured with Aaliyah at a release party for her last album, the self-titled *Aaliyah*. She was talented, gorgeous, and surprisingly modest. I really miss her as an artist and as a positive role model. *Johnny Nunez*

Here's a shot of me and Timbaland, also from Aaliyah's party. His partnership with Aaliyah was groundbreaking, and his artistic influence is still felt throughout the music industry. Plus, he's a cool guy to hang out with. *Johnny Nunez*

Russell Simmons is very soft-spoken, very funny, and very, very sharp. I liked his laid-back yet handling-his-business vibe from the moment I met him. *Personal Collection*

This Polaroid was taken during a photo shoot for *Honey*. LL Cool J and Gabrielle Union were promoting their movie, *Deliver Us from Eva*. Gabrielle's killer sense of humor kept the day moving while LL lived up to his name as he flexed his muscles for the camera. That man looks like he hasn't had a french fry since 1998! *Roger Erickson*

Wendy Williams and I hanging out in her studio at WBLS. That year (2003) she'd made a triumphant comeback to the New York City airwaves and we'd just put her first-ever magazine column in *Honey*. Now she's a nationally known radio and television superstar. *Jayson Keeling*

This picture was taken at a listening party for Beyoncé's first solo album. The whole room erupted after the last track ended because we all knew the release was going to be a hit. It was clear that Beyoncé was next up for title of reigning diva, and no one has yet to truly challenge her.
Personal Collection

Hanging out with Kimora Lee Simmons after a Baby Phat runway show. I'm no doubt congratulating her on how hot Baby Phat's spring collection looks and trying to get my orders in early, before the rush. Trust me: in person, Kimora really is that *fabulous*.
Johnny Nunez/WireImage

Same shirt, different event. Here, Macy Gray and I got caught by a photographer having a chat in the stairwell at an American Music Awards after-party.
Arnold Turner/WireImage

This was an awesome night. Amerie, Q-Tip, and Pharrell came to a screening of the movie *City of God* that I'd helped put together as a fundraising event for a nonprofit organization dedicated to children. *Dimitrios Kambouris/ WireImage.com*

Hilary Duff has changed so much in just a few years! I must say that I'm really digging her current rock 'n' roll vibe. *Dimitrios Kambouris/WireImage.com*

Jessica Alba and Andre Harrell stopped by a *Teen People* party to say hi. They were congrat-ulating me on being featured in a fashion story in that month's *Essence* magazine. *Dimitrios Kambouris/ WireImage.com*

Here I am with Andre 3000 and Big Boi. This shot is from a post-Grammy party that OutKast had in L.A. one year. The cops had to shut it down early because we were partying so hard! *Arnold Turner/WireImage.com*

This picture was taken at *Teen People*'s Artist of the Year party. Kanye West's CDs are in heavy rotation in our home— Max LOVES to dance to "Heard 'em Say." *Arnold Turner/WireImage.com*

I've always liked Usher—in the midst of the craziness at the events where I normally see him, we always manage to have a brief, real conversation about life. In this picture, he's greeting me at the Artist of the Year party. *Arnold Turner/WireImage.com*

This picture was taken at *Teen People*'s annual What's Next party. That night Lindsay Lohan was gracious and calm, and she looked absolutely gorgeous. *Dimitrios Kambouris/WireImage.com*

Jay and I were about to hit the stage to introduce an intimate showcase of the newest members of his talent roster, including Rihanna, Ne-Yo, and Teairra Marí. Cohosting with Jay was a little nerve-racking, but he is one of the nicest and most considerate celebrities I know. *Johnny Nunez/WireImage.com*

7

GET YOUR MONEY RIGHT

Manhattan's Fifth Avenue, that little stretch between Forty-ninth and Fifty-ninth streets, can be a very dangerous place. Saks and Tiffany and Gucci, oh my! A friend and I were window-shopping there recently, and after a few blocks of drooling, my girl could take it no longer. She pulled me into Bergdorf Goodman and proceeded to get busy. For every item I put back, she bought two. Each time I decided I liked something but didn't love it enough to justify the price tag, she would try to talk me into it, then have one in her size brought to her dressing room. After a couple of hours, I walked out of the store with one shopping bag; she staggered out with three. Over an early dinner later that evening, my friend confessed that between student loan payments and credit card bills, she couldn't seem to save any money, much less the down payment for the house she'd been fantasizing about for years. I didn't want to say anything, but I couldn't help glancing down at the Bergdorf bags. She followed my eyes and laughed. "C'mon, girl. That's different," she said. "You know I got to look good."

Too many of us share her attitude: We're *kinda* concerned about the future, but not if it means sacrificing that Prada bag or gas-guzzling SUV. We want to look like we got it like that while our savings accounts collect dust and we rent our homes instead of owning. Many of us are "hood rich," but we have no idea what true wealth is.

I don't want to act like I'm not guilty of occasionally overpaying for little letters on my bags and shoes. And I've definitely charged things I knew damn well I couldn't pay off at the end of the month. But I've been saving and investing for years. Even when I was living from teeny paycheck to teeny paycheck, I still found a way to put aside a little money. With the money my mom left me, I bought a small apartment (something that would *appreciate*) instead of a fancy car (that would *depreciate* the minute I drove it off the lot).

Don't get me wrong. I've bought myself a few treats over the years. But I've always watched carefully how my rich friends (from my fancy college) would dress discreetly, live reasonably, and hold on to their money so they'd have some to pass on to their kids. Plus, my mother was a terrific example of how to manage money. When she got her first big job in academic administration (and her first six-figure salary) she could have drastically changed the way we lived. Instead, she started aggressively saving money until she had enough for the down payment on a Harlem brownstone. After she renovated it, the proceeds from its sale paid for my college tuition, the down payment on another investment property, and a donation to the United Negro College Fund. Mom had nice clothes and took vacations, but she never drove ridiculously expensive cars, wore pricey jewelry, or otherwise flaunted her wealth. She had a great life and still managed to give back to her community and take care of her family.

> "It's incredibly important for women to be independent and to have our own assets."

In general, I've found that the less I obsess about money, the more money I earn. I went from a high-paying job in banking to a lesser-paying job in fashion to an even less-well-paying job in journalism. Everyone around me thought I was insane to keep putting my lifestyle at risk by venturing into fields where my earning potential was lower. But I just knew that if I wasn't happy getting up every day to go to the office, nothing else would matter. Turned out I was right: The happier I am, the harder I work, the better I perform . . . and the more I money I earn.

But earning is not enough. It's incredibly important for women to be independent and to have our own assets. Call your savings your "screw you" money. If you ever find yourself in a really bad situation, personally or professionally, you have the ability to say "You know what? Screw you," and walk out the door. You may never have to touch that money, but just knowing it's there, accruing interest, will make you feel empowered.

Of course, you can't drive your bank or brokerage house statements, much less wear them around your neck. That's why it's so tempting to buy expensive cars, jewelry, and designer handbags—to display "how you're livin'." But real wealth doesn't mean being laced in the latest gear. Wealth means owning your own home and getting your bills paid off. It's being able to send your kids to the best schools, ensure that your parents are living comfortably, and know that your community reflects what you've given back. It's having the money to retire early while being able to live nicely now, whatever that means for you.

To build that kind of wealth, you've got to compromise. Want to get your hair done every week? Put down the Louis Vuitton wallet. Need the LV? Forget about going out every night this week. Got to hit the club? Skip that weekend in Miami with your girls. While I've made it clear that I'm not into self-deprivation, I have learned to consider my long-term goals whenever I'm tempted to splurge on something I want instead of saving for something I need. I urge you to do the same. Do you want to work until you're eighty years old? Do you want your kids to start out with debts instead of assets? Do you want your man holding the purse strings? Just make smart choices, girlfriend.

Quiz: What's Your Wealth IQ?

Everybody wants money, power, respect—but accruing real riches takes the right mind-set. This quiz will show you where you stand when it comes to personal prosperity—earning it, keeping it, and truly enjoying it.

1. A sorority sister invites you to her out-of-town wedding. You
a. RSVP that you cannot attend and send a nice gift from her registry.
b. fly out, book a five-star hotel, and rent an Escalade.
c. take the train and stay with a cousin, splurging on an elegant dress you'll wear again.

2. A friend wants to start a business and asks you to be a silent partner. Of course you'd like to, but ultimately must say no because
a. the odds are so stacked against a single black woman's business venture.
b. your research shows there's little demand for that kind of enterprise in your area.

c. you blew your "silent partner account" on a very noisy weekend in South Beach.

3. When you get some extra cash, you put it away for

a. a down payment on a condo.

b. a rainy day.

c. next year's Gucci.

4. You get a package from your employer concerning your 401(k) plan. You

a. ask your girl in the next cube how she's investing and copy her portfolio.

b. take the weekend to read it carefully until you understand all your options.

c. mail the package to your financial adviser and do whatever she says.

5. Every time a "preapproved" credit card application arrives in the mail, you

a. feed the darned thing into the paper shredder immediately!

b. fill it out and send it in—you can always use a backup card.

c. read the details in case the interest rate and/or bonus options are better than those offered by the card you primarily use.

6. All saving and no shopping makes you a dull girl! Your binge-buying philosophy is to

a. allot 3 percent of your total yearly income to "me" money that you can spend however you choose.

b. charge whatever you really want and pay it off over time.

c. never, ever pay retail—if it's not on the sale rack, it won't go on your back.

7. An aunt passes on, leaving you an inheritance. You

a. buy a piece of "serious" art that you find beautiful and inspiring.

b. plow through it in a few months, splurging on bottle service at clubs and designer gear.

c. deposit it in your savings account until you can figure out what to do with it.

8. Brown bagging to work instead of getting the five-dollar lunch special

a. makes no sense—saving five bucks a day won't make you rich!

b. makes total sense—saving five bucks a day comes out to thirteen hundred dollars a year!

c. makes sense when you have time to fix your own lunch, but time is money!

9. Of these famous quotes on prosperity, the one that makes the most sense to you is

a. "Wealth is the ability to fully experience life."

b. "A penny saved is a penny earned."

c. "You can't take it with you."

10. Plans for your financial future include

a. putting 10 percent of every paycheck into the bank.

b. a diversified investment portfolio.

c. marrying a rich man!

THE SCORE

Give yourself points as follows:

1. a = 1, b = 3, c = 2   **6.** a = 2, b = 3, c = 1

2. a = 1, b = 2, c = 3   **7.** a = 2, b = 3, c = 1

3. a = 2, b = 1, c = 3   **8.** a = 3, b = 1, c = 2

4. a = 3, b = 2, c = 1   **9.** a = 2, b = 1, c = 3

5. a = 1, b = 3, c = 2   **10.** a = 1, b = 2, c = 3

HERE'S THE DEAL

Wealth Worrywart (10 to 16 points) With your slow and steady approach to prosperity, you'll no doubt have money to retire on and may even have something to leave to your grandkids. Your smart spending habits and strait-laced saving strategy were probably ingrained by hardworking, lean-living parents. But being slightly less financially conservative now may serve you—in the short and long term. Real estate, for example, can be a wiser invest-ment than putting all your money in a low-interest savings account—not only does property tend to increase in value, but you'll be able to live in a home you own rather than pouring rent down the drain. Start playing a more ac-tive role in your future fortune: Instead of blindly following a broker's advice, hit a financial Web site or peruse the financial pages of the newspaper. You may just find you have a healthy passion for prosperity.

Affluence Activist (17 to 23 points) Guess what? You're already a wealthy woman! Oh, your bank statements might not show numbers Donald Trump would envy (yet), but you balance saving and investing with spending so well, you're able to reap the most out of life right now while planning for the future. You're taking responsibility for your own riches, learning the ropes rather than stuffing every penny in a safe but low-yield savings account or saying "uh-huh" when your broker babbles. You've acquired a working knowledge of the investment world, aren't afraid of calculated risks, and treat yourself well without maxing out your plastic. Keep it up, girlfriend! Read the *Wall Street Journal* regularly, and consider backing a black-owned business in your community (your own, perhaps?).

Bank Burner (24 to 30 points) Okay, girlfriend—time for a reality check. Looking fly and splurging freely may make you an object of envy, but the people who admire you aren't around when the bills arrive at the end of the month. Come on now: You *know* living paycheck to paycheck under a mountain of debt is a fool's paradise. First, you need to make a commitment to getting debt-free—and there are helpful nonprofit agencies to help you do so (drop the word "debt" into a search engine). Next, analyze the weaknesses that stand in the way of wealth. Are you a sucker for shoe "sales," a spa or salon junkie, or simply the type who fritters away funds on costly cappuccinos and designer water every day (hey, they add up!)? Now ask yourself: Is that pair of boots, full body scrub, or daily mocha latte worth sacrificing your dreams?

START **TODAY**, GIRLFRIEND!

Turning thirty was a major defining moment for me. That year, I became the editor-in-chief of *Honey*, got married, sold my apartment, and used the profit to buy another (bigger) one *and* an investment property. And, oh, yes—I finally got my diamond earrings.

For years, I had wanted diamond studs. I would tear Tiffany ads out of magazines, window-shop endlessly, even try on the ones I really liked. When I learned how much those glittery little rocks would cost, I held that figure in my mind, hoping to find a way to get there. In the meantime, I poured any extra cash I had into renovating my apartment to increase its market value. I gutted, then remodeled, the kitchen and the bathroom, and added a floor-to-ceiling shelving unit in the bedroom closet. Instead of new shoes, designer jeans, and ten-dollar cocktails, I bought nice faucets, a granite kitchen counter, and light fixtures. When the apartment was finally finished, it looked fabulous—a million times better than when I had moved in.

> "Call your savings your 'screw you' money. If you ever find yourself in a really bad situation, you have the ability to walk out the door."

When my then-husband and I were planning our wedding, we decided to sell my one-bedroom apartment to buy a two-bedroom in the same neighborhood. I knew that my apartment had increased in value, partially because of my extensive renovations, but I had no idea how much: I couldn't believe it when the real estate broker told me the value had tripled! With the profit, we were not only able to get a spacious two-bedroom, we also bought a studio apartment that we planned to rent out. And when we'd finished all of the transactions (the sale and the purchase of the two new apartments), there was a little cash left over—just enough for my diamond studs.

Of course, I debated for a long time whether I should make a purchase so extravagant for myself. My ex-husband told me to go for it, but I still wondered if they were just too frivolous. Then I decided: Not only had I achieved a major professional goal that year, but through hard work I had also increased the value of my home so that I could buy a new home *plus* an investment property. And I turned thirty years old! So the earrings became my birthday present to myself—recognition that I had just come through a challenging decade, had still worked successfully toward my dream, and was entering a whole new era. And to this day, whenever I wear those earrings I feel good about who I am, what I've done, and what I know I can accomplish.

Financial responsibility does not need to be all self-sacrifice. Yes, you must consider long-term wealth over short-term desires. But you should also reward yourself for a job well done. Today, I want you to think of one thing you'd like to save for that would make you happy (a vacation, a car, a nice watch). Then start a "fun fund" to save for your dream item. Of course, you have to prioritize paying down your debt and putting money aside for retirement. But money is like everything else: If you forbid yourself from ever spending it, you'll crack, and wind up splurging on some stupidly expensive silver stilettos that you'll wear only once. Be careful and smart about your future—then have some fun!

Today ...

- **Know your credit rating.** Ignorance is *not* bliss, so find out how good (or not so good) your credit score is. It determines so much more than you think (credit card interest rates, mortgage eligibility; some prospective employers may even check your rating before hiring you). Also, checking out your credit score helps ensure that you haven't become a victim of identity theft. Experian, Equifax, and TransUnion are the only credit bureaus from which to get your free credit report (watch out for scams that promise these reports and are really looking to rip you off).
- **Get a lower rate.** Call your credit card companies to ask for a lower rate. Yes, you *can* just call and ask—and most times, they'd rather do it than lose you as a customer. Aim to get all your credit card rates under 12 percent.
- **Begin a cash-only policy.** Take your credit cards out of your wallet and stash them someplace safe (for emergencies only). Then go the ATM once a week and live on that cash until your next scheduled withdrawal.
- **Stop sabotaging your savings.** Girlfriend, you're killing your budget with unnecessary expenses like pricey restaurants, designer sunglasses that you lose every month, and a ride that costs more than your apartment. Ironically, the things that make you look rich are the most insidious savings-suckers there are.
- **Brown bag it!** Does twenty-six hundred dollars sound like chump change to you? Well, that's what you'd have if you cut back ten dol-

lars every workday. Little things add up, so start saving money by bringing lunch to work twice a week. Lose those six-dollar lattes and make your own coffee. Check out some generic products as opposed to the stuff with the fancy package and price tag.

• **Cut costs painlessly.** It's not that hard to make a sandwich in the morning, and there are so many more little things you can do to bulk up your bank account. Give it a little thought and you'll figure out lots of ways to save without sacrificing. Do you like to knit, cook, or engage in some other creative endeavor? Make the most of your holiday gifts. Are you a serious exercise addict? Great, the local YMCA is no doubt as well equipped as that expensive gym. You're a serious shopaholic? Fine, shop—just make a list of what you need and stick to it instead of roaming the aisles racking up random purchases. Or, better yet, get a side gig as a mystery shopper (a freelance professional shopper whom major retailers hire to check up on their local stores, making sure the stores are well maintained, the customer service is good, etc.).

MAKE **THIS YEAR** COUNT

Years ago, I attended the lavish black-tie wedding of one of my Delta sorors. She had pulled out all the stops. The three-hundred-guest reception was in the ballroom of an expensive hotel. There was a live band, the dinner menu boasted lobster, and you know my girl was wearing Vera Wang! While she was planning her extravaganza, I kept wondering how her family was affording it. Her parents were lovely folks who both worked to support their middle-class lifestyle and send their three kids to college. They had a Honda and a Saturn parked in their driveway, and I had never heard my friend mention an expensive vacation or anything else her family had splurged on in the past. Her fiancé was still in business school, and my friend was an assistant designer for a shoe company (sounded glamorous, but paid little).

Over lunch after she got back from her honeymoon (in Maui!) she finally confessed that she and her man had gone way over budget with the wedding. Every time they were faced with a choice—from flowers to menu to invitations—they picked the pricier option. Apparently, both sets of parents had contributed what they could, and the couple had put the rest on credit cards. The opulent affair had cost three times as much as they had planned, and minimum payments on their debt were becoming a major burden.

"Aren't you worried about catching up?" I asked when she told me how much she was spending each month just to keep her creditors at bay.

"Girl, please," she said. "When Michael graduates from b-school and I get my promotion, we'll be all good."

I didn't say anything further (what would have been the point—it was too late), but I worried about my friend starting her married life so deeply in debt. Unfortunately, my concern was warranted. It took a long time for her husband to find a gig in his highly competitive field, and not only did my friend not get promoted, her division was shut down by the company's investors. She lost her job and had to freelance for almost a year before finding another assistant designer position. Four years later, my friend and her husband are getting divorced—and they *still* haven't paid off their costly wedding. As you can imagine, it's a hot mess.

> "Real wealth doesn't mean being laced in the latest gear."

I'm not going to tell you not to have any fun, but I am going to recommend that you get real about your financial situation. This year, start with a home budget. Figure out your necessary expenses and your real income. If, after you take off at least ten percent for your personal savings, your expenses are higher than your income, you have a problem. It may take you several months to get the numbers right, but once you figure out what costs you can shave and what you need to do to make the budget work—stick to it! That is how you work toward your financial goals every month and avoid the traps that my girlfriend and her man fell into.

This Year . . .

- **Clean up your credit report.** Commit to getting out of debt. Look at your finances and figure out the most you can pay each of your creditors. Try to pay more than the minimum amount due, even if it's just a few dollars. If you're in a serious credit crunch, consider consolidating all your bills into one monthly payment. There are nonprofit organizations out there that can help. Surf the Net (plug "get out of debt" into your search engine) to see your options.

- **Start investing.** Okay, so you're saving ten dollars a day and that means $3,650 a year, right? Um, only if you're stashing it under the mattress. If you put it in an account that earns only 4 percent interest, in twenty-five years you will have $158,088 (that's called the power of compound interest!). If you invest in mutual funds, stocks, and/or real estate, there's an excellent chance you will have way more. To make saving easier, just have your employer direct-deposit a portion of your salary (10 percent is ideal) into a separate savings account. If you never see it, you're less tempted to blow it on that fabulous white leather bag that everyone's jonesing for this season!

- **Find an accountant and financial adviser.** Let's face it, not everyone is good with numbers or wants to decode the *Wall Street Journal* every day. So hire professionals to help you get your taxes and investments straight. Ask friends, family, business associates, or your mentor for recommendations. Also, check out The Garrett Planning Network Inc. (www.gfponline.com) or Cambridge Advisors Inc. (www.cambridgeadvisors.com). Both cater to clients of all levels of wealth.

- **Establish some goals.** So many stilettos and so little time. Who wants to think about retirement when those strappy suede heels are calling your name? Girl, I get it. But with Social Security up in the air and fewer businesses offering traditional pensions, you need to wrap your mind around the idea that you alone are responsible for your future. Consider what you want your life to look like in one year (debt-free with money in a savings account?), in five years (living in a home you own?), in ten years (head of your own business?), in twenty years (spending weekends at your vacation home in the country?), when you retire (in Florida? Atlanta? the Caribbean?). Those dreams should become your short-, medium-, and long-term goals.

- **Save for an emergency.** Build toward having an emergency fund equal to six months of your current income. I know, it seems impossible to put so much away, but start small (pay for lunch with a twenty-dollar bill and put the change toward your emergency fund). Anything is better than nothing.

- **Sell some stuff.** I bet if you take a good look in your closets and around your house, you'll find at least a few things that you never use and could easily do without. Sell the panini grill or silver-plated picture frame, or pink leather blazer on eBay or Craigslist. Put the extra cash in your emergency fund or your savings account.
- **Consider a second job.** A few nights a week at a temporary part-time gig can really help make a larger dent in your debt. Remember, the sooner you pay it down, the sooner you can start working toward the rest of your goals!

GET YOURS **FOREVER**

A few years ago, on a trip to Los Angeles, I spent some time with an old friend. She and I used to run the streets of New York, party hopping and acting crazy. However, while I would occasionally roll into my office somewhat hungover but functioning, she would hit snooze ten times, then call in sick. As I was trying to finish my master's and get my career in journalism started, she was diligently filling up her Rolodex with the numbers of eligible (read: powerful job, expensive ride, fat bank account) men and working on her M.R.S. degree. Sure, I was dating around, too—and looking for a special guy. But I was building my career at the same time. My misguided friend just kept hoping a man—the bigger the baller, the better—would rescue her from her entry-level job, tiny apartment, and what she considered her boring life.

Eventually, she hooked up with a West Coast millionaire and moved to California, where he set her up in a luxurious apartment and gave her a car and a weekly allowance that, at that time, was more than my monthly salary. Yes, he refused to marry her, and he was often MIA, but she had what she'd always wanted: a rich man to take care of her every monetary need, want, and whim. The first time I visited her in L.A., my girl picked me up in a shiny new car, drove me to her 90210 crib, and we chilled by her sparkling pool.

Fast-forward a few years. My friend's baller boyfriend dropped her for another girl with a longer weave and a tighter ass. She had to give back the car, move out of the apartment, and make her own way without a career or any savings. The next time I saw her, I drove to her small studio in my rental, took her to lunch, and gave her money to get her hair done since she didn't have the extra fifty dollars to hook up her 'do. "I feel so stupid," she kept saying. "I'm starting over with nothing."

On the plane back to New York, I kept thinking about how grateful I was for my mother's lessons about remaining independent. She cautioned me never to put myself in a position where I couldn't take care of my own needs. While my friend was living on borrowed time in a house she didn't own, driving a car that wasn't hers, and talking on a cell she didn't pay for, I was slogging away in grad school, working at magazines, and writing a novel in my spare time. I drove a thirteen-year-old car and couldn't even afford the Gucci that fell off the back of the truck. But I kept at it, getting better and more interesting gigs and eventually landing the job (and, later, the man) of my dreams. I have achieved success on my own terms, and I can enjoy it with a man who considers me his equal in every way. (Trust me, girlfriend: No guy really wants a chickenhead who's just after his wallet. Independence is very sexy!)

Now my friend is rebuilding her life. She's started a whole new career, cut her hair into a funky short shag that's easier to maintain, and is starting to date again. She just told me she feels better about herself than ever, and I know exactly what she means. Sure, it's fun to have a man treat you like a princess, but it's much more fulfilling and cool to get things for yourself. You know you're worth it!

Always . . . ～ℓℓ◯

- **Understand wealth versus cash.** I've carried on quite a bit about this in this chapter, so what I'll simply say here is to remind yourself of the difference. Especially when you get a windfall like a year-end bonus or get lucky in Vegas. You can blow it—or use it to reach your goals.
- **Buy what you can afford.** Stop abusing plastic—making purchases in cash feels so much more real. If you're not sure about an item, give yourself twenty-four hours to think about it. If it was meant to be yours, you'll go back and get it.
- **Don't be afraid to invest.** It doesn't matter if you have twenty-five

dollars or twenty-five thousand dollars to invest—do not get too intimidated by the stock market to start reaping the benefits. Yes, it may go up and down, but overall the market has outperformed the inflation rate by approximately 8 percent for more than eighty years. Stay the course, girlfriend, and don't panic when it dips. In the long run, the rewards will be generous, and the earlier you start, the more time your cash has to compound!

- **Keep your finances neat, literally.** Buy a small file cabinet, or at least an accordion file, for your bills, receipts, and documents. Having everything organized will help you stay on track.

- **Don't borrow from friends and "forget" to pay it back.** That's just no way to live—and no way to treat people.

- **Work your tax returns.** Usually hiring a tax accountant pays for itself many times over, so consider getting a professional to do your return. Computer programs like TurboTax do make it temptingly easy to save a few bucks through DIY. Keep in mind: All your business expenses are tax-deductible. That includes business-related entertainment like taking clients out to dinner, gifts to clients, transportation to meetings, education that furthers your career, home office furniture, etc. Use your tax refund to pay down debt, invest toward your future, or, if your finances are already in order, pay for that dream item.

- **Think about the future.** I know: Retirement seems, literally, a lifetime away. But the fact of the matter is that you can't depend on Social Security, most companies have stopped offering pension plans, and the national life expectancy has gone up. Translation: Unless you want to work until you're eighty years old or you want to be a very poor senior citizen, you need to save some money. The great news? The earlier you start, the easier it is. Check out *Girl, Make Your Money Grow* by Glinda Bridgforth and Gail Perry-Mason for some great ideas.

- **Give back to the community.** Contribute to local charities. Volunteer in your hometown. Support minority-owned businesses. You'll be doing the right thing, and that will make you feel like the richest woman on earth.

- **Know that you deserve to live an abundant, fulfilling life.** Be grateful for what you have, work for what you want. Dream big and go for it!

BASIC BUDGET

It's hard to create a household budget unless you know what you're actually spending. It may be a harsh reality check, but you need to know the real deal in order to figure out a financial plan that makes sense. Here's where you start. For an entire month (this works only if you're really consistent!) write down everything you spend in each of these categories: Food and Groceries, Shelter, Utilities and Cable, Phones, Entertainment (movies, music, games, etc.), Transportation (car insurance and gas and/or metro and bus costs), Clothes and Accessories, Personal Care, Debt Repayment, and Miscellaneous. Don't freak out if you're spending more than you earn. At least now you know, and you can figure out where to cut back. The goal is to spend less than you earn so you have some money to sock away. Keep modifying your spending until you can save *at least* 10 percent of your paycheck toward your future.

WAYS TO PROTECT YOURSELF AGAINST IDENTITY SNATCHERS

While consumer awareness has actually caused a decline in identity theft, don't sleep! Thieves are growing increasingly sophisticated and keep coming up with new ways to get ahold of your name, Social Security number, passwords, and other info that lets them pretend to be you—and rip you off.

1. **Check your credit report.** Once a year, obtain your free credit report from Experian, Equifax, or TransUnion. It will show whether you've been defrauded by ID theft.
2. **Invest in a shredder.** ID thieves often Dumpster-dive to get info on their victims, so never just toss papers from your bank, brokerage house, or insurance company, credit card receipts, or offers from credit card companies. Any documents that contain personal info should be passed through a shredder first.
3. **Play it smart.** Never give out personal info over the phone to unsolicited callers. You never know who's really on the other end taking it

down. Don't leave your wallet lying around in the workplace. Keep personal documents locked up at home.

4. **Review your credit card statements carefully.** Most people don't even know they've been ripped off till they see a charge they didn't make on their statement.

5. **Protect your computer.** Arm yourself against "phishers" with computer programs that keep these thieves out of your business, and make sure to update them regularly. Use different passwords for different Web sites. Don't use your credit card on unsecured Internet servers.

6. **Watch your back.** Use your body as a shield so nosy thieves can't read your PIN code as you type it in. And remember that the ATMs in bank branches are way more secure than the one in your local drugstore or gas station. Some merchants unknowingly rent ATMs from crooked companies that make their money by stealing information off the machines.

7. **Banish credit come-ons.** Have your name removed from credit card mailing lists. All a thief has to do is grab one of these offers with your name on it, fill it out, and start charging away. Besides, you don't need the temptation of getting yet another card.

MELLODY HOBSON ON WEALTH

As president of Ariel Capital Management, LLC, a Chicago-based investment management firm with more than $21 billion in assets, and the financial contributor to ABC's Good Morning America, *Mellody Hobson, thirty-seven, knows money. I first met Mellody at an event in Chicago. She is a slight woman with palpable energy, fierce intelligence, and incredible drive. And unlike many of her fellow finance industry executives, Mellody is chic from head to Manolo' Blahniked toe—so much so that* Vogue *even featured her in a spread on the country's most stylish successful women. I liked her immediately! She's here to impart some vital financial info, so take note.*

Amy: **Would you please fill us in a bit about your background?**
Mellody: My story is pretty simple. I grew up in Chicago, the youngest

of six kids. I went to college at Princeton, and was a summer intern at Ariel. My full career has been at Ariel, which is going to be fifteen years this summer. So I've only had one job.

AB: *In terms of rising up the ladder, were there moments that changed your career?*

MH: One big one was when we decided to split off from the mutual fund company that was distributing our mutual funds. That was something that I initiated. I was twenty-five years old at the time. It was a major investment for the firm and major business revenue. It was a platform for us to become an independent mutual fund company. At the time when we did that, we had about four hundred million dollars in mutual finance assets that dropped down to three hundred million. Ultimately, today, we have just over eight billion. So I think it worked out, but back then it was very scary.

The other big moment for me was helping Bill Bradley run for president. I think it is a real good idea to get involved politically. I only did it because he was my friend, and I thought he was best for our country. But I didn't realize the side benefit, which was putting me in contact with leaders around the country. It was not only gratifying, it exposed me to things that I didn't know anything about, and it got me noticed.

AB: *What does wealth mean to you? And how does wealth differ from just having cash?*

MH: I'm working toward tremendous wealth, but I have certainly not achieved it. The way I would describe it is freedom. Wealth is about giving you lots of choices. I have a friend who always says, "Money talks and wealth whispers." That is something that has always stuck with me. Wealth is not an outward sign of success or financial security. It is the sense of security that you have inside that wealth gives you. I think it is a great relief to know that you are going to be okay financially.

AB: *Do you think it is important for women to create their own wealth and keep it?*

MH: Absolutely. I tell women all the time no one is coming [to save them]. So you want to prepare yourself for a life where you can always be self-sufficient regardless of who does or doesn't come along. You need to maintain a level of financial independence. Even if you are married, you should have something in your name, and a credit history, in case something happens to your husband or if you are no longer married. Also, you have to be aware of where the money is and where it is going, even if someone else is paying the bills. Women generally make their biggest financial decisions when there is great emotional stress—death or divorce. You do not want to be making life decisions when you cannot think clearly.

AB: *In general, how can women achieve financial stability?*
MH: The first element would be not getting into debt. If you are in debt, get out of it. Make sure that you save for retirement. That's very important. Most elderly people who are poor are women. Also, by raising our children, we step out of the workforce. This reduces our salary, promotion, increases, and Social Security payout—this is the mommy tax. Over the course of a lifetime, the typical woman who has graduated from college loses about one million dollars in raises and promotions and the like due to the time that she is out of the workforce raising her children.

AB: *Do you have any tips for getting out of debt?*
MH: Have one credit card only. If you are going on a diet, you do not have cookies in the house. If you are trying to get out of debt, you don't have a wallet full of credit cards. It is too tempting. The second thing I say is—the three Cs. You call, you cancel, and you cut. You call the credit card company and try to renegotiate your interest rate. After they agree to take your rate down, you pay it off, cancel the card, and you cut it up. You commit yourself to not reopening the account. Your one credit card is for emergencies only. You do not buy what you can't afford. Try to live off your income, which is something that is very hard for Americans.

AB: *How helpful do you think budget planning is?*
MH: The best thing to do is to focus less on budgeting and more on where your money is going—it's sort of a back-door way to budgeting. You can't save unless you know what you have and what you are

spending. Once you understand what you are spending, you can start to figure out where to cut corners and save. The average American eats lunch out five times a week. Is there a possibility of taking your lunch two days a week? The average person spends eight dollars a day on lunch. Over the course of a year, that is just over two thousand dollars. If they split the difference, that is already one thousand dollars in savings.

AB: *Every little bit adds up. Do you have any other easy money-saving tips?*

MH: A lot of people drink bottled water. In America, we have the best [tap] water in the world in terms of its purity. If you don't like the water in your town, get a filter for thirty dollars, versus buying it at two dollars a bottle. A lot of people buy magazines on the newsstands; getting subscriptions saves a lot of money. One of the best things you can have is a library card. The library has so many things—the latest music, DVDs, the latest video games—that you don't have to pay for.

AB: *What are some financial goals for women in their twenties and thirties?*

MH: Retirement. If we get that piece right, especially black women, it will change the whole paradigm in terms of the wealth gap in this country. Also, the wealth that we will leave to our children, so our children will not have to take care of us in our old age.

AB: *What kind of financial pitfalls do you think we keep falling into?*

MH: Thinking that the stock market is too risky. Women tend to be too conservative. By being too conservative, we miss out on growth opportunities.

AB: *What is the best way to grow your capital?*

MH: There are a number of mutual funds out there, Ariel included, that will allow you to invest small amounts of money, as low as fifty dollars a month. Eventually, you will get more comfortable with stock-market investing. Ultimately, if you find your money growing, it becomes addictive.

AB: *How important do you think it is to own your home?*

MH: It is clearly the American dream, [but] not always best for everyone. A lot of people have been stretching, getting what I call "extreme" mortgages. This will have an impact long-term. If you buy a home, don't stretch. For example, interest-only mortgages are a very bad idea. You could easily find yourself foreclosed upon.

AB: *How can novices understand how to invest their money?*

MH: Read your local newspaper, and begin reading the business section. Get familiar with the terms and ideas that are thrown around. *Black Enterprise* does a great job with personal finances and investing. I think that is a good magazine to read. *Money* magazine and *Kiplinger's* are really good publications that provide real-life scenarios. If you are working with a financial adviser, ask him or her a thousand questions. Just as you would ask a doctor about something that you did not understand that involved your health.

AB: *How important is it to give back to your community?*

MH: Philanthropy is incredibly important. We get what we give. I am a big believer of that. At the end of the day, we recognize all that has been done to get us here and we have an obligation to give it back.

AB: *Let's talk about you for a moment. How have you "gotten yours" in your life?*

MH: I have gotten more than I could have ever imagined, but I also hope for much more as well. I have gotten it by being very open-minded, being willing to take risks and willing to stand out from the crowd.

PROMISE PAGE

My dreams and goals for my financial
future are:

_____
_____
_____
_____
_____
_____

I promise that today I will:

_____
_____
_____
_____
_____
_____

This year I promise to:

_____
_____
_____
_____
_____
_____

I will always:

_____
_____
_____
_____
_____
_____

8

GET HIM

College was an interesting time for me. I was challenged by my classes at Brown University but did well, nurturing the notion that I could excel in this world. I also had an active social life. Let's call college a time of reading, writing, and romance. However, though I dated quite a bit, many of my boyfriends didn't treat me right. And in retrospect, I understand why.

I'd grown up with both grandmothers bitter over their adulterous husbands. My parents had a rocky relationship—and my father's hasty wedding to my stepmother right after my parents' divorce was final never sat well with my mom. Our rootless way of life during my youth made it difficult for me to forge firm bonds with my peers, girls or boys. So although my mom tried hard to keep my mind open about the male species, I couldn't help the vague feeling that no one was safe in love. I felt a fundamental mistrust of guys—which, of course, meant that they usually met my low expectations.

But because I was insecure, I felt it was my fault. If only I was cuter, nicer, more understanding, had bigger boobs or longer hair, they would love me right. So I hung in there—to be taken for granted, lied to, cheated on, and, eventually, dumped. Despite my heartbreak and all the tears I shed, this continued to be my romantic MO throughout much of my twenties. Except for my period of mourning after my mom's passing, I dated pretty consistently—some great guys, some knuckleheads—but I was still too unsure of myself to demand the treatment I deserved. Even as I embarked on my positive path toward a full, happy life, I kept repeating the same pattern when it came to men.

Then, in my late twenties, I met a great guy. He was well educated, well paid, professional, tall, and good-looking. We shared common interests, values, and goals. Plus, as time went on, he proved to be absolutely devoted to me. He became my best friend and partner-in-crime. It was the first time I ever felt safe with a man, and when he proposed after a few years of dating, I said yes. Only problem? This nagging feeling that our chemistry didn't quite measure up. What did I do? Ignored it! We married in a lovely sunflower-filled outdoor ceremony, and so many people told me how lucky I was to have found this amazing man, I smiled through the fact that I simply didn't feel passion in my heart.

After only a year of marriage, I began to feel a fundamental distance between us that only grew worse. Eventually, I had to have a conversation with myself about what I was doing. I'd learned to live every other aspect of my life as an adventurous, self-confident woman. Why couldn't I do the same in my romantic relationships?

It's easy to talk about taking risks and never settling, but sometimes it is truly hard to do. One of the worst moments of my life was telling my husband that I wanted to move out. It was incredibly painful for both of us. There I stood, ready to walk away from a stable, supportive situation, when ahead of me was the unknown and behind me a heap of bad breakups. But I knew that if I didn't leave then, I would never find the true love and partnership I was meant to have.

Shortly after I separated from my first husband, I went to my ten-year college reunion. Of course, I plucked and pedicured and otherwise prepared to make sure I was looking my absolute don't-you-wish-you-hadn't-dumped-me best. I didn't know whether any of my former flames would be there, but a few actually did show up. While they were all somewhat impressed by what I had achieved professionally, most seemed more excited by the results of all my copious primping. At one point, one of my exes held me at arm's length and let out a low whistle. Just as I was starting to feel a little too good about myself, he said, "Too bad I didn't know you were going to turn out so well. I would have treated you better in college."

> "Have high expectations of men as human beings."

And with that, the air was quickly and decisively let out of my oversized balloon. It was clearly time for some necessary introspection. His callous remark brought back all the years that I had accepted subpar treatment from men. Like many of my friends, I assumed with every relationship that if I stuck it out my boyfriend would eventually see the light. I thought that if I were patient enough, he'd grow to appreciate and love me. But the guys who walked all over me just kept walking—right out of my life, leaving me to wonder what I'd done wrong. Then, in a move of drastic overcompensation, I'd married a man who loved me to death, but it didn't *feel* exactly right.

> "The more you focus on feeling good and living life, the better the men who will come your way."

After my ex's comment, I sulked for a little while, feeling really stupid and more than a little embarrassed for myself. Then it hit me: That was my *past* self. I would adopt a new lease on life when it came to men. I'd date my way—I'd put myself first for a change. If a guy liked me, great! If not, that was cool, too. I may not always have a man around, but that was preferable to being with the wrong one.

As soon as that new attitude took hold, I began to go out with some truly great men. I literally had more guys than I could handle because I'd finally figured out that the less you need a man, the more he'll want you. The less you tolerate bad treatment, the more he'll appreciate you. Trust me, a healthy splash of gutsy independence in a woman is a *very* attractive quality. In the middle of my hot streak, I even defied the unwritten black girl rule that says you must grow your hair as long as you possibly can—I chopped off my shoulder-length curls for an easy-care "Halle Berry back in the day" pixie . . . and I got even more dates!

The only new pitfall I found was the occasional rich guy who tried to buy my love with vacations and jewelry. Please! I didn't need their money. But even if I had still been struggling financially, my mind-set would not permit me to entertain that nonsense. Girlfriend, it was not even tempting. I'd seen friends flip from being treated like princesses to being treated like property by ballers. Not for me!

I value my independence above all else. I never want a man holding the purse strings and deciding how much I can spend and on what. And having come out of a marriage that couldn't sustain deep love, I had no desire to enter into a relationship for the wrong reasons. Last, I wanted to be responsible for creating my own dream lifestyle—that way I could enjoy it even more. Those ballers who were so sure all it would take was an expensive bag or diamond watch to get me to roll over (literally and figuratively) got no play from me.

During this period of plenty, I met Jeff, the man who would eventually become my second husband and the father of my child. I fell in love with his heart, soul, mind, and smile. He is warm, kind, fun, smart, ambitious, stylish, and gorgeous! Most important, he respects who I am, what I do, and only wants to see me achieve everything I possibly can. Immediately, I dropped everyone else I was seeing, because in him I finally saw (and felt) the deep love and true partnership I had come to envision for myself.

Unfortunately, when I look around me, I see that there's been too much repetition of the myth that there aren't enough good—that all-purpose, all-encompassing adjective—black men to go around. Too many men have watched booty-shakin' videos depicting women of color as pole-dancing trophies to be used then thrown away. Too many women believe men are supposed to lace us in jewelry and designer gear, *and* pay our cable bill. Many of us have trouble finding love because we want to be rescued by a brother who's "paid"—and the men we're interested in feel they have too many options to settle down, or don't want the burden of our bills. Since we're often frustrated with this situation (and may have difficult or nonexistent relationships with our fathers), we're often too hard on the men in our lives. At the end of the day, black men and women often have unfair expectations of each other—and it's damaging our relationships and our families.

The easiest way to break this cycle is to have high expectations of men as human beings—not their ability to hook you up with a Prada bag, but how much they will cherish and respect you. Of course, they won't do that unless they know how much you value yourself. That means you must have—and meet—high expectations of yourself. Be the sort of woman who does not need or want a man to take care of her, who has a full, fascinating life, and who knows how to have fun, and those good men who seem so hard to find will suddenly start popping up all over the place. The more you focus on feeling good and living life, the better the men who will come your way.

Quiz: Are You Looking for Mr. Right or Mr. Very Wrong?

You don't need a man. But being in a solid, sexy, honestly loving relationship sure does round things out nicely! Take this quiz to see if you're on point about finding and securing the brother you really belong with.

1. For a man to measure up to your "must" list he's got to have

a. a good heart and a good job (or at least prospects for the latter).

b. money, looks, brains, and mo' money.

c. what "must" list? You consider such things too limiting.

2. On Friday night, you and your girls go out on the prowl—uh, to town. What scenario best describes what typically happens to you?

a. you work the club, collecting free drinks and phone numbers.

b. no one really talks to you—your flashy friends attract most of the attention.

c. you chat with a few different guys, and get the digits of the one who seems most promising.

3. Your idea of a great date is

a. cocktails at a hot new place, followed by front-row-center seats to a sold-out concert.

b. an afternoon stroll in the park or through an art gallery.

c. going to the movies, which is always fun, but you're happy to just hang out.

4. When it comes to meeting men, you

a. prefer to be fixed up by someone you trust.

b. hit clubs and parties, visit dating Web sites, work it at the car wash— you're always on.

c. go where you know you'll have fun, whether you hook up with anyone or not.

5. Your friend thinks you and her cousin would hit it off. Your first question is

a. what's he like?

b. what does he do?

c. why would he like me?

6. Your boyfriend cancels a date at the last minute. You

a. understand that these things happen. You're cool as long as he doesn't make it a habit.

b. are so disappointed. He must not be that into you.

c. tell him this is unacceptable and if he's not at your door in twenty minutes, he's out.

7. The guy you've been seeing calls at eleven o'clock on a Thursday night and wants to come over. You

a. bust out the La Perla, and tell him to bring the Veuve.

b. tell him you're about to turn in, but to give you a call tomorrow to make a plan for the weekend.

c. tell him sure and heat up some leftovers in case he's hungry.

8. This smart, funny, cute guy is chatting you up at a party—but he doesn't share your ethnic background. When he asks you out you say yes because

a. he's smart, funny, and cute—nuff said.

b. a good black man is so hard to find.

c. he's wearing a Rolex and an Armani suit.

9. When it comes to first-date fashion you

a. err on the side of modesty—you don't want him thinking you're easy.

b. pull out all the stops—high heels, low neck, lotsa logos.

c. go casual-sexy—jeans, a cute top, your favorite necklace that's such a conversation piece.

10. You thought your man loved you as much as you love him, but now there are subtle signs that he's losing interest in the relationship. To deal with this you

a. say nothing about your fears but snoop around discreetly to find out if he's cheating.

b. plan a weekend away together and, when you're both relaxed, draw him out about his feelings.

c. make yourself unavailable to him for a few nights, even weeks. Absence makes the heart grow fonder!

THE SCORE
Give yourself points as follows:

1. a = 1, b = 3, c = 2   **6.** a = 2, b = 1, c = 3
2. a = 3, b = 1, c = 2   **7.** a = 3, b = 2, c = 1
3. a = 3, b = 2, c = 1   **8.** a = 2, b = 1, c = 3
4. a = 1, b = 3, c = 2   **9.** a = 1, b = 3, c = 2
5. a = 2, b = 3, c = 1   **10.** a = 1, b = 2, c = 3

HERE'S THE DEAL
Step Up Your Standards (10 to 16 points) A sweet, warm, generous woman like you—you're a prize for any man. Trouble is, as far as you're concerned, any man will do. Before you can find a guy who will treat you with respect, you have to believe you deserve it. Make a list of your qualities—emotional, spiritual, and physical—and memorize it. This will remind you that you are entitled to the best. It will also help you gain confidence. It's not enough to be out there; you have to have fun out there. If no one at the club immediately starts talking to you, spark a conversation with the guy who looks good to you. Consider going out without all your girls so you'll stand out more. And if things don't work out, it's not you—it's him.

Keep on Glowing (17 to 23 points) Because your life is so full and rich, you're not desperate to meet a man. That's exactly what draws men to you! You're comfortable in your own skin and know how to have a good time, whether there's a guy in the vicinity or not. Plus, you're open-minded and you follow your heart, not a list of criteria or a set of rules. When flirting you never try too hard—you're just yourself. And when dealing with a bump in the relationship road, you're honest and understanding. If you haven't met the man of your dreams yet, you're cool with that. You know you will, and in the meantime you're having a blast.

Take It Down a Notch (24 to 30 points) You're a man magnet, no doubt—but if it's a genuine, satisfying relationship you want, think quality, not quantity. Of course, with your nonstop workin'-it attitude, list of things a man must possess in order to date you, and set of lines he'd better not cross, you believe you *do* demand the best. Reality check: Your priorities are off. It's not what he has (translation: what he can give you) that counts, it's who he is. And at the bottom of all your rules is a deep-seated sense that a man is bound to let you down—you need to let go of that negativity to win at love. Rather than dazzle a guy with supersexy presentation, let your guard down and give him a glimpse at your inner goddess (a.k.a. the real you).

START **TODAY**, GIRLFRIEND!

When I was in my early twenties, I dated a guy who was really into golf. And when I say "into golf," I mean that homeboy seriously thought he was Tiger. He'd wake up at 5:30 AM Saturday and Sunday to squeeze in his eighteen holes. He regularly went to the driving range and to the putting green to practice. He even took golfing vacations with his buddies so they could play from dawn to dusk.

> "If you're single, celebrate these fun, fabulous years, and never let a man validate who you are."

At first, I thought it was great that he had a serious hobby. I was impressed by his knowledge and thought his skill was sexy (I know it's *golf,* but he could regularly hit 275-yard drives—that requires some nice hard arm muscles). Plus, he'd go from preppy collared polo shirts to Tims without missing a beat. Figuring he'd appreciate my effort (and wanting to spend more time with him), I signed up for golf lessons as a surprise. When I told him, I should have known from the pained expression barely concealed beneath his superfake "Okay, cool!" that there was a problem. But I was so sure it would be great for our relationship that I pressed on. Over the next couple of months, I suffered through endless weekends on the links, whacking the ball in water, rubbing gunk from the sand traps out of my eyes, trekking the walk of shame from hole to hole after blowing past par (by twenty strokes!). Try as I valiantly did to convince myself I was having fun, the truth is I was just attempting to enter his world and prove that we were meant to be.

After gamely putting up with me for a while, my boyfriend began to avoid me, claiming he had road trip plans with friends, telling me his cell was broken—once he even "lost" me on a particularly woodsy golf course. Eventually, he broke up with me because I was smothering him and, frankly, embarrassing myself.

A couple of years later, I met another golf junkie. No way would I make the same mistake twice! I realized that pretending to be interested in something to get a guy is fruitless (and in my case, left me with some pretty corny golf gear). So I let my new boyfriend go off on weekends while I hung out with my girls. While he was at the driving range, I would take a dance class or get some writing done. We spent less time together, but the time we did share was quality. We remained really tight, right up until his company relocated him to Dallas. Neither of us was into a long-distance relationship so we broke up amicably. Besides, as much as I liked him, I knew he wasn't "the one," and I was way beyond trying to talk myself into believing he was.

Start today on a path to get the man you want and deserve by writing a list of all the things you regret doing in past relationships. Even though they may be mortifying in retrospect, just put them on paper. Okay, girlfriend, read the list, remember how ridiculous you felt at the time, and promise yourself never to let history repeat. Just think about what you learned from your mistakes, and act on that. This is a new day, and you are armed with the knowledge and power maturity bring.

Today . . . ⌐ℓℓℓ◯

- **Stop believing the man-shortage hype.** First of all, it doesn't exist. According to the U.S. Census Bureau, by 2010 there will be just over one million *extra* men aged twenty to forty-four. Besides, as a unique and exceptional woman, you don't expect the right man for you to be a dime a dozen. So quit complaining about how bad men are; that just invites bad men into your life.
- **Give him breathing room.** If you're in a relationship now, quit hovering, smothering, and clinging. You think you're being loving and "there for him"; he no doubt sees it as desperation. And you're not desperate. So treat yourself to a fab girls' night out!
- **Quit searching for Mr. *Exactly* Right.** Want to ruin your chances of meeting a great guy? Compose a list of qualities he has to have.

These "must" lists limit you, and tend to include superficial things about age, education, income, and appearance, instead of soul qualities like warmth, sensitivity, honor, and humor.

- **Expand your dating pool.** Whatever strategies you use to meet men, multiply them by doing things you've never done. Try Internet dating, go to singles' events, agree to sensible fix-ups. If those methods aren't yielding results, go further—track down an old crush, throw a singles' soiree, dress up and dine alone at a hot spot. Just get out there!

- **Accept that it's over.** I'm not saying get over your ex *this minute,* but at least acknowledge the breakup. Stop calling him for whatever irrelevant reason you can think of. In fact, remove his number from your speed dial. Put his pictures out of sight; do the same with anything else (gifts, concert ticket stubs) that causes you pain to look at. You will feel better. I promise.

MAKE **THIS YEAR** COUNT

I used to live near Brooklyn's beautiful Prospect Park. Every now and then, my sportier friends and I would take our bikes or in-line skates to the park and get moving. Of course, we weren't getting that much exercise. It was more about hanging out and enjoying the afternoon. Still, we suited up in our workout gear, did a couple of loops, then sat on a bench to gossip. One day, while we were "taking a break," a guy rolled up to our group. He knew one of my girls from undergrad, so we all chatted for a while. He raved about a recent trip he took to Cuba—the friendly people, the fabulous food.

He seemed really cool and I could see a couple of my friends checking him out. But when he gave in to our lazy mood and took off his skates, it became obvious that, minus the wheels, he was barely my height. That was the kiss of death for my friends (and I'll admit, I *do* like a tall brother), but I was still interested. So when he asked for my number as we all left the park, I gave it without hesitation. After he took off, my girls mocked me for a good fifteen minutes, telling me not to wear heels on our date, laughing that we'd better not go to a concert or I would lose him in the crowd, cracking that at least we could share clothes. But I found him compelling, so I ignored them.

The next weekend, while my girlfriends were making plans to see some chick flick on Saturday night, I was pulling out cute dresses (and, yes, heels) to wear on my date. He showed up on time, dressed to kill in a black designer suit. He took me to a hot new Cuban restaurant—in his chauffeur-driven Benz. Turned out that he was a well-regarded studio musician. Okay, even though I'd never been with a guy just for his bank account, it sure was fun telling my friends later that, yes, we did go to a concert that night, but I didn't have to worry about losing him since we were seated in the VIP area, and partied backstage with the band afterward.

The relationship wasn't meant to be, but he was a cool guy and we stayed in touch off and on for years. And our first date was definitely one for the record books—something I wouldn't have experienced if I'd blown him off. This year, go out of your way to give a chance to guys whom you wouldn't normally consider. I don't mean settle for a man who doesn't interest you—just don't listen to what other people say is desirable. So what if he's not built like The Rock or wears a uniform (that isn't scrubs) to work. So what if you don't feel "sparks" immediately. If you think he's interesting, go for it! See what develops. Trust me, girlfriend, it's all about how a man makes you feel.

This Year . . . ⁓ℓℓℓ)

- **Give chemistry a minute.** Many women (and men) erroneously believe that the first three seconds of laying eyes on someone must crackle with intense electricity. Relationship experts will tell you otherwise. And any woman who ever realized she was in love with her best male friend will say ditto. Besides, if you were meant to be with the guy you were superhot for from the get-go, you'd have married what's-his-name from eleventh grade. Sometimes it takes a while to get over your nervousness, to stop fronting, to hit on a shared passion or just "feel right" before lightning strikes.
- **Never look back.** If you get that feeling—in your heart, your gut, your head, and your senses—that a relationship is not working, make a clean break and don't look back. Do not stay in the wrong relationship; it's not fair to you or to him. And if it's a bad scene (as in physically or verbally abusive), *get out now!*

- **Don't kid yourself.** Men are not very complicated, so if he tells you he's not looking for a relationship or doesn't want to settle down, believe him. He's not lying. He's not testing you. He's not just in need of the love of a good woman (i.e., you) to prove otherwise. You're wasting your time at best, setting yourself up for heartbreak at worst.

- **Google him!** Nowadays it's just plain smart to plug his name into your trusty search engine to see if he's all he says he is. (You can find out where someone is employed, where he went to school, if he is or was married, and lots of other information.) Also, listen to your intuition—if you get a sense that something's wrong, you're probably right. Some surefire signs that he's playing you: He hangs with players, his schedule changes dramatically, he's often MIA, you have only his cell number, and he's never introduced you to a close friend, family member, or business associate.

- **Embrace your sexuality.** Okay, you want to talk about getting yours? Let's talk about *your* orgasm. You cannot expect him to "give" you one; that's your responsibility. Besides, beyond all the sex skills you may be an expert in, the most exciting for a man is seeing you lose your mind with pleasure. So open up sexually. Indulge your fantasies (just think about those turn-ons; you don't have to act them out). Expand your sensuality with a massage class. Try some sex toys. Experiment with different positions. Explore having sex in risky places, like a restaurant bathroom (or at least your own kitchen!). Adopt a ladies-first mentality and do for self—in front of him.

- **Relax about interracial dating.** There are plenty of fish in the sea, and they come in all colors. Just make sure you're realistic about the potentially unenthusiastic reaction of your parents, his parents, and the public.

- **Get that second date.** If you want to see him again, clinch it on the first date. Do something where you get to talk, but also be involved in some sort of fun activity (riding bikes, gallery hopping). Let him know you're interested in him by asking questions, but also show how interesting you are by bringing up your passions. Relax, be honest, and don't talk too much (or at all!) about relationships. At the end of the evening, tell him you had a great time, but don't press him to commit to another date. He'll be so intrigued that he will have to call you to hang out again.

- **Date like a man.** When it comes to romance, women let men call the shots. Flip the script once in a while and date on your own terms. See a few different guys at once; wait a day to call him back and end the phone call first; lean over and plant one on him!

GET YOURS **FOREVER**

When Jeff and I moved in together, people would ask when we were getting married. Once we got engaged, they wanted to know if we'd set a date for the wedding. After we jumped the broom, the question became: When are you starting a family? Even in these supposedly enlightened times, many still consider women incomplete until we get hitched and give birth. My single friends with fabulous careers and fulfilling social lives get pestered all the time about why they haven't "settled down"—as if being single, successful, and happy is somehow unstable.

Why are women expected to be Desperately Seeking Stability (husband, kids, house in the burbs)? We're pitied if that's not the life we have—even if we don't want it. And if you're single on Valentine's Day, forget about it! You must endure your attached friends crowing endlessly about flowers received and dinner plans made.

One year I got really stressed about Valentine's Day and decided to rebel. Some girlfriends and I got all dressed up and went to a club. We rejected every man who stepped to us because we'd decided in advance that this was *our* night and no man was going to compromise our fun. To this day, that night remains one of the best I've ever had. We stayed out until the morning, drinking champagne, dancing, and turning away the hordes of fascinated men who just could not get over the spectacle of a group of women preferring to spend time with one another rather than collect guys' cell numbers.

If you're single, celebrate these fun, fabulous years, and never let a man validate who you are. You are unique and terrific with or without a guy. And whether you're single or in a relationship, *always* make time to have a blast on your own and with your girls. Call it a perk of a well-rounded life: The more fun you have on your own, the more guys will flock to you. On Valentine's Day and every day, be your own true love first.

Always . . . ~ℓℓ𝒪)

- **Refuse to settle.** Expect that you will get the guy you want. After all, he's what you deserve.
- **Don't mess with someone else's man.** Whether he's married, engaged, or has a girlfriend, steer clear. It's bad business, bad karma, bad every which way. Besides, if he does leave her for you, doesn't that make him the type to leave you for someone else?
- **Let him know how lucky he is.** Your behavior around him should always indicate your feeling of self-worth. It will remind him that you're by his side because you *choose* to be, that you have other options, that he'd better treat you right. You are the best thing that ever happened to him. Believe it, and he will, too.
- **Accept imperfection.** Nobody's perfect—not you, not him. No relationship is perfect either. Learn to compromise. Agree to disagree (and when you do argue, fight fair). Don't expect him to follow your script or your orders (you'll never respect him if he does). Realize that he may come with some baggage (don't we all).
- **Trust and be trustworthy.** Trust is the backbone of true love. You should never have to doubt him, nor he you. Do not cheat! What does that mean? *Anything* you wouldn't want him to do with a third party.
- **Communicate effectively.** Men are not from Mars, but there can be misunderstandings between the sexes. So don't expect him to "just know" what you want; tell him. Don't talk around your main point. Give him some time to absorb what you are saying. Don't play passive-aggressive. Avoid giving unsolicited advice or criticism—ask first.
- **Keep your kids in mind.** If you're a single mom, be cautious when it comes to dating. See a new man discreetly, and don't disrupt your children's schedule so you can date. Wait until you know for sure that your relationship is going somewhere before introducing a man to your kids (dating for *at least* six months first is a good general rule). Avoid arguing with your boyfriend in front of the kids.

Allow your children to have a relationship with their biological father, and don't confuse them by treating a boyfriend as a replacement daddy.

- **Be with him—but be yourself.** It's nice to be open to your man's interests and opinions, but if you find that you don't share them, let him pursue them on his own! Don't start TiVoing the U.S. Open just because he keeps a tennis racket in his trunk.

- **Treat him like a king.** If you've got a good man, make him feel special. Dress up for him. Tell him that you love him. Be supportive. It doesn't make you a doormat to do for him. It makes you a lucky woman who knows what she's got!

- **Don't overanalyze.** A healthy relationship is organic. If you find yourself constantly analyzing what's going on between you and your man, either you need to relax and lighten up or something is amiss. Try the former first. If you find yourself plagued by doubt, suspicion, or insecurity, you two might not belong together.

- **Don't confuse breakups with failures.** The media bombards us with the notion that there is only one true love for everybody. But the reality is, not every relationship is meant to last forever. You may want different things when you're sixteen, twenty-six, thirty-six, and beyond. As long as each relationship teaches you something, it is a success.

- **Protect yourself.** Please, girlfriend, *please* use a condom. I get so upset every time I think of you needlessly putting yourself at risk just because he insists or you get caught up in the moment. I really want you to have fun—just please respect your body, your spirit, your uniqueness, and your purpose on this planet. You are too valuable to risk your health for no good reason.

ROMANCE AND FINANCE

Once a relationship moves beyond the courting phase, couples tend to have misunderstandings about money. Before you move in together or start planning the wedding, get on the same page so you won't clash when it comes to cash.

- Figure out what is yours, what is his, and what you own together.

- Discuss who'll pay for what. Some couples simply deposit two paychecks in a joint account. Some determine a monthly household budget, then figure out how much each can contribute based on earnings, put that amount in a joint account, and pay bills from there. Others determine who'll pay which bills (she gets the rent; he gets everything else). Whichever you choose, agree and stick to it.
- Get your financial goals in line. Will you want to buy a house in the next few years? Will one of you want to go back to school or start a business sometime soon? What kinds of investments do you feel comfortable making?
- Discuss major purchases together. A plasma flat-screen—or a new washer/dryer? A second car—or an exotic vacation?
- Decide who will be responsible for paying the bills and balancing the checkbook.
- Don't lose sight of the fact that you're together for love, not loot!

5 THINGS YOU *CAN* GET HIM TO DO

Of course, you should accept your man for who he is. But here are some "fixes" for a few *minor* improvements. If you want him to . . .

1. **Dress better.** Shop with him, show him *why* certain things suit him, and flatter him when he looks sharp.
2. **Stop staring at other chicks.** Look captivating and be charming, and should his eyes wander, call his attention back to you with an "Over here, baby."
3. **Share his feelings.** Draw him out when he's relaxed (not exhausted) and has time to talk. Reveal something about yourself and ask him how he feels about that. Give him time to express himself, and listen.
4. **Cut his mama's apron strings.** Align yourself with his mother. Once she's on your side, you won't have to do anything—she will tell him to go home to you!
5. **Pick up after himself.** Assign him specific household chores (and then don't do them for him). Also, make it convenient for him to be neat by setting up your home with organizing systems.

HILL HARPER ON RELATIONSHIPS

Want to know what men really feel about love, lust, and relationships? Talk to a man! I decided to go to one of our most exciting leading men (and, at press time, one of the most eligible bachelors!): the talented Hill Harper, a star of CBS's CSI: NY and author of the terrific empowering book for young men Letters to a Young Brother: MANifest Your Destiny. Hill and I were cool from having gone to Brown together, but we became tight years ago over our two-way pagers. He and I used to have these random long discussions about our lives and dreams over short notes that we'd type back and forth all day. I really knew we were destined to be friends forever during a trip I took to Los Angeles for the MTV Video Music Awards show. Hill and I hung out the night after the show. We started out at some swanky L.A. restaurant, but instead of continuing the night at an equally high-profile club, he took me dancing at a small local lounge—a place where it was obvious that no paparazzi had ever stepped foot. We had the best time, and to this day I think Hill is one of the coolest guys I know.

Amy: **What should women look for in a man?**

Hill: Women should be looking for a man they are truly, truly, truly attracted to. I think most of us end up dating people that we think we are attracted to or that we are told we should be attracted to—the person who looks good on paper or has all those things that advertisers and music videos say you should be attracted to.

AB: **What do men look for in women? I find that a lot of men just look for the physical.**

HH: The problem is we have all been bombarded with the idea of what success or beauty is. These definitions can be very specific to communities. Meaning in one community the woman with the big earrings and the little baby hairs gelled down is what is sexy.

AB: **What defines a solid relationship for you?**

HH: It's the relationship where two people love each other so much, they are willing to do anything and everything for the other person. You love unconditionally. You want to know who they are, what they want out of life, and how you can help them manifest that—and they are doing that for you. It is a pluralistic relationship, rather than "I am just going to keep her" and "I am just going to keep him." We are all about keeping, particularly men, and women need to recognize this. Men will keep you around; they will keep you on the hook. They don't want to be with you but they will treat you well enough to make sure that you stay around.

AB: *Do men want what they can't have?*
HH: Yes, and that includes sexually. Oftentimes the woman will be like, "He was a little less interested once I gave it up. He called five times a day before, and now he just calls once a day." That is part of the whole chase.

AB: *Just to be real, finding a man who does not think that way is challenging! If a woman wants a mutually fulfilling, respectful, monogamous relationship, what do we do?*
HH: Find a man who is mature enough to have a relationship like that. Because if a guy feels like there is something else out there for him, he will be out there.

AB: *Do you think the state of black male and female relationships is in trouble?*
HH: Yes, huge trouble. But I think it is more the problem of what happens before we get into relationships. Listen, we as black people have self-worth issues that are serious. Unless we are addressing those, the idea of having a healthy relationship is out window. Rather than being comfortable about who we are, we look for value outside of ourselves. So with men it will manifest in terms of a trophy wife, creating manhood by sleeping with as many women as you possibly can, collecting women, dating women who look or dress a certain way. Women, on the flip side, would rather in many cases ignore truth and their intuition just to have a man who *looks* like the right man.

And if you really want to get *real,* there are sex issues with regard to black women that I think are societal—and that affects things.

AB: *What do you mean?*
HH: I think many black women are very conservative with regard to their sexuality. Black women exist in some type of strange spectrum

where she is either the stripper or she is ultraconservative, and that affects sex, dates, and relationships. Many black women have had tough experiences—with the father who may not have been around, with guys cheating on them. And society saying you are a "ho" because you are black. There is a callus that builds up in the soul that I believe starts to suck life out of you in the relationship area.

A lot of guys take a sister out and she is heavy—not heavy in weight but in mood. Her being-ness is heavy. And it is like, "My life is tough enough, I don't want to date a woman that brings me down even more. Why can't she just throw some shots down and party and dance on a table like Paris Hilton?" The most incredible black women I know are all of those things—sexy and sexual, serious and light—but they don't show it enough. They will show it with their girlfriends. If sisters can bring their same level of joy and fun that they have with their friends to relationships with men, you would see relationships among black men and black women improve.

AB: *Women have a lot of trust issues. It makes it difficult for us to let our guard down with men. What can we do?*
HH: You can't have it both ways. If you truly want to have the life that you say you want, you have to have the courage to step out, and live that life. Yes, there are trust issues. Yes, you have historically been the martyr, been beaten down, and things have been tough. But at the end of the day, if you really want to find that guy that is equally yoked with you, you need to bring it all to the table, too.

When you are overly serious, there is no wonder a guy does not want to date you—you are no fun with him. When you're with your girlfriend, you're like, "Girl, let's have a martini!" But with a man, you are totally different. Your girlfriend cannot understand—"How can you not have a boyfriend? You are the greatest girl I know!" Well, not when she is with a man.

AB: *Okay, if women need to relax and unclench their teeth, what should men do?*
HH: Men have the equal burden and responsibility to be honest with a woman from the get-go. Men have set women up so many times, and that is why women have gotten hurt. They will analyze the woman and

figure out what she wants to hear for him to be able to get with her, and he will present that. If she wants to hear, "I am looking to have a girlfriend, and I want to get married in the next couple of years," he will say that, knowing that is not what he is interested in at all. Men are dishonest because they have a goal—to collect women—because they feel inadequate.

AB: *Are there any other big mistakes that women make in dealing with men? Is there anything else that we can do to try and make things better?*
HH: The whole game-playing thing, women need to stop it. There are no rules if you are attracted to somebody. You are attracted—allow yourself to be. You don't have to tell yourself, "I need to date him this amount of times before I do this with him, and I am going to do this, and not do this." No! Let your intuition speak. If your intuition is telling you this is a guy that you don't need to be giving it up to, then don't give it up, whether it is the first date or the fiftieth date. Applying arbitrary rules and timetables is meaningless.

AB: *Do you think that men and women should have roles in a relationship?*
HH: I don't think the woman has to be the one to cook the meal every night and the guy should be the one to always think of what to do. If I can give one dating tip, it's women need to come up with some ideas—as a guy, it gets very tiring to always be the one that plans the dates. It should be equal. This pluralistic idea of two people bringing things to the table, I think this is huge. Analyze the tone of the conversations you have—are you telling him, or is he telling you? Or are you asking questions: "What do you want to do? What are you passionate about? What makes your heart beat faster?" If you are not hearing those types of questions from a potential partner, he is not for you. The most powerful relationships involve questioning. Each person is trying to serve the other.

AB: *Do you think a relationship is necessary to have a balanced life?*
HH: Everyone has their own journey, and things happen in time. My mother has been single for years and she has a wonderful and beautiful life. I believe she is happier now than when she was actually in a so-

called relationship. So I do not think it is required. If it is a positive relationship, then it is a positive addition to your life.

AB: *What makes you happy in a relationship?*
HH: I am a touchy person, so I personally like a woman who likes to touch. Little touches, hands on the shoulder, like that. If the woman brushes my hand, it is not sexual, but it is intimate. Those little touches—I call them touches of endearment. That is one thing. A light-spirited sense of humor. I want to enjoy life, so when we go out, let's have fun, joke around, act silly. I want to laugh. That is a turn-on to me. Seeing a woman laugh, and laughing with her, that is a turn-on. The other turn-on for me is confidence—in how you dress, and how you present yourself.

AB: *Do men want women to always be done up?*
HH: Absolutely not. They want them to be themselves in whatever way that that is. You don't have to be done up or wear the most popular gear or the cutest outfit. But whatever is special about you, always bring that to the table. It is more about the spirit—represent yourself in a unique way. Women feel like they have to dress the same, like the person they see in the magazine. Men are attracted to uniqueness. Be an original. You will shine and glow as the prettiest, most unique woman in the room.

AB: *Define* sexy.
HH: Sexiness is that internal sparkle behind your eye that you just know who you are, that you are comfortable with it, and you know how to share all of yourself with others, without giving yourself away. What I mean by that is that you can be totally present and like, whoa!—but you don't feel like someone is taking anything away from you. You are so confident that you can be here, be present right now, with this moment right now. That is sexy!

AB: *What's the best way to deal with a breakup?*
HH: A lot of people beat themselves up over relationships, whether it worked or not. What they did or what they didn't do. But timing has an impact on a relationship, where the two people are in their lives. You

can't go beating yourself up. That relationship with you two just wasn't right—it came to its organic end.

AB: *Do you have any other words of advice for women?*

HH: Keep your curiosity about new people, new places, new things, and new experiences. Don't be afraid to do things alone. You don't need someone else to take you to the museum, to go to see that movie. The point is to stay curious and keep putting input in. It doesn't mean that you need to go out to the club. But don't sit in your room and say there's just nothing out there for me. Experience life and live it.

PROMISE PAGE

My dreams and goals for a romantic
relationship are:

_____
_____
_____
_____
_____
_____

I promise that today I will:

_____
_____
_____
_____
_____
_____

This year I promise to:

_____
_____
_____
_____
_____
_____

I will always:

_____
_____
_____
_____
_____
_____
_____

9

GET YOUR CHIC ON

My mom, bless her heart, must not have wanted a vain daughter. She styled my hair in pigtails way past the appropriate age, bought me huge round beige glasses when she learned my vision was poor, and dressed me in colorful ensembles that defied trends and, frankly, good sense. When I hit my early teens, I added braces and bad skin, creating a trifecta of awkwardness that my self-esteem was built on. Mm-hmm, I was a sight to behold. And my awkward stage lasted most of the way through high school. I did, at least, discover fashion early—when I was ten years old, I pestered my mom until she bought me a pair of Sergio Valente dark-blue jeans and a gold-flecked purple sweater with matching socks so I had the perfect outfit for the all-important first day of fifth grade. By the time I got to junior high school, I was putting together some pretty elaborate ensembles, swinging wildly from preppy to punk to prissy, often in the same week (hey, at least I was creative!).

My beauty regime, however, lagged far behind. Every time I tried to make myself up, I just made the situation worse. My makeup choices were totally embarrassing: iridescent purple eye shadow and matching lip gloss that I would slather on in a thick, goopy layer. As if that wasn't bad enough, I made particularly gruesome errors with my hair, chopping it myself to create weird styles that looked like Edward Scissorhands had been practicing in my do. In college, I also developed a predilection for dying my hair bizarre shades, including a red so intense someone said I glowed in the dark. At my frequent salon visits with Mom and Grandma, various stylists would attempt to fix my misguided efforts at creating a "look," but usually the damage was already done and all they could do was wash and set my bright shorn head. The bottom line was that I kept experimenting because I had no idea who I wanted to be or what I really wanted to look like.

> **"You have to *feel* attractive to be attractive."**

And then, in my early twenties, I had a resonant and life-altering discovery. I still remember clearly that sunny afternoon a girlfriend and I wandered into the M.A.C. store in downtown New York City. Makeup mecca! Though by that time, I had already given up my sparkly purple face paint, frosty peach was now my staple lip color, and I was still using my blush as eye shadow. Having some style sense, and a year of classes in fashion design and merchandising under my belt, I'd honed my wardrobe. But my makeup game was terrible. The M.A.C. consultant took one look at my peachy palette and immediately sat me down in his chair for a total makeover.

> "Comfort and confidence is pure allure—it's what being sexy really means."

Though he spent a good fifteen minutes of our hour-long session lecturing me about how crazy I looked ("I mean, you're making your face all *red* and *orange* for no *reason,* and just *look* at your *bushy* brows . . ."), he had enough time to pluck my eyebrows into an actual arch and teach me a few things—how to contour my cheekbones, line my lips, apply concealer over as well as under my eyes, etc. By the time he had finished, I looked better than I ever had. Mercifully, I had just grown my hair into a cute shoulder-length bob and it was a nice chocolate brown (mostly because I was too lazy and poor at that time to keep up any high-maintenance style). The simple dark curtain of hair framed a face that suddenly seemed more angled and chic. The consultant, possibly angling for a juicy tip, even said I resembled a model he'd recently done for a fashion shoot. I tried to play it off, but in my mind I screamed, "He said I look like a *model!*"

Later that evening, my girlfriend and I went out to a club. We were convinced it was our new sophisticated look that got us past the bouncer in record time! That night ushered in a new era: my period of plenty. It wasn't an instant change, but the positive impact looking great had on my self-esteem carried through to everything else I was working out in my life. I started to feel like I'd truly arrived as an independent, single-and-lovin'-it career woman who was not afraid to do stuff like run off to a foreign country for half a year, throw fiscal caution to the wind to apply to grad school, scrap for unpaid writing gigs until someone finally paid me for my words, and party like a rock star when the mood (and the Möet) hit me. I felt confident—and confidence breeds confidence.

At first, I gave M.A.C. cosmetics *all* the credit. After all, the positive change in my appearance was so dramatic that, literally, everyone noticed. But it wouldn't have mattered if the polished exterior still covered an insecure wimpy woman. Yes, my new look helped me hold my head higher when I walked into a room, but I was also getting to know—and truly like—the real me.

For the record, my inner geek is always with me. I still look in the mirror and see her blinking back, the messy half 'fro, frosty lipstick, and big square eyebrows. But I can smile at her now with love, since I have become okay with my flaws and comfortable within my own skin. I have tapped into the secret and the true power of style and attractiveness: At the end of the day, you have to *feel* attractive to be attractive.

Next time you go out, take a good look at which woman gets the most attention. You'll notice that it's not always the prettiest woman in the room or the one in the skimpiest outfit, but often the woman who exudes confidence and looks like she's having the best time. That comfort and confidence is pure allure—it's what being sexy really means.

Urban women have been the source of many of the hottest style trends over the past two decades. We've always known how to hook ourselves up, but we often lack the confidence not only to work our external look but also to achieve the self-acceptance that makes us *truly* sexy. And trust me, girlfriend, beauty is temporary and fashion is transient, but sexy and stylish are forever. So your mission may not simply be a matter of scoring a new pair of stilettos, but being able to walk in any shoes like you rule the world!

Quiz: What's Your Style Profile?

Of course you've got style—I never met a sister who didn't. But are you truly working your innate sense of the fly and the fabulous to your best advantage? This quiz will hone in on your fashion and beauty assets, and help you take them to the next level.

1. When you walk into the club, heads turn because your

a. outfit is the exact same one Beyoncé wore in *Essence* last month.

b. look is pure class.

c. ensemble is completely unique.

2. You run into an old college friend at the mall, but she doesn't recognize you at first—probably because

a. you wore your hair longer in college, and almost always in a ponytail—it's a sleek bob now.

b. you change your hair every few months, and that day you're wearing a long, red, curly weave.

c. your sexy side-swept bangs are draped over one eye.

3. Like every woman, you consider jeans a wardrobe staple. To you, this means

a. thrift-store Levi's you've adorned yourself with patches from an old brocade jacket.

b. pairing them with a Ralph Lauren polo and Ferragamo loafers.

c. the latest pair of Sevens with a Marc Jacobs top and Jimmy Choo stilettos.

4. A friend is having a pool party. You wear a(n)

a. mix-n-match bikini in contrasting prints, platform sandals, and a bright headscarf.

b. sleek black one-piece under a pair of khaki shorts, tennis shoes, and a straw hat.

c. Etro swimsuit with matching cover-up, Chanel shades, and a sign that reads: SPLASH ME AND DIE!

5. When your man rings your doorbell to pick you up for a date, he wonders

a. how long you're going to keep him waiting while you finish dressing.

b. just what kind of look you'll have pulled together for tonight.

c. if you're going to scold him for wearing sneakers and jeans.

6. Your new job requires you to get to the office by eight every morning. You

a. wake up at five-thirty so you'll have time to do your hair.

b. bite the bullet and get a short, low-maintenance do.

c. devote some of the extra cash you're earning now to getting your hair done twice a week.

7. You look at fashion magazines to

a. get ideas for ways to update your look every season.

b. pick perfect ensembles for yourself, from shoes to 'dos.

c. suck your teeth over the foolishness some women will wear.

8. Your everyday makeup

a. takes five minutes—a dot of foundation to even your skin tone, mascara, and a sweep of lip gloss.

b. takes half an hour—it's not easy looking this flawlessly natural!

c. depends on your mood—black liner and red lips one day, deep purples and blues the next, an eighties-style rainbow the day after that.

9. It's not like you have unlimited funds to spend on your look, so you

a. would skip a few meals if there was something you simply had to have.

b. shop at flea markets for distinctive stuff you can afford.

c. invest in well-made, quality classics that never go out of style.

10. When dressing for a job interview you think

a. What would Oprah wear?

b. Comfort is key!

c. Will it work against me if my outfit costs more than my prospective boss's?

SCORE

Give yourself points as follows:

1. a = 3, b = 1, c = 2	**6.** a = 1, b = 2, c = 3
2. a = 1, b = 2, c = 3	**7.** a = 2, b = 3, c = 1
3. a = 2, b = 1, c = 3	**8.** a = 1, b = 3, c = 2
4. a = 2, b = 1, c = 3	**9.** a = 3, b = 2, c = 1
5. a = 3, b = 2, c = 1	**10.** a = 1, b = 2, c = 3

HERE'S THE DEAL

Cool, Classic, Collected (10 to 16 points) Let other women drive themselves crazy over the fickle whims of fashion—you have good taste, an unshakable sense of understated chic, so you don't worry about what's in or out. This is a great guiding principle for getting dressed, and it no doubt connotes what kind of smart, solid person you are inside. You'd no sooner wear clashing patterns and piles of bling than scream at someone to get your point across. But safe and conservative can get a little boring. If you ever feel hemmed in by your to-the-knee hemlines, or a trifle envious of that girl in the froufrou party dress, it's okay to give your fanciful side some play. Remix your classic look with a lingerie top under a blazer instead of a blouse, some funky-chunky beads against your cashmere T, a vintage wool suit from the forties. Come on—why not?

Unique, Eclectic, Chic (17 to 23 points) Do people have trouble recognizing you from one meeting to the next? Probably, since you're always changing up your look. Your style runs the gamut from classic to boho to, well, kooky—and it reflects your open-minded, free-spirited, adventurous personality. Sure, you check the fashion mags for inspiration, but you're not about to follow anyone's rules but your own. As long as you're comfortable and get a kick out of what you're wearing, that's all that counts—and this extends to your beauty routines as well as your wardrobe. You want your hair, nails, and makeup on point, but you're not willing to miss out on life for a high-maintenance image. Just remember to keep the appropriateness factor in mind when it comes to pulling yourself together for a job interview (no jeans, please!) or to meet your new man's parents (save the fishnets for another night).

Fierce, Fabulous, Impeccable (24 to 30 points) Fashion is a high-stakes game, and you play to win. You don't just flip through fashion magazines, you study them like you're trying for a PhD in Diva. Designer logos, jewelry from the finest stores, an "it" bag every season are your goals, if not your musts. This is just the kind of person you are—someone who deserves the best. Only trouble is, your dedication to always being at the height of fashion doesn't leave much room for creativity or comfort. The most amazing outfit is really amazing only if it looks great on you—so if long skirts are in, and you've got killer legs, why hide your assets just to mirror the pages of *Vogue*?

Also, consider what having every hair in place may cost you, not just in terms of money but in missed opportunities to have a blast. You're very high-maintenance, and I bet the air is pretty thin up there! Come down a few rungs, breathe easy, and have fun!

START **TODAY**, GIRLFRIEND!

I was running errands one Saturday afternoon and found myself with an hour to kill in midtown Manhattan. I decided to go to an upscale department store to look for a new lip-gloss shade for the summer. Next on my to-do list was a trip to Bed, Bath & Beyond to shop for bathroom accessories. Clearly, I was not dressed to kill. I was rocking a sweat suit (not even a cute Juicy, just an old gym tracksuit) with flip-flops and a scruffy tank top. I hadn't bothered to put on any jewelry and I'd pulled my hair into a fuzzy ponytail.

As I entered the posh store, I could see the security guards' eyes rivet on me, then chart my every move as I made my way down the aisle. I kept it moving, but when I rolled up to a cosmetics counter, I could also feel the disdain of the overly made-up saleswoman. After ignoring me for several minutes, she slooowly finished straightening the display case, made her way over, looked me up and down, sighed deeply, and asked if I needed help in a tone that indicated she thought I was *beyond* help. I was so turned off by her attitude that I turned on my heel and went to another counter. There, it took me several minutes to get the women gossiping behind the counter to notice that they had a customer. I kept thinking how ironic it was that I was the editor-in-chief of a national magazine that beauty companies begged to place their products in, yet I couldn't get anyone to sell me a stupid lip gloss!

When a saleswoman finally heard me say "*Excuse* me," she rolled her eyes at her friends and leisurely sauntered over. She didn't even bother to speak, just looked at me with raised eyebrows and a smirk. Girlfriend, you know I wanted to tell her about herself, but my husband and I were going to a dinner that night and my time was running shorter than my patience. While I was waiting I'd already checked out a couple of shades I liked and just handed the floor samples to the saleswoman with a matching smirk. As I dug cash out of my wallet, I watched her casually root for the boxed lip glosses in a drawer and toss them into a bag. I went home, did my hair, put on a cocktail dress and heels, and reached into the small shopping bag for a lip gloss to finish the look. Of course, the salesgirl had thrown the wrong colors into my bag. I was so mad, I made my husband leave early so we could stop by the store (okay, I'm not *totally* crazy—it was on the way).

It was a totally different story when I went back all dressed up in designer gear. The guards smiled and waved me in. I was offered endless spritzes of perfume and free samples of makeup on my way to the area where I'd bought the lip gloss, and when I walked up to the counter, the woman who had treated me so poorly earlier rushed over to serve me. When she realized who I was, she got flustered and apologized profusely for her mistake. I didn't read her the riot act, but simply smiled and exchanged my purchase.

Now, on the one hand, salespeople should be polite to whomever walks into the store, regardless of how they are dressed. On the other hand, I took it as a personal lesson. Clearly, the saleswomen were way out of line, and I'm not trying to justify their behavior. However, I really do believe the care we take with our own appearance is a signal to others of what kind of treatment we expect—especially as women of color. You don't have to spend a ridiculous amount of money on your clothes and hair to get some respect, just know that you control how people see and, therefore, act toward you.

These days, I try to look my best at all times. I'm not saying I put on a full face of makeup for the gym or wear a designer gown to the car wash, but I just know how differently I'm treated depending on my appearance. Today, whether you're going to work or to a party or on a date, think about how you want to be treated and dress for it. This doesn't mean buy the most expensive clothes or dress up every day. Just wear an outfit appropriate for the situation and walk through the world looking like you love yourself. The world will react accordingly.

Today . . . ~ℓℓ◯

- **E-windowshop.** Do some online browsing at several fashion and beauty Web sites. It's a totally free way to get ideas for sharpening your look. You don't have to buy everything (or anything, really)—this is just for inspiration.

- **Stock up on beauty bargains.** Here's a secret I learned during my long association with beauty professionals: The cheap stuff often works just as well as fancy products in glossy packages. For example, I cannot tell you how many top makeup artists swear by good old Maybelline Great Lash. Check out the deals you can get at the drugstore.

- **Evaluate your closet.** Donate or dump anything that shows signs of wear and tear, colors and cuts that don't suit you, items that don't make you feel fabulous when you put them on. Then reorganize your closet so that you can find stuff easily. Opening that door—the door to your personal style—should give you a serene, supremely confident feeling. That can't happen if your closet is a wreck.

- **Build a look around an accessory.** Often we throw on clothes, grab earrings, and go, but for a truly original style statement, try the reverse approach. Choose a treasured accessory, then select an outfit that shows it off.

- **Commit to skin care.** Evaluate your skin (oily, normal, combination, or dry) and purchase a regimen of products to treat it (again, no need for hundred-dollar jars of moisturizer!). Get or give yourself a facial (and "chestial/backial" if you need it). And no matter how bone-tired you are when you get home tonight, wash off your makeup.

- **Hook up your brows.** Treat yourself to a professional eyebrow shaping (either a waxing, threading, or tweezing). If you don't want to bother with weekly salon visits for upkeep, DIY by following the shape the pro gives you. Consider bleaching your brows a shade lighter than your hair. It sounds weird, but slightly lighter brows make your eyes look huge and brighten your whole face.

- **Invest in good beauty tools.** Buy a sturdy pair of tweezers and an eyelash curler. Also get a good set of makeup brushes (the ones that come in the compact generally don't do the trick). Wash makeup brushes regularly with mild soap and water to banish nasty germs.

- **Find your best foundation.** Finally, cosmetics companies are acknowledging women of color! So get the shade that matches perfectly and blends flawlessly. Use foundation only where you need it, not necessarily all over your face.

MAKE **THIS YEAR** COUNT

Several years ago, I got a weave. I was going to a televised awards show, and a hairstylist I'd profiled for *Essence* (where I worked at the time) offered me a freebie. She wove a two-foot-long, thick, straight mane into my own shoulder-length hair. And for the next week and a half, men would *not* leave me alone. I got more whistles and stares than ever before, and was even followed by one overly persistent loser until I led him to a parked police car and knocked on the tinted window.

While I didn't totally dislike all the weave-generated attention, I was fully annoyed by its source: someone else's hair. It was the first time I seriously began to consider cutting off my own locks. At the very least, I couldn't wait to get the weave out. The hairstylist was shocked when I appeared two weeks early to have it removed. Don't be mad, girlfriend—I've got nothing aginst a good weave. It just wasn't for yours truly.

I was already accustomed to receiving different levels of male attention, depending on my hairstyle. When I wore my hair straight and loose, I'd get tons of it; when I pulled my natural curls into a ponytail, few men looked my way. That weave only emphasized the point: Men tend to respond strongly to women with long, straight hair. Perhaps that's why, preweave, I really did crave long hair. Unfortunately, a bad dye job had so damaged my 'do, it would grow to about an inch or so past my collarbone and split. I took hair-strengthening supplements, got expensive deep conditioning treatments, used hair sunscreen, and slept in a silk scarf every night. The whole process was extremely frustrating. I started to ask myself: Why was long hair so important to me? And why did I want to attract men who preferred fake hair anyway?

A black woman cutting off her naturally curly semilong hair is an act of rebellion, empowerment, or stupidity, depending on whom you ask. For more than a year I tortured people with endless questions about whether short hair would flatter me, if I had a funny-shaped head, and how I'd deal on bad-hair days if a ponytail was not an option.

What ultimately pushed me over the edge? One day, I heard someone I had thought was enlightened and cool say of a woman with long, loose curls, "She'd be nothing without her hair." Hearing this from another woman's mouth, I couldn't believe that I had bought into the long-hair nonsense, too. Right then I realized that I was expending way too much energy worrying that I would be somehow diminished with short hair. I am so much more than my hair! I called that day to book an appointment with my trusted hairstylist to cut off my hair—cut it *all* off.

Despite my resolve, I was really nervous on the day of my appointment. I made my best friend hold my hand while my stylist snipped away. But when the cutting was done, I felt incredibly free. And when I walked out of the salon with my supershort shag, I got just as many stares and remarks from men as I did when I had the weave. This time, they were responding to my excitement and confidence.

I kept my hair short for several years. I dyed it blond, then reddish brown. I wore it curly, straight, spiky. And I had a great time. Eventually I grew it again because I wanted to try some new looks, but now I change my hairstyle every few years. Personally, I believe that every woman of color should go short at least once, just to detach from all that long hair drama. You can always grow it back—it's just hair. Not ready? That's cool. But at least experiment with some aspect of your appearance this year: Switch your hairstyle or color (or try braids for a vacation with your girls). Buy an all-black outfit if you're used to wearing color, or a bright jewel-colored dress if black is your wardrobe staple. Just do something new, and know that people's reactions will depend much more on your confidence than on the actual change. Most important, have fun!

This Year . . .

- **Style yourself like a pro.** Secret insight: Whenever you see a celeb step onto the red carpet, remember that she had a team of professionals devote hours to everything from her pedicure to the part in her hair. Not that you should hire a stylist before a night on the town, but a single consultation with a pro (or a friend with great style) can pay off. If there's an aspect of your look that you're not supersolid on, be it hair, makeup, or fashion, get some advice. Ask questions and take notes; then use this knowledge to put yourself together like you're ready for your close-up.
- **Minimize your maintenance.** The problem with a high-maintenance

look is you can't get back the time you put into it. And what would you rather do—get ready, or have a blast? So put yourself on speed style! Develop a hair-and-makeup routine that doesn't take forever.

- **Look like a million within your means.** Figure out how to look hot without blowing your budget. Buy clothes a month or two into the season so you can hit the sales. Learn how to give yourself a facial (plug "at-home facial" into a search engine for how-tos). Get a hairstyle you can manage inexpensively.

- **Host a clothes exchange.** Want a new wardrobe without spending a cent? Invite several of your most stylish girlfriends over for a clothing swap. Each invitee must go through her closet and bring a shopping bag full of stuff that no longer works for her. Then swap till you drop!

- **Get a great tailor.** Nothing makes an outfit look better than a perfect fit—but since no one has a perfect body, a tailor can make all the difference. A sewing machine maven is your secret weapon— whether you need something taken in at the waist, let out around the hips, or hemmed to the ideal length.

- **Take on a DIY project.** Nothing says distinction like something you made yourself. Learn to knit or crochet. Take a jewelry-making class. Design an emblem of your own and embroider it onto a pair of jeans. Find a vintage dress in a thrift store and use the funky fabric to make a sash or scarf. Let your imagination go!

- **Find your best jeans.** Finding great jeans can sometimes feel like an impossible mission, but the perfect pair is out there. Search until you find the cut that works your assets. Then buy two pairs—hem one for heels and one for flats.

- **Declare war on obvious beauty busters.** While I advise accepting who you are and what the good Lord gave you, that doesn't mean you should tolerate ashy skin, acne, damaged hair, or a bad weave. Even out your skin tone and banish pimples. Trim your hair, renew your weave, and get your roots touched up regularly. Have your teeth cleaned, and whiten them using an at-home kit. Exfoliate your body skin so you're smooth all over. And, above all, shave!

GET YOURS **FOREVER**

When I was at *Honey,* I'd do periodic photo shoots to change the picture I put on "Personal Space," my monthly column. Usually the shoots were a major production, with a stylist, makeup artist, photographer, and assistants. Imagine trying to look relaxed and natural in borrowed clothes with a crowd watching you pose. Not so easy! One photo shoot in particular was really nerve-racking for me. The photographer was a high-strung *artiste* with a crew of bored, chain-smoking assistants who were visibly irritated that they weren't spending the day on a "real" fashion shoot. When the photographer shined a superbright light on my face and told me to pout for the camera, all I wanted to do was throw my own jeans back on and rush out the door. I settled for a nervous chuckle. "I don't know how models do this all day," I said, stalling. "I never love the way I look in pictures."

That's when one of the photographer's assistants decided to weigh in: "Yeah, well, it's not like you're twenty-two anymore," he casually announced.

There was dead silence, then a flurry of hasty apologies and I-only-meants. But I just started laughing. That was exactly what I needed to hear to help me shake off my anxiety! The guy was right—I was thirty-one and I loved my age. See, I didn't have the traditional thirtieth-birthday crisis so many women go through. In fact, I was psyched to enter my thirties. I'd done so many crazy things in my twenties, I remember thinking that now that I had some real experience under my belt, the next decade would be cake in comparison.

Most of my friends, however, had been petrified at the prospect of turning thirty. During one memorable girls' night out, a few of my friends started to complain: "I'll never look as good as I did at twenty-five"; "The chicks my boyfriend stares at on the street are all younger than me"; "My boobs are sagging"; etc. Even the most accomplished, respected professionals in our group admitted they'd begun to obsess about gray hair and wrinkles.

In our youth-driven pop culture, it's hard not to feel past your prime by the time you've hit your late twenties. Models, singers, actresses, even sports stars, are younger than ever. And, I can't lie: When my guy friends point out how hot some barely legal party princess is,

I do get a *little* aggravated. True, men also experience forms of appearance-based discrimination, but usually guys are judged on their achievements. (We all know that if we see a Steve Urkel look-alike with a supermodel, he's got to be paid!) Besides, men are deemed "distinguished-looking" when they get crow's-feet and turn salt-and-pepper.

Well, I'm thirty-seven years old as I write this and have no wish to turn back the clock because the secret to true beauty has little to do with how you actually look. It's all about how you carry yourself and how you feel. There's nothing more attractive than a secure woman who's not afraid to command attention. (However, there are few things less attractive than an attention-grabbing ego-tripper. It's a fine line—do not cross it.) The icing on the cake? Being observant, intelligent, and kind. Guys may not be initially drawn to your big, beautiful brain, but that is what keeps them. Clearly, I believe in looking your best, but let me assure you, the combination of being confident and interesting is very, very sexy—at any age.

"Define beauty on your own terms."

It took me most of my twenties to figure this out, and now I feel better about myself than ever before. I know that because I'm happier, healthier, and more knowledgeable, I am a much more attractive person as I head into my late thirties. I'm even looking forward to my fortieth birthday—I can only assume that by then I will understand and appreciate myself even more. Embrace the idea that you are as attractive as you feel and that sexiness is about confidence more than your actual appearance. You will stay hot forever!

Always . . .

- **Define beauty on your own terms.** It's difficult when you're bombarded by media images of skinny models and teen starlets, but you know who and what you are. Remember, too, that as much as we would like it, there is no photo retouching in a three-dimensional world.
- **Work what you've got.** Rather than obsess about your flaws and spend time and money trying to reverse them, push your power

points. That great smile, those gorgeous eyes, your gravity-defying booty, etc. They will never let you down!

- **Develop a timeless personal style.** Understand the difference between fashion (fleeting) and style (forever). Don't be a fashion victim—accept that some trends may not flatter you and avoid them, even though "everyone" might be wearing them. Choose cuts and colors that not only look good on you but make you feel great, too.

- **Clear out your closet.** Take those bundles of clothes you no longer wear down to the thrift store and get a receipt you can write off on your taxes. Or, better yet, go to the Dress for Success Web site, dressforsuccess.org, to get information about where to donate your gently used suits and separates to women who are trying to get ahead and may not have the funds to buy the appropriate gear.

- **Invest in your bag and shoes.** Don't just buy a pricey purse or pair of kicks because of the logo, but because these items hold up—in terms of stylishness and sturdiness. Shabby shoes and bad bags do not reflect well on you. Oh, and please, please, go for comfort! Shoes that squeeze your feet put a grimace on your face, and too-high heels make most people walk funny.

- **Go bright at night.** The little black dress is fine, but it's not your only option for evening wear. Hot colors look great against brown skin, and will help you stand out in a crowd.

- **Shop smart!** Buy clothes during sale season. November's the time for fall bargains, February for winter clothes, May for spring merchandise, and August for summer steals. If you're a catalog or online shopper, remember that these outlets offer discounts, too. Sign up at your favorite stores and they'll send you coupons (but avoid opening charge cards for stores, even if they try to lure you with discounts for signing up). All that said, never buy just because something's on sale; only buy clothes you love.

- **Be proud of who you are.** It never fails to amaze me when I hear gorgeous brown-skinned women talk about how they don't like their skin color. Please, please, love your skin . . . and hair and features and shape. There is no such thing as "pretty for a dark girl." There is only confident or not—and I truly hope, after reading this book, you will commit to being fabulous you!

7 WAYS TO PUMP UP YOUR STYLE

Look like you, only even more fly!

1. **Get inspired.** June Ambrose (the famed celebrity stylist who's worked with Mary J. Blige, Mariah Carey, Jay-Z, and Kelly Ripa, just to name a few) has written a fabulous book called *Effortless Style*. She makes looking good look easy!

2. **Accessorize bold.** Large beads or a wide belt with a big buckle will get you noticed. Just stick to one chunky piece; don't pile them on.

3. **Shop when you travel.** Expand your wardrobe as you broaden your horizons. Buy interesting items wherever you go so you'll stand out at home.

4. **Shine on.** You needn't drop megabucks on bling. Go for fabulously fake rhinestones or metallic details on shoes and bags. Try makeup in gold or even silver hues.

5. **Do an updo.** Sweep your hair into a chignon, French twist, or simple sleek bun for instant glamour.

6. **Play head games.** Keep a few hats you like on hand to change up your look and help you deal on bad-hair days.

7. **Grab alternative "accessories."** Drink the chic cocktail of the season. Carry a fab foreign magazine under your arm. Stock your iPod with buzz-worthy tunes.

10 WAYS TO FEEL GORGEOUS— NO MAKEUP REQUIRED

Want to feel really pretty, right now? Here's how:

1. Luxuriate in a bubble bath.
2. Buy some silky sheets with a high thread count.
3. Meditate or do breathing exercises.
4. Talk to someone who loves you.
5. Have your man wash your hair or polish your toenails.

6. Get long braids for a vacation.
7. Treat yourself to a spa day.
8. Lie naked in a sauna or steam room.
9. Have a vigorous workout.
10. Make a child smile.

KELIS ON STYLE

The thing about Kelis that's so ridiculously attractive is that she simply does not give a damn. As long as I've known her, she's never cared about what others think of her, her music, her style, whatever. The proof? The first single off her debut album, "Caught Out There," in which she yells, "I HATE YOU SO MUCH RIGHT NOW!" Over the years, Kelis has carried off long curly multicolored hair, short straight pink hair, mod minis, eighties leggins, hippie skirts, punk rock spikes—and even a bright green wedding gown. (Her husband, rapper Nas, has said of his wife, "She's the hottest one out here. Point. Blank. Period.") Clearly, when Kelis sang, "My milkshake brings all the boys to the yard," she wasn't kidding. Now she's four albums into being a funky alternative to a sea of generic R&B divas.

I've interviewed Kelis in the past and spent time with her at photo shoots, but we hung out only once. I was with some friends at a nightclub in Manhattan, sitting around a raised circular banquette that overlooked the rest of the club. In strolls Kelis, rainbow hair, artfully ripped shirt, bangles up both arms. We said our hellos, ordered some drinks, and got comfortable. Next thing I knew, Kelis heard her jam, jumped up, and started to dance. And I don't mean the self-conscious hip wiggling of a celebrity who's hyperaware that an entire nightclub is checking her out. No, Kelis was dancing—and she has skills. My friends and I stared for a moment, and then joined in. And then the whole club went crazy. I don't think a single person was sitting down by the end of the song. Kelis was having such a good time doing her thing that she became the hottest person in the club—whether you were into her look or not. Now, that's sexy. Here, she shares her style secrets.

Amy: *You're such a trendsetter. Have you always been ahead of the curve?*
Kelis: I'm just really honest with my look. I trust myself and I believe in what I'm wearing. I wear what I feel like that day: It might not work any other day, but on that particular day it feels perfect. A lot of times I'm on the worst-dressed list of gossip magazines and I never care. I never apologize for anything I wear.

AB: *What are your inspirations?*
K: My mom. I have three sisters, and my mom let us wear what we wanted and encouraged us to be ourselves. I'm sure my mom thought I looked crazy sometimes, but she gave me the style confidence I have today. Plus, I like to wear a lot of her old clothes. I also believe in themes. Some days I might look like a goth, other days I look like a hippie, but I always feel like myself.

AB: *Do you think that clothes can help to shape a woman's image?*
K: Sure. My clothes reflect my personality. I like to have fun and I don't take myself seriously.

AB: *And I believe that people treat you according to how you look.*
K: Absolutely. Appearance is everything for a woman. Even in business. The male head of a Fortune 500 company can look sloppy, but a woman has got to be put together.

AB: *What are some basic things a woman can do to look good?*
K: I used to be a salesgirl and I noticed that many women didn't know what looked good on them. You have to know yourself and how to dress for your body. Some clothes I think are really fly, but I know they wouldn't work on me. I have really long legs so I'll wear shorter things to accentuate them. Other areas of my body I don't love as much, so maybe I don't show them off.

AB: *What's more important: developing a personal style or looking like you know what major trends are hot?*
K: There's a big difference between fashion and style. Fashion is all about art, the whole process of creating and showing a line of clothing. Style is about who you are and how you make that look yours.

Someone can tell you the fashion trends, but no one can tell you how to have personal style. That's all about who you are.

AB: *So many stars these days look and dress the same, but you always stand out in the crowd. What do you do to add a personal spin to your outfits?*
I don't just take a runway look and wear it—I make it my own. You could take a really formal designer blazer and rock it with jeans and sneakers. Anything that makes a look unique.

AB: *What style details do you think are most important?*
K: I think people overlook accessories. Every woman should have at least one killer bag and some great shoes. Even if you're on a budget, just get one amazing pair of black shoes and another brown—so every day your shoes and your bag are tight. Also, the color you choose to wear can be powerful. People loved me when I dyed my hair pink. But when I dyed it green, they thought I was a freak and treated me really badly.

AB: *Do you have any more suggestions for women on a budget?*
K: Check out old glamorous stars for style ideas. Or go to a vintage store. I wear vintage stuff all the time. I don't like to look like I'm wearing old clothes, but you can find really cool and cheap things in vintage stores that no one else will have.

AB: *Do you think that makeup and hair are as important as clothes?*
K: Absolutely. A lot of times people see your face and hair first. Some days I go crazy with my makeup just because I feel like it. You can really express yourself with makeup if you want to.

AB: *I love that you cut off your hair. When I chopped off mine several years ago, people thought I was insane!*
K: People were surprised when I cut mine off, too. So many women think that you have to have long hair to be sexy. Well, I don't think so. I think you can have short hair or long hair or curly hair or straight hair and be equally hot. It just depends on the person.

AB: *What does Nas think about your style?*
K: I don't know. I've never asked him! I guess he likes it. I know he thinks I'm sexy.

AB: *Do you think it's necessary to dress for your man?*

K: Absolutely. I don't know why people think that it's a problem to dress for your man and to look sexy, like you're doing something negative. Some days I totally dress for myself and other days I want Nas to think I look good. Sometimes he looks at me and he's like, "Damn, you look hot." And I like that. I think it's important for your man to enjoy the way you look.

AB: *How much of feeling sexy is about self-confidence?*

K: A lot of it. You have to know what looks good on you, but you also have to feel like you look good and know that your outfit reflects who you are.

AB: *Black women tend to like to get dressed up. Do you think we overdo it?*

K: We *do* like to dress up, but I'm not mad at that at all. I will say that I think it's really important to dress appropriately for an occasion. I don't think you should wear a cocktail dress to a ball game. I drive my manager crazy sometimes when I'm getting ready to go to an event because I want to know where it's going to be, who will be there, will I be mostly sitting or standing . . .

AB: *What have been your most important life lessons?*

K: Be true to yourself and be honest about who you are. Also, I don't worry about today because I believe it will take care of itself. I leave most things up to God and I don't stress. I always try to have fun—and I know my style reflects that.

PROMISE PAGE

My dreams and goals for my personal style are:
_____
_____
_____
_____
_____
_____

I promise that today I will:
_____
_____
_____
_____
_____

This year I promise to:
_____
_____
_____
_____
_____

I will always:
_____
_____
_____
_____
_____
_____

10

GET YOUR PERSONAL SPACE

Not too long into our apartment hunt, my then-husband and I lucked into a beautiful space with two huge bedrooms, a windowed eat-in kitchen with a walk-in pantry, and a sprawling living room that overlooked a garden. It was fabulous, and I wanted so badly to have the perfect newlywed apartment that I spent months decorating it. I studied various shelter magazines for influences and created a space as close to a designer showcase as I could get on my budget by renovating the kitchen and bathrooms, buying fancy Italian furniture, and painting every room a different understated color. I added some signature splashes of color (more on that later), but only within a palette I'd researched and charted on a board with little paint chips. Everyone who visited complimented us on how beautiful it was.

Secretly, I couldn't stand it.

For a while, I tried to pretend, even to myself, that I was as in love with my apartment as everyone else seemed to be. I would walk from room to room, admiring the sophisticated colors, the little finishes, the shiny hardwood floors. Yet somehow it left me cold and I just couldn't shake the feeling that I didn't belong there. Even before my marriage started to noticeably go south, I had concerns in the back of my mind. Why, I kept thinking, doesn't our apartment feel like home? Looking back, I sometimes wonder if our straight outta *Architectural Digest* abode contributed to the demise of the relationship. Maybe we just couldn't get comfortable in our "impeccable" space.

Fast-forward to the first time I visited Jeff's place. It wasn't particularly fancy or decorated or even, well, neat. But it was warm and colorful, with simple dark furniture, and photos of his family and friends, and amazing artwork (by his father) on every wall. I felt instantly comfortable and I just *knew* . . . Now he and I have an apartment that means more to me than anyplace I've ever lived. It's not huge, nor did we spend a fortune decorating it. But we have large, beautiful windows, artwork from both of our collections and from our trips to the Caribbean and Asia, and a great deck that we hang out on almost every night as long as the weather allows. We've even started gardening, filling the deck with different plants for every season. Just being in our apartment relaxes me and makes me feel happy.

And every time I curl up on the sofa or lounge around the kitchen (watching Jeff cook!) or snuggle with our baby I feel so blessed to be here, since I truly believe your living environment deeply affects you—spiritually, mentally, and physically. Your home can clear your head, soothe your soul, define your world, show your appreciation for yourself, and enhance your private and family time. Now, I don't mean that you have to live in a palace with pricey furniture and trendy finishes. In fact, some of the loveliest homes I've seen belong to friends who don't have a lot of money and were forced to be creative. You just want to make sure your home reflects your taste and your spirit. You want it to be a space that you're not only proud to show off during a dinner party but makes you feel content when you're sitting around in your sweats drinking coffee on Sunday morning.

> "Make sure your home reflects your taste and your spirit."

I believe it's important for all women to have a beautiful home so we can stay calm and happy, no matter where we happen to be in our relationships. In fact, if you are currently single, I urge you to put together your personal space as a testament to your independence, to ensure that your highest expectations are met before you even consider moving in with a partner.

Quiz: Does Your Space Suit You?

Your place should give you comfort, please your senses, and reflect your personality. Take this quiz to see if where you hang your hat really is your home.

1. Your dream house is
a. a big, rambling place with a different style of decor in every room.

b. an airy condo in a modern high-rise with all the amenities.

c. a warm, cozy place filled with books, knickknacks, and framed photos.

2. The most important piece of furniture in your home is

a. the bed—basically, you're there to sleep.

b. the large, comfy sofa strewn with plush pillows.

c. your find of the moment—right now, a hexagonal leopard-print coffee table you bought in an antique shop.

3. Your idea of entertaining is

a. a dinner party for half a dozen close friends—five courses, linen napkins, the good china.

b. a simple preparty before a night on the town—chips, dips, and beer.

c. great jams, gourmet finger food, and colorful decorations for a lively crowd.

4. After a long, rough work week, you come home Friday evening and

a. put on your sweats, pop some popcorn, and forget your troubles.

b. vent your aggressions by painting the bathroom.

c. jump in the shower, change your clothes, and head out to the club.

5. You've *got* to clean the house on Saturday. That means

a. an hour, max, of running the vacuum and sanitizing the bathroom.

b. an all-day affair of dusting your collections and scrubbing your tiles with a toothbrush.

c. several hours of straightening up all the piles before you even get to the nitty-gritty cleaning.

6. Your date arrives to pick you up, but you're not ready yet. When you finish primping, you find him

a. wandering around, checking out all your stuff.

b. sunken into your couch cushions, eating candy from a cut-glass bowl.

c. sitting stiffly in one of the two chairs.

7. When it comes to home improvements, you know how to

a. fix a leaky faucet.

b. change a lightbulb.

c. call the super.

8. You'd like to spice up your space but need some inspiration, so you
a. breeze through the Ikea and West Elm catalogs.
b. visit your grandmother's home.
c. roam the design and fabric districts of your city.

9. The last time you cooked in your kitchen was
a. dinner Thursday night.
b. breakfast this morning.
c. Does making coffee count?

10. You're considering reupholstering your old sofa. Your eye is drawn to
a. soft microsuedes in rich colors similar to the hues you've already scoped out in home decor magazines.
b. lush patterns and prints, just like your mom and grandma have in their living rooms (maybe minus the plastic covers).
c. Teflon-coated gray and beige fabric, like the functional furniture in your office lobby.

THE SCORE
Give yourself points as follows:

1. a = 2, b = 3, c = 1	**6.** a = 2, b = 1, c = 3
2. a = 3, b = 1, c = 2	**7.** a = 2, b = 1, c = 3
3. a = 1, b = 3, c = 2	**8.** a = 3, b = 1, c = 2
4. a = 1, b = 2, c = 3	**9.** a = 2, b = 1, c = 3
5. a = 3, b = 1, c = 2	**10.** a = 2, b = 1, c = 3

HERE'S THE DEAL
Cozy in the House (10 to 16 points) Home is where your heart is! You're a genuine nester, and you feel happiest and most comfortable snuggled up in your own space. Not that you necessarily intend to be there solo (what man wouldn't fall for your housekeeping and cooking skills?), but your place is about *you*. It's your haven, your retreat. You maintain it lovingly, and that shows how much you love yourself. Even if it's not the biggest house on the block, or in the choicest zip code, it is beautiful. Spending time at home helps you reenergize and relax, get away from the mad, mad world. That said, bear in mind that there *is* a whole wide world out there—your place is great, but you don't want to be isolated inside it like a princess held prisoner

in a castle. Next time someone suggests a Saturday adventure, don't turn it down in favor of dusting knickknacks!

Lively in the House (17 to 23 points) Though you're too much of a doer to spend tons of time at home, you do enjoy being there—and having friends share it with you. An independent woman with varied interests, your choice of neighborhood and funky home reflect your personality. And your take-control attitude extends to the fact that you know your way around a screwdriver (the tool, not the cocktail)—you actually like tackling a home-improvement project. Only caveat: Your crib can get a bit cluttered, even messy. That's not good for your personal clarity. Either cut back on the stuff, or buy some storage containers that will help you stay organized. And before things get too out of hand, consider hiring a cleaning service.

Simplicity in the House (24 to 30 points) As long as there's a closet, a bathroom, and a bed, you're cool with your crib. The very words *cozy* and *homey* make you feel claustrophobic. A minimalist with a busy schedule, you feel that the fewer rooms, the less furniture, the more built-in conveniences, the better. Maybe you'd simply rather stay out and party than curl up with a good book, or you've got so many roommates the crib is more hectic than the club. Or your not-into-nesting attitude could stem from a less-than-nurturing environment growing up. That doesn't mean your home life should be devoid of personal pleasure. A few simple things like fresh flowers on your nightstand, scented candles in your bathroom, or high-thread-count sheets will sweeten your existence. Who knows—soon enough your mantra may be "There's no place like home!"

START **TODAY**, GIRLFRIEND!

Many years ago, while I was still living single in Brooklyn, I had one memorably hideous day. A work project I'd been struggling with for months fell through, I got into a terrible fight with the guy I was dating, and I lost my umbrella after getting my hair done. By the time I walked into the lobby of my building that night, I was exhausted, cranky, and had a huge frizzy 'fro. A mailbox filled with bills didn't help the situation. I got off the elevator on my floor, ready to crawl into bed and pull the covers over my head. But then I saw a beautiful bouquet of bright flowers sitting in front of my door. I knew they weren't from my man (a cheap creep who ended up getting the boot soon after that day). Turned out, they were from my neighbor. A couple of weeks earlier, I'd done her a major favor, and she'd left me the flowers as a thank-you.

It was a simple arrangement, but the colors were striking—lots of reds and purples. I put them on the coffee table in my living room and took a few steps back to survey the effect. I'd never realized before how dull the colors in my apartment were. It was all cream and brown; I was going for simple chic, but the splash of color from the flowers made my space look bland and generic. I threw myself onto my tan sofa, ready to sink into my well-earned sulk, but as I gazed at the lilies and roses and snapdragons in front of me, I felt my mood suddenly lighten. Instead of wallowing in my setbacks, I decided to end my day on a positive note. I went online, found a resource for cute home accessories, and ordered some red and purple velvet pillows for my sofa and two red vases for my bookshelves. The items were such a small (and cheap—under fifty dollars!) addition, but when they arrived, they changed the look of my whole living room.

> "Discover your personal decor sensibility—just as you figured out your personal style."

More important, that small incident changed the way I felt about my space. I was happier coming home because I appreciated it more. Because I appreciated it more, I spent more time finding little things for my apartment that made me smile. I had very little money at the time, so nothing I bought was expensive, but it really doesn't take much to add some fun and personal style to your home.

I'm not saying red and purple is the be-all and end-all. But for me, splashes of color against simple furniture in muted shades do the trick. For you, it could be the opposite or something totally different. The point is to discover your personal decor sensibility—just as you figured out your personal style—and begin to transform your living space into something that makes you happy.

Start today by doing something simple: Buy yourself some flowers (they don't have to be pricey—a five-dollar bunch of daisies will do). Put them in a vase and set them in the center of your home. Now, just take a moment to appreciate what they add to your surroundings. Do the colors please you? Does the fresh scent make you feel like you've done something nice for yourself? Imagine all of the possibilities in your home and start to get excited about loving where you live.

Today . . .

- **Evaluate your current place.** Decide which decorating changes will have the most positive impact on your lifestyle and which can wait. Go from room to room and ask yourself questions about what fits your lifestyle, and what enhances or detracts from your overall level of happiness.
- **Get more decor for less money.** Browse eBay and Craigslist. Hit tag sales on the weekend. Check out discount decor stores like HomeGoods and the home section of Marshalls.
- **Dump the duds.** Hey, we all make mistakes—the home decor equivalents of that fake-fur miniskirt. But while sartorial wrongs can hide in the closet, furnishing fiascos are right there in the living room, staring at you. You don't have to endure them—unload them on eBay or Craigslist, donate them to the Salvation Army, or put them on the curb (I guarantee someone else will love them and snatch them up).
- **Start collecting swatches.** Even if you have the cash to start an extreme home makeover tomorrow, don't. Redoing your place shouldn't be a hasty decision; give yourself plenty of time to decide on the shades, fabrics, and other materials you want to live among.
- **Go for the green.** Yes, flowers are nice, but flowers die. Plants won't, if you treat them right—and they add so much. Visit a nursery and explain your environment (Do you have a lot of light? Do you want things that sit in the window or hang from the ceiling?) to the salesperson, who should be able to help you find a potted companion that's hard to kill.

MAKE **THIS YEAR** COUNT

After my divorce, I moved from Brooklyn to Manhattan. While I stayed in a temporary sublet, I searched for an affordable space I could rent while we sold our two-bedroom apartment. It was crucial to find the right environment after the emotional upheaval of my breakup. I was looking for small one-bedrooms, but couldn't find anything that seemed like *me*. Finally, an agent showed me an apartment that instantly felt like home. It was a junior one-bedroom (read: big studio with a "separate sleeping area")—smaller than I had hoped for, but somehow perfectly proportioned, with a modern kitchen and bathroom and tons of closet space. But the real reason I took that lease? There was a long wall with oversized windows that ran the length of the apartment. Because it was on a high floor, my view was basically sky and clouds. I loved the airiness and the light—it actually made me *feel* lighter, and helped blow out my blues. I brought in minimal furniture in pale, cool colors, added my now signature splashes of color (some lavender pillows, a maroon throw). Mostly, though, I kept the accents minimal and let the windows and light define the environment.

I was happy in my tiny new space, but soon after I moved in I got really busy at work. I started leaving the apartment earlier, coming home late, and working most weekends. I could never keep up with my dirty laundry and dishes. Bills and unread magazines piled up in corners. I was also traveling a lot for my job, and it seemed like I never fully unpacked my suitcase. There were stacks of clothes and books everywhere. Girlfriend, my place was a wreck! I even canceled the monthly book-club meeting I was supposed to host because my crib was so crazy and I didn't have enough time to clean it. When opening my front door went from relaxing to even more stressful than my day, I decided to make a change in the way I lived.

> **"**Imagine all of the possibilities in your home and get excited about loving where you live.**"**

I made a commitment to organizing my apartment and keeping it neat. The following weekend, I found some plain, inexpensive shelves and created a system for my books and CDs. Next, I bought some desk organizers for loose papers and bills. Then I tackled the closet: I stacked my shoes on shelves, hung cubbies for T-shirts and sweaters, draped my belts and scarves over hangers. It took about two months, but finally my apartment was perfect again—clean, bright, and airy. And it was totally worth the effort. Waking up every morning to my space the way I liked it was a much better way to start each day. It even helped me clear my head, preparing me for those long workdays.

Come up with at least one home-improvement project and commit to completing it by the end of this year. Even though it may seem like a pain (unless you're like my superhandy girlfriend who keeps spackle, paintbrushes, and an electric drill in her hall closet—yeah, me either!), it has the potential of changing your whole outlook on life. Try to make the project fun. Invite friends over to help and promise them a home-cooked meal—or at least a pizza—for pitching in. Just get it done, so you can feel the gratification of having done something for yourself, and the happiness of having a home you can be proud of.

This Year . . .

- **Work toward your dream home.** Figure out how much you'll need for a down payment on a home of your own, then see how you can tweak your budget to start saving for it. Attend some open houses (Realtor-speak for viewing places on the market without an appointment), or cruise neighborhoods you might like to live in.
- **Organize your space.** Make it easier to keep your crib clutter-free by buying closet organizers, shelves, and storage units that can slide under the bed or double as furniture (a wooden trunk or a side table with shelves, for example). Set a housekeeping plan you can deal with—either devoting a few hours of your weekend to neatening up, or ten minutes every night before bed.
- **Putter!** Of course you should have an active social life, but you don't have to be out every night. Spend one or two evenings a week at home. Whether you revel in a warm bath with candles all around, work on a craft project, try out a new recipe, or simply catch up on your TiVo, you'll begin to realize how good it feels to be alone in your own space. Ahhh!
- **Buy a great mattress.** It's the basis of a good night's sleep and the

main reason you'll love your bedroom. Shop around for the best price and the best "fit"—lie down and roll around on the mattress before you make a purchase. Consider calling 1-800-MATTRES. They really do have great deals and will deliver immediately.

- **List your projects—then pick one.** Perhaps you want to print, frame, and hang favorite photos. Or paint the interior of your place. Or refinish some old pieces of furniture. Or make your kitchen a more efficient place. To choose what to do first, think about which room you'd like to spend more time in, and start there.

- **Enlarge your environs.** Got a small space? Think about hanging a mirror for the illusion of space and light, using floor cushions instead of bulky chairs, or getting a large sectional sofa for maximum seating. Think of ways you can make your rooms multipurpose (a kitchen home office, for example), and find "secret" storage areas.

- **Rearrange your rooms.** Got wide, open spaces? Consider using furniture to create separate areas in a large room—an entertainment area, a cozy nook for reading, a place where kids can play.

- **Redo the bathroom.** This is a great place to start—you can probably tackle it in a weekend. Paint the walls a pretty color that looks good with your skin. Find a great shower curtain and bath mat, then add a few unusual touches—a framed piece of artwork, a collection of seashells, etc.

- **Liven things up with lighting.** Nothing works so subtly on your mood—or your looks!—as lighting. Consider installing dimmers or track lighting. Place candles strategically (like around your bedroom . . .).

GET YOURS **FOREVER**

I live in New York City, tiny-apartment capital of the country. Those of us who love it here gladly accept that residing in such an exciting place means our bedroom is barely big enough for the bed and dresser, much less a chair and a desk. Forget about rec rooms or pianos or lawn furniture (things our suburban friends often remind us we could easily have if we simply packed up for the nearest cul-de-sac). Not a chance!

We crazy New Yorkers will do what we have to do in the never-ending quest to find a place for our stuff. Who knew an oven could double as shoe storage?

Recently, I went to a dinner party at a girlfriend's studio apartment that was so small, we all ate on the floor, sitting on cushions. You would have thought the space would be uncomfortable—especially with ten people packed in—but it was lovely and homey. The walls were painted rich shades of red and orange, her furniture was upholstered in buttery-soft fabric, there were candles everywhere, and she'd hung African and Asian textiles on her wall and draped them over her floor. The best part? In one corner, next to a small brass lamp, my girl had piled Moroccan pillows around a small round wooden table. She explained that this was her meditation/reading/writing/relaxing corner, and it transformed her studio from cramped to a warm and welcoming home that she clearly loved.

Which goes to prove that it doesn't matter how large your space is—if it doesn't feel like home you won't be happy there. So whether you live in a rented room or a four-bedroom house, create a relaxation area for yourself. It can be as simple as a comfortable chair and a side table where you read magazines at the end of the day or a bathroom as inviting as any spa. Or, if you have a big house or apartment, devote an entire room to your pleasures—a place where you hang out, make scrapbooks, write in your journal, listen to music . . . in other words, be you!

Always . . .

- **Love your space.** It's essential to your well-being to have a home that makes you happy. If yours doesn't, figure out why and fix the problems—anything from a leaky faucet to a dull color scheme. It may not be your dream home yet, but there's no reason why you can't be content where you are right now.
- **Invest in pieces that will last.** Okay, I've been going on about how you don't have to spend a lot to lively up your home, but the truth is quality pieces should last you for many years. Skip the pricey pony-skin rug and pony up for a sturdy, beautiful sofa or bed instead.

- **Start a collection.** It can be serious, it can be kitschy, it can even be corny—but if it makes you smile, bring it home. A collection should be about finding pieces that truly touch your soul, not simply amassing as many items as possible. Display your treasures proudly.
- **Let your home reflect you.** You're the one who has to live there, not some high-priced decorator. So your home should match your personal style, and as you grow and change, so should your surroundings.
- **Create a mood.** Think about what you'll want to do in different areas of your place and fill them with the colors, fabrics, and items that help you achieve those goals. A bright and cheery kitchen will fire you up to cook, while a clean, serene office will help you get things done, and a sumptuous, sensual bedroom will enhance the way you . . . you know!
- **Reclaim housekeeping.** Okay, no woman in her right mind is going to tell you she loves vacuuming under the bed. But bear in mind, taking care of your home is an extension of taking care of yourself. Keeping the place in order maintains an environment where you can think more clearly and relax more fully.
- **Loosen up about art.** Beauty is in the eye of the beholder. Think about hanging scarves, road signs, posters, enlarged prints of vacation pictures, a collage of vintage wallpaper or postcards, pretty textiles, etc.

10 WAYS TO ENJOY YOUR PERSONAL SPACE

Call this Homebody 101—a crash course in nesting like a natural!

1. Spend an entire day in your pajamas, or your underwear.
2. Spend an entire day in bed with *him*.
3. Invite your family over for Sunday brunch.
4. Cook an amazing meal for yourself—and set the table with good dishes, linen napkins, candles, the works.

5. Organize your CD collection.
6. Dance around from room to room while singing into your hairbrush. (You might want to close the blinds for this one.)
7. Throw a small house party for no damn reason. Wear some funky "hostess attire."
8. Get a pet and snuggle with him.
9. Take a mental-health day from work and give yourself a facial and a pedicure.
10. Watch all the *Godfather* or *Harry Potter* films, or have some other kind of movie marathon. Don't forget the popcorn!

IDEAS FOR DECORATING ON A BUDGET

Here's how to hook up your place like a palace without going broke:

1. Use a mix of rich and subdued colors—they look expensive.
2. Think minimal—place just a few items on a shelf or coffee table and they'll look like rare museum pieces.
3. Throw a housewarming! Accept gifts!
4. Don't call it secondhand—call it vintage.
5. Create your own art. Go online to learn how to make a mosaic or do decoupage.

Read this before you rent or buy!

PREVENT RENTER'S REMORSE

Where you live is one of the biggest decisions you can make. Take your time, do your research, ask a million questions, and live happy!

- Think about whether you really need a Realtor. On the one hand, she will cost you an average of at least one month's rent—for most of us, that's a lot of money. On the other hand, do you realistically have the time to pore through the hundreds of classified ads (many of which are totally bogus) in your local newspapers? If you do decide to go it alone, search Google and Craigslist for no-fee listings. Make sure you save yourself some time by asking the landlord very specific questions to make sure the apartment is worth a visit.

- Do NOT spend more than 25 percent of your gross (before taxes) monthly income on rent—even if the place is amazing, even if you think you *might* get a raise soon, even if a hot guy lives upstairs.
- Ask yourself these questions: Is the apartment near your place of work? Is the neighborhood safe? Is it near public transportation? What are the parking regulations or costs? Is it near stores, banks, the post office? If you have kids, ask: Is it close to a good school?
- Before you sign the lease, make sure all appliances work, the water turns on, the windows open, the locks and smoke detectors work, etc. Ask who is in charge of repairs when something goes wrong. Check out the neighborhood at night and find out what type of security is in the building and/or the area. Find out if the neighbors are noisy (Do they have young children? Are they recently graduated frat boys who still love to throw keggers? Are they musicians? Do they have pets that get lonely and loud during the day?).
- Read your lease carefully before you sign it, then have an attorney read it. There are many things the lease spells out (like subletting rules, who pays for utilities, what physical changes to the apartment or house you may or may not make, etc.). You need to understand and agree to all of it.
- If you have a dispute with your landlord, go online to familiarize yourself with your local landlord-tenant laws and contact your state rental or housing agency to find out what your options are.

BUT I REALLY WANT YOU TO *BUY* A HOME!

Owning your own home is, hands down, the smartest investment you can make. Instead of disappearing in the pocket of your landlord, your monthly housing payment will go toward building equity (the difference between what you paid for your home and its market value when you sell it). Plus, your tax bill will decrease as you'll be able to deduct a portion of the interest on your mortgage and your property taxes. And there's just nothing like the overwhelming feeling of pride and accomplishment you get when you open the door to your own apartment or house.

- Before you do anything, you need to get a handle on your financial situation. Find out what your credit score is and work on raising it, if necessary. Also, figure out your net worth (what you have minus what you owe) and your disposable income (what you earn minus what you spend). Any lender is going to want a complete picture of your finances, so you'll need to get all of this information together.
- Figure out how much down payment you need to get a decent starter home. Most lenders want you to put down 20 percent of the purchase price of the property, but will accept as little as 5 percent under specific circumstances. The more down payment you fork over, the less your closing costs and monthly payments will be. Contact your local Housing and Urban Development Office as well as any other local housing bureaus to see if you qualify for any first-time-buyer programs in your area.
- Now calculate how much you can reasonably afford to pay every month. Because you'll get a larger tax break with a mortgage, you can afford to pay a little more than you would for a rental, but not much. Try to limit yourself to paying 30 to 35 percent of your gross monthly income. When you start looking at different mortgages and their monthly payments, remember to add in the cost of home maintenance. In *The Money Book for the Young, Fabulous & Broke,* Suze Orman says that in a house (versus an apartment building with a maintenance staff) that figure can be as high 40 percent of your basic mortgage cost. In other words, if you calculate your mortgage payment to be one thousand dollars, add four hundred dollars for all the stuff that can go wrong in your home that you are now solely responsible for fixing. If you are looking to buy in an apartment building, that cost is normally fixed and billed to you monthly.
- Find an experienced mortage broker who can help you figure out which mortgage makes the most sense for your budget and goals. For example, if you know you are going to move in a few years, you could consider a hybrid mortgage that offers you a fixed rate for three, five, seven, or ten years. But if you plan on staying in your home indefinitely, you should try to get a thirty-year fixed mort-

gage. The longer term your interest rate is fixed, the higher your monthly payments.

- Get prequalified. In other words, have your mortgage broker ask a lender to give you a letter that says you are qualified for a mortgage of the size you desire. This will speed up the process, and will prove very helpful if you find yourself in a bidding war with another buyer. The seller will always choose the buyer who is prequalified because that person has a better chance of following through with the deal.

- On to the good part! Find a Realtor you trust (word-of-mouth is the best way) and tell her specifically what you're looking for. Instruct her not to take you to any open houses for homes that are outside your price range or that don't meet your standards. Ask all the questions I list in the section above. Also, consider the overall value of property in the neighborhood. Has it gone up or down? Is it a rising neighborhood or is its prestige decreasing? Basically, you want to make sure that in addition to buying a home you'll love, you're making a good investment.

- Bid smart. Ask your broker for sales in the area over the last six months and for recent comparative sales. Try to get less than the asking price, but don't go above your ceiling.

- Have the property inspected carefully, find a real estate lawyer to help you close the deal, get homeowner's insurance, move in, throw a party, and dance in your own living room until the sun comes up!

COURTNEY SLOANE ON HOME

A self-made woman of incredible vision, Courtney Sloane is one of the most fabulous interior designers I know. She has helped create a stylish sense of personal space for celebrities, athletes, and captains of industry, yet her view of what a home should be is down-to-earth and real. I directed a photo shoot at her apartment years ago and loved the warm, inviting space so much, I didn't want to leave. Courtney's gorgeous home was filled with color and art, but it wasn't at all cluttered or kitschy. There were oil paintings and African masks, Italian glass vases, and an amazing zebra-fur ottoman; but there were also books and comfy sofas and a huge, friendly, fluffy chowchow. Not only does Courtney work on interiors, she creates functional, high-design products and is a host of the show Material World *on TLC. I haven't even mentioned the truckloads of design awards she's won. Yeah, Courtney's no joke!*

Amy: *Tell me about the scope of your design firm.*
Courtney: I started my company, Alternative Designs, in 1991 in Jersey City, New Jersey, where I was born and raised. Queen Latifah became the first entertainment person I worked with. I have worked with Puffy, Jay-Z, different athletes, and a host of other music industry executives and corporations as well. We recently completed the Carol's Daughter store in Harlem. We also did the *Essence* show house; it celebrates the thirty-five-year anniversary of the magazine.

AB: *Why do you think it is important to love your personal space?*
CS: Because your home is the cornerstone of your life. We run around all day and then we come back to home base to regroup, reenergize, refresh, and rejuvenate ourselves.

AB: *Is it important that your home is stylish? Or should it reflect who you are?*
CS: I think it should be more of a reflection of the person you are. It should embody each individual spirit, not necessarily be the most stylish. What is most important is to be comfortable in your own skin.

AB: *What can you do to personalize your space?*
CS: Through really simple things that we can all do—for example, you can use paint to articulate your personality through different colors. I'm also a big believer of bringing texture and different sensory things into a space. You can interject your own personal sense of being with things that are you—that empower you and make you feel good. Because it is *your* space. That can be a wall, a piece, a painting—something that just strikes a chord.

AB: *Do you have any inexpensive ideas for making an impact on your living space?*
CS: Paint is definitely one. Fragrance is another—candles, natural sprays, and incense. Textiles that you can pick up and touch like pillows and throws add to the room. Those are simple things available at any price.

AB: *Let's talk about details. What details are important in a home?*

CS: Accessories make a big difference and help to warm a space up and personalize it. I am a big box person; I love boxes of all different sizes and textures. You can also start some sort of collection, like figurines, hourglasses, different type of vessels—tall, short, wide, elliptical, circular. Having plants or fresh-cut flowers could be it. Family photos, magazines, things that you want to share, special things. This is when you begin to tell the story of who you really are.

AB: *Give us some cool DIY project ideas.*

CS: Sometimes you can present things from different events in your life simply with framing. So many of us have great family photos, and there is such an abundance of picture frames in the marketplace. Or you can frame personal notes and letters. That is a small project.

AB: *Do you have any ideas for unusual color combinations or style patterns that maybe we have not thought of?*

CS: Step out of the monochromatic world we know. Don't be afraid to push yourself. Be inspired by a photograph or piece of art to push you further.

AB: *Do you believe in changing the home a lot? Redecorating frequently?*

CS: I am big on seasonal things. Changing throws, pillows, rugs. In wintertime, use warmer, darker, deeper things, then pare down in the summer. Go lighter and more bare.

AB: *How can you make a small space larger?*

CS: Mirrors are great. Lighter colors—select a color palette that feels cooler. The fewer things you have on the floor, the better off the overall environment is—look for wall-hung cabinetry and shelving to keep the floor as spacious as possible. Try to keep a sense of openness from down below.

AB: *Do you have advice for when people move in together and blend styles?*

CS: Before you leave the old place, there needs to be an inventory and a purging. After the purge, you have what you will build on. You are allowed to keep certain sentimental things, but you must pare down so you can start over.

AB: *Where can the average person get professional home decor advice?*
CS: A lot of the retailers now have a design studio in-store. People can consult with a designer without having to hire their services. Many designers or decorators will do an hourlong consult with you. That is part of how my business dynamic has changed—I am doing more consulting and helping people figure it out themselves.

AB: *Your career and life is such an inspiration to me and to a lot women. Do you have advice on how a woman can really "get hers" in terms of career, family, relationships, personal satisfaction?*
CS: A lot of hard work and continuing to believe and focus on your dreams. But mainly, I think you really need to love and honor yourself.

PROMISE PAGE

My dreams and goals for my personal space are:

_____
_____
_____
_____
_____

I promise that today I will:

_____
_____
_____
_____

This year I promise to:

_____
_____
_____
_____

I will always:

_____
_____
_____
_____
_____

11

GET CREATIVE

When I first began taking dance lessons as an adult, I found a fabulous studio called Steps. They had all different kinds of classes, so I could experiment with what made me feel good (jazz and modern) and what made me feel stupid (ladies, it's *really* hard to begin ballet in your midtwenties). One day I saw a notice for a new African movement class and signed up. When I got to the class early the next day to warm up, I found myself alone in the room with the instructor. She was kneeling in front of the stereo with her back toward me, fiddling with the volume knobs, but called out a friendly hello when she heard me enter. Her voice sounded vaguely familiar, but since the music was already pumping I couldn't quite place it at first. Once she turned around, I couldn't believe my eyes.

"Denise?" I said incredulously. The human resources administrator at the Wall Street bank where I used to work, she'd helped process my exit papers—and was one of the most conservative, buttoned-up sisters I'd ever met! "I, um, I didn't know you teach dance."

"And I never would have pegged you for a dancer," she replied with a laugh.

"I'm not, so please don't make fun of my moves," I told her, slightly embarrassed. "I'm just playing around."

"Well, I'm glad to hear it," she said, twisting her hair into a colorful headwrap. "Trust me, this will clear your head and relax your body. I know if I didn't have my dance classes I'd go stir-crazy!"

The image of Denise in that class remains with me to this day. I still think about how joyous and free she looked. Being able to express herself through dance enabled her to be who she was in the office and still be happy, in touch with and tapped into her creative side. I knew she needed an outlet, and I believe we all do—even if, *especially* if, such "nonsense" wasn't encouraged when we were children.

My parents, both hard-core academics, didn't exactly value creative expression. They did insist that I study piano—which I was decidedly mediocre at—but that was all about what they deemed a well-educated, well-rounded girl *should* have under her belt. No one really cared about my true passions: I loved writing and I desperately wanted to take dance lessons. Everyone complimented me on the short stories I penned and proudly read aloud at every opportunity, but clearly thought they were part of a passing phase—like every young girl's obsession with poetry. As my parents debated enrolling me in ballet, a well-intending physical education teacher who taught some movement classes at my school made the colossal error of telling my mother that I had real talent as a dancer. That was that! My mom decided right then and there that dance lessons were out. The logic? "No daughter of *mine* is going into show business!" All I knew was that certain types of music compelled me to get up and move, but the image Mom had of her only daughter in a skimpy feathery outfit, shaking her booty at sleaze-bags on some dusty stage in Nowheresville, could not be dispelled. No, it was endless piano scales for me.

I spent many years without a true creative outlet. I quit writing short stories in high school, thinking they were childish and stupid, and after a while I gave up on agitating for dance classes. I absorbed the idea that those activities were unnecessary, a waste of time. Finally, in college, a friend convinced me to join a casual dance group that toured the schools around my college town, entertaining kids. It was silly, but I loved every minute!

Of course, when I actually started taking formal dance classes, I was very nervous. Most people start training before they hit grade school, and here I was, in my twenties, out of shape and still weaning myself off a diet of Twizzlers and Chinese food. Just putting on the required outfit was mortifying. Still, I squeezed my thighs into the tights, pulled the leotard over my round frame, and got myself to class. I couldn't chicken out when I finally had the opportunity to do something I'd talked about my whole life. And how bad could it be?

Um, real bad.

It took a few classes before I could even follow one simple routine, a couple of months before my body got used to the movement and effort, and almost a year before I felt free and comfortable. But it was one of the best years of my life. I started holding myself better, walking with more confidence, feeling more comfortable in my own skin. And not just because of the skill I was learning or the way my body was shaping up. No, it was mostly because I had a new passion.

Identifying and pursuing your true passions is crucial to living a full life. There's nothing more important than living with purpose and conviction—and how can you possibly do that if you're ignoring the stuff that makes your pulse race faster? I don't care if it's flower arranging, jewelry making, calligraphy, or furniture restoration. Just do it! And if you're lucky, one of your passions might even become your career. It did for me. Dance has been a wonderful hobby, while the written word ended up changing my entire life. I would never have had my successful career in journalism (or written this book) if I hadn't rediscovered my love of writing.

> "Every woman can find power and peace in doing or making something beautiful."

Creativity can come in so many different forms (cooking, sewing, drawing, writing . . .), and every woman can find power and peace in doing or making something beautiful. Once I tapped into my creative side, I realized that there were entire elements of my personality that I had never truly explored. Through dance classes and writing workshops, I found interesting new ways to express my ideas and emotions—and I learned self-acceptance on a whole new level.

I've been very fortunate that my main creative outlet ultimately became my career. Most women, however, must make time to pursue their passions—which are often the first things to go in a busy schedule. That's a shame, since I believe stretching your imagination is extremely valuable to every woman, particularly black women, as we are less frequently encouraged to develop in this area. Sure, it may be easier to zone out in front of the TV than pick up your guitar or sketchbook at the end of the day. But true happiness comes when you enhance a strength and feel fulfilled as a result. If you have a natural talent or strong interest, think of ways you can delve into it. You will be happier as a result.

Quiz: What's Your Creativity Quotient?

The more you nurture your creative spirit, the more fulfilled you'll feel. This quiz will help you discover where your self-expressive leanings lie, and how to stoke—not stifle—these passions.

1. When waiting on a long line, you
a. sing your favorite songs to yourself—the ones you know all the words to.
b. read a book or magazine.
c. let your mind wander freely into daydreams.

2. While making dinner, you realize you don't have a few key ingredients. You
a. improvise, adding different spices and throwing in that leftover chicken.
b. invent your own dish, using just one of the original recipe's ingredients.
c. toss a simple salad, order a pizza, and call it a night.

3. It's Latin night at the club, and you don't know your salsa from your rhumba. So when a hot guy asks you to dance, you
a. say your feet are killing you, then invite him to sit down and chat.
b. accept, as long as he promises to be a patient teacher.
c. get on up on the floor and shake your tail feather freestyle.

4. The celebrities you admire most are
a. Renaissance women—those do-it-all types who sing, act, dance, design.
b. women with talent who also seem to have it together in terms of finances and family.
c. absolutely the best at what they do—the ones with a collection of Grammys or Oscars.

5. Someone at a party suggests charades. You're game, since
a. you're really good at figuring out what people are acting out.
b. you just love getting up in front of a crowd and playing a role.
c. you're great at coming up with clues—even though you do get irritated when people don't guess your charade quickly enough.

6. If you were asked to draw a picture of your family, you would

a. pull a family snapshot from your wallet so you can capture everybody's features just so.

b. sketch stick figures with name tags reading Mom, Dad, etc.

c. draw cartoon animals that represent your family members.

7. A friend gives you a beautiful journal for your birthday. Soon you fill it with

a. to-do lists, ideas, reminders, and "notes to self."

b. the details of your days and nights—and your innermost thoughts and feelings.

c. poems, drawings, jewelry designs, half a screenplay...

8. You'd been using a vintage crocheted shawl to cover a chair, but when you notice the shawl showing wear and tear, you

a. make it into a miniskirt.

b. lovingly repair the damaged spots.

c. buy a piece of new fabric for the chair.

9. Your boss asks you to attend the most boring meeting in the history of your field. On your pad you

a. doodle surreptitiously.

b. jot down some notes for your novel-in-progress.

c. plan your sister's baby shower.

10. To add a special touch to your boyfriend's birthday celebration, you

a. bake his favorite cake.

b. draw his portrait on a handmade card.

c. write him a song and belt it out for him at dinner.

THE SCORE
Give yourself points as follows:

1. a = 1, b = 3, c = 2		**6.** a = 1, b = 3, c = 2	
2. a = 1, b = 2, c = 3		**7.** a = 3, b = 1, c = 2	
3. a = 3, b = 1, c = 2		**8.** a = 2, b = 1, c = 3	
4. a = 2, b = 3, c = 1		**9.** a = 1, b = 2, c = 3	
5. a = 3, b = 2, c = 1		**10.** a = 3, b = 1, c = 2	

HERE'S THE DEAL

Artistic Perfectionist (10 to 16 points) You're gifted in many areas, and you take pride in your artistic abilities. When you master something—a new dance, for instance—or complete a creative project, you feel a real sense of accomplishment. In fact, you like to display your work so others can admire it, too. There's probably a photo you took or drawing you did framed on the wall of your home, or maybe your favorite sweater is the one you spent six months knitting yourself. The only obstacle to getting more out of your creative powers is your need for everything to be just right. I bet you always colored inside the lines as a kid! Persnickety perfectionism can inhibit you. Try having a looser hand, a freer mind—without worrying so much about the results. Stop being your own harshest critic and let yourself go!

Creative Inferno (17 to 24 points) You're so full of ideas, imagination, and unbridled energy, you could no doubt transform folding laundry into an avant-garde ballet. You trust your creative instincts, and you really have fun letting 'em rip—even if the outcome doesn't earn raves. (So the tuna-and-raisin couscous you served the other night didn't go over well—big deal!) For you, it's all about the process, and you give yourself permission to make mistakes. Occasionally, they're brilliant ones! However, wildly creative people like you sometimes have trouble completing projects. You're going like gang-busters on your hip-hopera, only to get distracted by a screenplay concept. Tell the truth: Isn't there at least one half-finished photo collage or armless sweater or abandoned guitar sitting around your crib? You know you have talent—now focus, and take a project to fruition.

Untapped Potential (24 to 30 points) Chances are you don't think of yourself as a creative person—and you're fine with that. You're a grounded, practical woman with a lot of real issues to contend with on the day-to-day, so "fooling around" with "artsy-fartsy" stuff has no place on your agenda. Newsflash: Creativity and productivity happen to go hand in hand. I'm not saying take a sabbatical from work to paint the next Sistine Chapel, but exploring some artistic avenues will do you good. Sing your head off in the shower, vent the frustrations of a lousy day in your journal, go dancing just for the pleasure of moving your body. Then take it to the next level—a course in flower arranging or Web design can help you stretch creatively . . . and may just lead to a second career.

START **TODAY**, GIRLFRIEND!

The first few months after I became the editor of *Honey*, I worked around the clock—literally *around* the clock. A week could pass where I wouldn't feel sunlight on my face. It was all good since I was living my dream, but I was exhausted from the physical effort and drained from the creative energy I expended every day. Finally, when my job calmed down a bit, I woke up one Sunday with the unusual realization that I did not have to go in to the office, nor did I have anything truly pressing in my briefcase. As I thought about the day, I kept coming up with stuff I should do (pay bills, clean out my closet, get my car washed, blah-blah-blah), not what I *could* do (take a dance class, catch up on my journal writing, take my dog to the park). It occurred to me that as much as I loved my job, I hadn't spent any time doing something that was purely for me in months. So, after paying the bills that were *this-close* to being overdue and straightening up my apartment enough so that I could see some floor again, I grabbed a blanket, my journal, and the dog and headed for the park. We hung out for a couple of quiet hours, and by evening I actually felt like *me* again. So what that my closet was still a disaster area! I'd composed a couple of sentences that I considered beautiful, and they were all mine, sprung from a place inside me that I didn't exactly understand yet knew I was (and am) blessed to have.

As go-getting, do-something sisters, we can so easily get caught in the mind-set that every waking hour of every single day must be "productive." There are always errands and household organizing and cooking . . . the list goes on, seemingly forever. The idea of taking time for yourself to do nothing but think, daydream, stare at the clouds, or make up rhymes seems frivolous, almost irresponsible. But I say it's the most productive time you can spend because connecting with your creative side recharges you to better handle what life throws at you. Besides, your ultimate responsibility in this life is to yourself. If you take care of you, you will do a better job with everyone and everything else.

Before you can even figure out what passions to pursue, you need to first feel comfortable with the idea that making yourself happy is the most valuable way to spend your time. So start today by doing something, anything, that's just for you. I don't care if you take half an hour to read a book, sit in a bubble bath, listen to a new CD . . . Just relax and hang with yourself for a short period of time.

Today . . .

- **Turn off the TV.** Don't get me wrong, I've got an ample supply of my favorite shows TiVoed, so I can watch an episode of *Ugly Betty* whenever I want! But girlfriend, you know that TV can't replace true experience. Just think about limiting the amount of time you spend parked in front of the tube. Trust me, it's preventing you from doing other, more interesting stuff.
- **Get inspired.** All the practical things you do day in and day out can stunt your creative growth. To stimulate your artistic side, immerse yourself in art—whether that means listening to your favorite tunes, touring an art museum, perusing your favorite fashion boutiques, walking down the street admiring the architecture, or sitting outside soaking up the most awesome of all art forms: nature.
- **Identify your strengths.** If you haven't come up with a passion you want to pursue yet, think about what you're good at and can develop. Then consider how to use that strength creatively every day. If you've got good handwriting, for instance, address your envelopes like you mean it, or hand-letter a sign for the lobby of your apartment building that will get everyone's attention for the upcoming tenants' meeting.
- **Tell yourself you're talented.** Maybe you just haven't figured out what your creative gift is yet, but it's in there . . . and you will!

MAKE THIS YEAR COUNT

About the same time that I rediscovered my love of dance, I also rekindled my relationship with the written word. Moving around so much as a child, my best and most consistent friendships for many years were with books. I used to stay up after my bedtime and read by flashlight under my covers so my mom wouldn't catch me. The next day I'd make up my own stories, taking inspiration from my favorite books but going my own way. (Okay, so I was more than a little geeky!) My passion for reading and writing stayed with me for years, and eventually I knew I had to explore my talent to see what I could accomplish.

Figuring out how to develop my writing was less obvious than dance. I started by writing short stories again—little one-pagers. I worked up to longer stories that were mostly autobiographical, then I began to really get into fiction. I saw an ad posted in a local coffee shop for a group of amateur writers who met to workshop their stories a couple of times a month. I joined them for a while and gained more confidence about my writing, then took it to the next level and enrolled in a real creative writing class. There I developed technique and refined my skills—and decided that this was something I wanted to pursue more seriously.

> "True happiness comes when you enhance a strength and feel fulfilled as a result."

I moved to Ireland and, for a semester, seriously studied writing at one of the great universities in Dublin. While there, I edited some of my best stories, built a portfolio, and applied to graduate school in creative writing. You know the rest: My love of writing turned into a profession that has brought me incredible satisfaction and joy.

This year, take the time to really develop one of your passions. Take a class, read a book on the subject, or join a group. Do it purely for yourself—don't even think about turning it into a money-making pastime at this point. Now is the time to reward yourself by developing your gift and having it give back to you. Talent is like a muscle—the more you work it, the stronger it gets. And hey, you never know. If you do find a way to turn a hobby into a profession or a cool side gig, all the better!

This Year . . .

- **Take a class.** Don't think of it as (*blech!*) school. Think of it as a mind-and-soul-expanding choice you make for yourself. Adult education courses don't necessarily mean a long-term commitment of time or money. Study the catalog from a local college or consider an online course. If you're interested in writing, for instance, go to www.mediabistro.com and you'll find loads of diverse classes taught by published authors.

- **Find others who share your interests.** It's common to think of an artist as someone who toils away, all alone, in a grim, cold garret—but in fact it's not that stimulating to work in a vacuum. Through structured classes, casual groups, and attending events like lectures, readings, and museum tours, you'll meet like-minded friends who'll energize you to do what you love.

- **Spend time alone.** The flip side of keeping creative company is making sure to enjoy being alone. Forget the stigma that people who hang with themselves are losers. Devote some precious moments to letting your thoughts and ideas run wild. You will surprise yourself.

- **Try something unusual.** So you've never been elbow-deep in clay or wiggled your middle in belly dancing or tasted Thai cuisine, much less cooked it. That's the point. Give it a whirl—you just may find you're great at it!

- **Start a journal.** Even if you're not especially interested in writing, keeping a journal can help you discover what you want to do. Consider it thinking in print. You'll never forget an idea if you write it down. Journaling can focus your thoughts, solidify your concepts, and allow you to organize your dreams in ways that make them real and doable.

GET YOURS FOREVER

My mom collected black memorabilia for twenty years. To be honest, as a kid I thought it was incredibly bizarre. Our house served as the showcase for her permanent display of Aunt Jemima cookie jars, posters depicting slavery auctions, ceramic figurines of huge-lipped black boys eating watermelon, etc. Now, of course, I recognize her collection as an important representation of what black folk have been through in this country (and a reminder to never let it happen again). At the time, however, it was just embarrassing to see my friends' eyes widen at those images of grinning minstrels, subservient mammies, and shuckin' and jivin' slaves. But my mom didn't care. For her, it was much more than a hobby—it was her greatest passion.

Few people are busier than my mother was during her life: A young, divorced college professor with a small child, she not only raised me but climbed the academia ladder to become a college administrator and, ultimately, a university president. I rarely saw her sit in one place and chill for more than an hour—she was always practicing a speech or reviewing a budget or writing an article. But almost every weekend, I'd go with her to at least one flea market. And if we were driving and she saw an antique store she'd never been in, she'd always stop to see if there was any worthwhile black memorabilia inside. It didn't even matter if we found anything—it was all about the hunt and her passion. As hectic as her life was, Mom made sure she consistently added to her awesome collection. It made her feel content, even when her work got overwhelming and stressful. Eventually, her collection became so impressive that it was exhibited in a New York museum.

> "Identifying and pursuing your true passions is crucial to living a full life."

Always make time for what you love, girlfriend. Don't abandon your passion when life gets complex and chaotic—that's when you'll *really* need a creative outlet to help you remember your priorities (you!) and be the best you can be.

Always . . .

- **Avoid the dreaded rut.** Whether you simply move from drawing in charcoal to pastel or decide to put music on hold for a while so you can dabble in photography, it's important to try new things periodically. Even if you ultimately don't excel at your latest endeavor, that's cool. The point is to stop stagnation in its tracks. When you return to your true passion, you'll feel renewed and eager.

- **Consider profiting from your passion.** The first and main reason to follow your muse is love. But there's nothing wrong with making money from your art form. If people ooh and aah over the adorable hats and scarves you knit, why not whip up a batch and sell them at holiday time?

- **Take creative vacations.** There are retreats and "camps" for almost every enthusiast under the sun. Take a weekend of cooking classes (check out www.naturalgourmet.com), write in solitude for a week (visit www.writersretreatworkshop.com), or try your hand at photography in a beautiful location (the Audubon Society has camps for adults throughout the country). You can even devote a few days to completing a scrapbook project at a quaint inn in Michigan (log on to www.gotta-scrapinn.com for more information). If this feels too rich for your budget, how about a "stay-cation," where you immerse yourself in a project for a weekend at home.

- **Remember your creative value.** Maybe you won't win a Grammy or a Pulitzer or a fill-in-your-most-coveted-statuette-here in this lifetime. Just do what you do for the satisfaction it gives you. Delight yourself—with your voice, words, rhythms, movements, ideas, and inventions—and that is bounty enough.

10 COOL CREATIVE WEEKEND PROJECTS

You don't need a decade to create a magnum opus! Pick a weekend and...

1. **Make a movie.** Grab a disposable video camera, gather some friends, outline a script (or strictly improvise), and then it's lights, camera, action! Put your flick on YouTube so the world can watch it.
2. **Build a birdhouse.** Knock out one of those pretty little feeders for your backyard or windowsill. The birds will thank you, year in and year out.
3. **Have a major Kodak moment.** Collect all your loose photographs and put them in albums. Consider interesting themes you can group the pictures in.
4. **Do kid stuff.** Write and illustrate a children's book. This is a project you can do with your kids, if you've got any. Watching their imaginations at work will amaze you.
5. **Cook creatively.** Get busy in the kitchen and concoct a signature specialty using some of your favorite ingredients. After giving it a trial run, invite folks over to devour it the following weekend.
6. **Cut a record.** Most newer computers come with music-making programs, like Garage Band. Lay down that melody you've been humming in the shower.

7. **Design a Web page.** Even if your HTML skills are next to nil, you can do a page with words and photos. Put up a page on MySpace and use their free graphics and music to jazz it up.

8. **Create your own invitations.** Or business cards, or even stationery. Search the Web for sites that will give you all the instructions, depending on what you want to design. Or check out Amazon.com and Barnes & Noble for tons of books on how to use your home computer for pretty paper projects.

9. **DIY denim.** Make a skirt from an old pair of jeans. Find the how-to at www.thread.co.nz.

10. **Write a poem.** It doesn't have to be a sonnet Shakespeare would envy. But devote yourself to form, rhythm, and language until you've nailed a piece of work you're proud of. Then read it aloud.

SARAH JONES ON CREATIVITY

The ultimate "solo artist," this Tony Award–winning playwright, actress, and poet has earned national recognition for multicharacter one-woman shows like her wildly successful Broadway debut, Bridge and Tunnel. *In addition to being brilliant, Sarah is also a really great person. She and I both went to the United Nations School in New York (okay, I'm a few years older), and she was close with my best friend's younger sister. We all used to hang out after school, thinking of creative ways to get in trouble that none of us was gutsy enough to pull off. Even back then, Sarah had great ideas and an interesting perspective. She's still a whirlwind of artistic energy, but I got her to slow down a minute to discuss the importance of creativity and passion.*

Amy: *Why do you do what you do?*
Sarah: The mission to become an artist is not something that takes a tremendous amount of courage. If you write, you will know that you should be a writer, because if you didn't, you would die. It is almost as if your passion is rooted in what is literally your lifeblood. Whatever is vitally necessary for you to do, you pursue.

AB: *Would it be possible for you to be creative without passion?*

SJ: Absolutely not. There would be no motivation. I would not be able to find the discipline to sit and listen to people. What can be less interesting than the details of some random person's life? But to me that person is totally important—the way they hem and haw, the little idiomatic expressions are little nuggets of gold. The passion turns those details into something urgent. I *must* accurately portray this person, and have others see that their story is relevant. Passion makes the rest of the work possible and pleasurable, and sometimes easy. Many people say, "I don't understand how you can mimic that person's accent." But for me it feels natural and wonderful, and that all comes from passion.

AB: *What inspires you?*

SJ: What stokes passion in me is this urgent sense of how much work there is to be done on a wide variety of issues that have an impact on more people on the planet than we like to think. We are nearly six billion people. I want to figure out how those of us who are more fortunate can feel compassion for everybody else, and understand how our luxuries are connected to their lives. That is what motivates my work, whether it is talking about issues of diversity, or women's rights, or the state of health care in this country.

AB: *Do you feel that your purpose is to edify or to entertain or both?*

SJ: I think it is some type of hybrid. Neither is worth my time without the other. To me there is no real line that can be drawn. It just so happens that I'm a woman, I'm a person of color, I live in the United States, and there is not a single part of my life that is not touched by the politics of the moment. [But] I could not make you believe that I am a small Jewish woman if I didn't care what her history is, such as the message of anti-Semitism in our world.

AB: *Has anyone ever asked you to compromise your passion to be creative?*

SJ: Sure. At this moment, I am contemplating a television deal that would be a wonderful opportunity for me, and at the same time it is TV and I'd have to sell soap. So if they say, "We don't like the way you say this; can you please compromise?" I would have to decide what it is worth to me as an artist to maybe have to [alter] some of what I would do. Ironically it is your passion that helps you find the compromises, and helps you accept that this part of what you believe to be deeply important might have to be sacrificed so you can continue with the overall goal.

AB: *Do you think it's important for all women to find a creative outlet?*
SJ: Oh, yeah. I have had some really rough times—I lost my sister when I was in my early twenties—but my creative pursuit saved my life. Anything—cooking, baking, gardening, anything that will give you a moment to yourself that does not belong to other people, which doesn't belong to getting your bikini waxed—is empowering. Creativity is the one thing that we can have control over in our lives that will enrich us and prolong our sanity.

AB: *This book is about putting yourself first and everything will come. Do you agree that if you prioritize your own happiness, everything will come into play?*
SJ: Yes. [But] just to contextualize it: There are so few people who have access to their personal happiness regardless of their gender. We live in such an oppressive and repressive time. We have these prescribed goals we have to fulfill since we were little kids. Since the time you are born, they are putting you in pink clothes or blue clothes, and telling you how you have to act. Access to who we might be is something that very few of us have.

AB: *What makes you feel happy and successful?*
SJ: I think I am still in the process of finding my inner ear, to hear what it is I need at the various points in my life. Do I want to have a kid? How did I know when it was time to get married? The practical ways that most of us don't have access to who we might be because of societal conventions or the roles that we are supposed to occupy, all of that is with me. Throughout my journey, I have been grappling with what happiness looks like. Is it money? Is it fame? Is it red carpet? Is it free clothes? For me the challenge has been: How do I define fulfill-ment? It is not easy and it changes day to day.

AB: *What helps you make decisions—creative decisions, personal decisions?*
SJ: Meditation clears the clutter. I don't want to call it clutter because our children and loved ones are extremely important, but clearing

space in your heart so you can hear yourself above everything else. That does not mean that you don't love the other people in your life. It doesn't mean you are a selfish, terrible person if you need to take the time to hear your voice. It means that you will probably have better access to who you are. And you know what? If you figure out, "Wow, I should have not married this guy out of high school. I'm not happy, and we need a divorce," that is progress. Sometimes what does not look like progress is. Sometimes what does not look like a direct route to happiness actually is. I think it is a life journey to get closer and closer to whatever your deepest desires are, and how in this life you can manifest them.

AB: *Can you relate that to creativity?*

SJ: Creativity is a conduit for that energy. Most of our life is: I got to do this, my husband needs this, my kids need that. Obviously there are important threads of love running through the obligations, but when we free ourselves through creative pursuit, to spend time not watching the clock or dropping off the kids to soccer, to just sitting and molding a piece of clay, or tampering with a recipe until you find something new about it, those impulses are a kind of exercise. Creativity, in whatever forms it takes—singing to yourself, making patterns or sewing clothes—offers you a little bit of freedom. It exercises those muscles that you can only train by attentiveness to yourself and your inner voice. The more you train them, the more you begin to think outside what might be the very narrow constraints in your life.

AB: *Who has influenced you most?*

SJ: My mother was a tremendous influence on me. She is an organic feminist and an example of what women's empowerment did to radically change the lives of so many people of her generation. She became a doctor while having three kids. She was this person who was able to find the courage to leave her family's house at age sixteen, and go off to college and discover an entirely new world, and figure out how to navigate that world fairly well. So that is tremendously inspiring to me. There are a lot of women like her who are the unsung heroes of our society, who keep families together, engender good self-esteem in our generation of girls. But there so many people I admire: Gloria Steinem,

Richard Pryor, Gandhi, Joni Mitchell, John Lennon, Bob Marley. I think of these artists and activists in the same category—they are people who have access to that voice inside them and found a way to amplify that voice, and help it reach other people.

AB: *What is the best piece of advice you have ever gotten?*
SJ: To trust myself. I know that is pretty generic and maybe cliché, but to say something like that to a little kid is sort of revolutionary. We are in a world where kids are coming through a public school system that prepares them for other institutions—whether it is the army because they can't afford school any other way, the prison system because we basically criminalize poverty on a lot of levels in this country, or whatever ways we do not try to motivate kids to be critical thinkers or trust their own instincts. To say to a kid, "What you are feeling is valid. You should listen to that voice, you should question authority when you can feel that what you know might be better." That is a radical thing. Knowing that I can trust my inner voice has been a tremendous resource for me as a creative person and as an artist.

PROMISE PAGE

My dreams and goals for my creative
spirit are:

I promise that today I will:

This year I promise to:

I will always:

12

GET SPIRITUAL

My mother came from a Baptist family. Growing up, she attended church every week, prayed before bed every night, took Sunday school classes, and even joined the choir. But once she reached college age, she was desperate to free herself from the confines of her conservative Lackawanna upbringing. She purposely chose the most liberal, unconventional college she could find and took off, determined to find herself. While doing so, she also found my father. Though his family is Jewish, he was raised with much greater cultural ties to his religion than spiritual ones.

When it came to me, neither parent pushed any particular spiritual approach, which meant I basically had zero religious education as a small child. My grandmother, appalled that my mom had shaken off many of the traditions she was raised with, would try to instruct me in the Bible. Family lore has it that she even snuck me away one weekend to get baptized without telling my mom and dad. But without reinforcement at home, nothing really stuck.

After my parents divorced, I think my mother regretted the total spiritual ignorance I exhibited and came up with a solution: the Mommy and Amy religion. She and I sat down one weekend when I was nine years old, and literally invented our own faith, complete with our own set of commandments. We decided that God was within us, and that it was our responsibility to bring him (or her) out into the world every single day. We felt that God was what connected us to one another and balanced our good and bad. We didn't have to go to church—we could talk to God wherever we wanted to because he was, after all, inside of us. Part of our religion's tenets dictated that we were citizens of the world and respected everyone's individual beliefs accordingly. We felt responsible if something good happened in the world because that meant *we* had done enough good. If something bad happened, we also felt somewhat responsible because that meant we weren't doing enough positive things to invite good for everyone.

It probably sounds silly, but our personal religion provided a very real base for my spiritual development. And I clung to it as a raft when I began to confront more "adult" moral dilemmas, often asking myself: Is this action bringing God into the world?

After my mother passed away, I struggled to find greater meaning in my life. Yet I resisted seeking spiritual comfort for my pain. I would even get a little angry when well-meaning folks would tell me that my mom was in heaven looking down on me. I didn't believe in heaven or hell or angels—and I just felt alone and frightened.

When I ultimately reconnected with my spirituality, it wasn't in a church or any other traditional place of worship—instead, it was on top of a mountain in New Mexico. I had just been accepted into the buying training program at Lord & Taylor. The only catch was that it didn't start for a few months, so I decided to spend some time (and, oh, most of my savings) traveling around the country with a friend, camping and hiking. I just wanted to go exploring and do something totally different to shake myself up; I had no idea it would lead to a new spiritual awakening.

> "Spirituality can be the purest form of self-understanding, empowerment, and freedom."

One day, after four hours of scrambling three thousand feet up a steep and rocky trail to the peak of the Guadalupe Mountain range, I bent over with my hands on my knees, huffing and puffing—and cursing my stupidity in agreeing to this mad excursion in the first place. Then I heard a strange whistling sound above my head and saw something streak by in my peripheral vision. Curiosity won, and I hoisted my backpack onto my aching shoulder again to venture closer to the edge. Looking out, I witnessed dozens of swallows darting back and forth across the sky so fast I could barely see them. I had scarcely caught my breath from scaling the peak, and here it was, snatched away from me again.

I began to take in my surroundings for the first time. I'd never been so high up and so far out in nature. The view was all mist-shrouded mountains, sandy valleys, patches of forest, and endless sky. Suddenly a feeling of great respect and belonging overwhelmed me. In that moment, I remembered details about the Mommy and Amy religion that I'd completely forgotten—most important, that we were all connected to and responsible for one another. Also, the idea that energy and spirit never dies. I stopped feeling so alone and instead felt a part of something much larger and more profound than myself. I still carry that sense of humility and true universal responsibility to this day.

Maybe my moment of spiritual epiphany seems strange to you. After all, women of color tend to be raised in traditional religious homes, and be very religious in general. But if my story intrigues you, perhaps you yearn to explore faith and spirituality as a way to feel connected not just to your own definition of God but to the world around you as well. A one-on-one dialogue with your God is wonderful, but I truly believe that spirituality can be more than that—it can be the purest form of self-understanding, empowerment, and freedom. I'd love for all of us to develop a larger spiritual understanding along with our religious faith, to feel more empathy for those with different beliefs, and to use spirituality to get in touch with our own needs and to feel better about ourselves.

START **TODAY**, GIRLFRIEND!

Starting a relationship with your higher power does not have to be difficult. I know that most people feel they need to be in a place of worship, or actively praying, to make that happen. But since my beliefs are more about God as positive energy and feeling a part of the universe, I can engage my spirituality whenever I want to. And I try to do just that every day. It's not that I've become obsessive or fanatic about it. Honestly, I just feel happier when I walk through the world in an unselfish and connected way. While I firmly believe that *you* (your happiness, your passion, your independence) must be your first priority, living only for yourself is an empty and lonely way to spend your days on this planet. Simply recognizing this and acting upon it will strengthen your relationship with your higher power.

Usually, I make my efforts pretty simple. They range from calling my elderly grandfather to doing a few yoga stretches to quietly appreciating my clear view of the tall spire and stained-glass windows of the church that sits next to my apartment building. As long as I feel a part of the world—nature or humanity—I believe that I am connected to my spirituality. When I act on this feeling, then I have strengthened my relationship with a higher power. Regardless of your individual beliefs, say hi to your higher power. And try to do it every day, starting today.

Today . . .

- **Count your blessings.** Before you get out of bed each morning, take a moment to be thankful for everything you've got. No matter what else is going on, even if you are struggling. Especially if you are struggling, because this simple act will help you deal.
- **Breathe.** Find a few minutes to focus on your breathing. Inhale deeply and exhale fully. This will make you feel centered and balanced, in tune with the world.
- **Meditate.** Take your breathing exercises to the next level and meditate. All this entails is trying to empty your mind of all thoughts, or concentrating on one thing (such as a sound or phrase, or an image). This allows you to develop your mind and spirit, and truly relax.
- **Be aware.** Read the international section of your newspaper and remember that those stories are about individual people with real lives—just like you.
- **Forgive someone.** Whether it's a pesky coworker who got in your business or someone who has harmed you in the past, release yourself from negative feelings about this person by absolving her.
- **Forgive yourself.** Beating yourself up for faults or errors accomplishes nothing. Accept responsibility, resolve to do better, then let it go.
- **Activate your inner peace barometer.** If you're not content and relaxed in any given moment, ask yourself what it is about this situation, person, environment, experience, etc., that is interfering with your sense of serenity. Then act accordingly, whether it means leaving the room or taking a drink of water or making amends.

MAKE **THIS YEAR** COUNT

After my mom passed away, I felt incredibly drained from the emotional strain of her illness, from dragging myself to a job I despised, from having to deal with family obligations that were far beyond my twenty-two-year-old scope of knowledge. I was tired and lonely and lost, without inspiration. I just couldn't seem to get out from under the weight of missing my mom. Just when I thought I might never recover, my best friend dangled a proposition. A year earlier, she had gone to a yoga retreat in the Bahamas for a week; she wanted to return, and asked me—more like begged me—to come with her. To be honest, I was going more for the beach than for the yoga, but she didn't care—as long as she could get me there.

I have to admit, I was a little freaked out at first by all the robed monks walking around and the big om symbols painted on the walls, not to mention the daunting schedule (up at 5:30 AM for an hour of chanting and meditation, then two hours of yoga, two more hours of yoga in the late afternoon, followed by more meditation . . . *whaaaat?*). But the retreat was on a lovely stretch of land with a beautiful sandy white beach and clear green water on one side and a sparkling, sailboat-dotted bay on the other. I figured, at worst, I could chill in the sun all day. But my friend urged me to keep an open mind and just *try* the retreat's program, so begrudgingly I crawled out of bed before dawn and made my way to the meditation area. I won't lie—I felt ridiculous at first, chanting while sitting on the floor in the dark. During the meditation session, I kept sneaking peeks at the people around me, wondering what their deal was. But the sound of om was soothing and we were gazing out toward the ocean. I'd never done yoga before, and that was equally hard to get a handle on. By evening, I was exhausted from getting up early and the endless contortions my body had forced itself into.

I was about to give up and just hit the beach the next day, but my

> **"You will have more energy and enthusiasm for everything else in your life if you are spiritually grounded."**

girl begged me to try once more. I still felt a little weird, but the chanting seemed more natural, and even had a calming flow that time. My body relaxed somewhat into the yoga, so I began to feel strong and centered. I even kept my eyes closed during meditation and actually managed to clear my mind of some distractions and harmful thoughts. By the end of the week, I felt like a completely new woman, energized and ready to move forward with my journey. The yoga, meditation, and even the chanting somehow helped me feel more connected to the rest of the universe. I still missed my mother, but I could feel her with me. That week turned out to be an extremely spiritual experience for me.

The trip was so rewarding that even though I did not continue to practice yoga seriously, it did make me realize how important it is to renew spiritual energy on a regular basis. I urge you to do the same. I'm not saying you have to go to a yoga retreat if it doesn't interest you. You can join a church, visit someone else's house of worship, participate in a Bible study class, read a book about positive living—just devote some quality time to your inner life. I promise you will have more energy and enthusiasm for everything else in your life if you are spiritually grounded.

This Year . . .

- **Wake up to watch a sunrise.** It's such an amazing experience and it happens every single day! It will make you feel enormously grateful for the gift of this beautiful planet.
- **Give back.** Join or launch a program at your place of worship that helps your community. Try to donate something more than money—give your time and reach out to work one-on-one with those in need.
- **Seek your true purpose.** Let go of others' expectations once and for all, and affirm your right to figure out why you are on the planet. It may take a while to find your purpose, but when you do—live it!
- **Let go of your baggage.** You've been lugging around painful stuff for so long, you may feel as though it's attached to you, like a limb. Therefore, it can be hard to let it go—if so, talk to someone who can help. But once you release it you will feel lighter, and be able to go so much further.

GET YOURS **FOREVER**

When I was growing up, my family was comfortably middle-class. We were far from rich, but I can't say I ever wanted for anything. I attended private schools, had plenty of clothes, went on vacations. In other words, I was very, very fortunate. My parents raised me to appreciate everything I had, and for the most part I did. They also raised me to be empathetic to people who weren't as lucky as I was. They encouraged me to have friends who weren't necessarily as financially well off as we were. It was their hope that I would grow up to be secure and happy, but also motivated to do better for myself and my community.

We lived in Harlem during my high school years, and while our street was lined with beautiful brownstones, most of the surrounding blocks were crowded with tenements and guys hanging out on street corners. Once, when I was going through my brattiest teen year, I made a comment to my mother about how lazy those guys had to be, and that maybe if they had jobs like everyone else, they wouldn't have to live in the projects. Girlfriend, let me tell you—I have rarely seen my mother *that* furious. After she called me ungrateful, high-and-mighty, and a snob, she grounded me for a month (my mother did not play!).

When Mom finally calmed down, she explained that I should never take anything for granted, and that we didn't have a nice home just because she worked hard. She told me that many people had sacrificed *everything*—including their lives—to make our comfortable existence possible. Then she gave me reading assignments on the civil rights movement, the Holocaust, Native American history, etc. She made sure I understood that I am named after W.E.B. Du Bois because he was a brilliant scholar and dedicated activist—not because I was part of some talented tenth that was more deserving than the rest of our community.

> **"Everything you do to help someone else heals the universe and is a profound act of spirituality."**

At the time, I thought her reaction was extreme and unfair. But looking back, she may have saved my soul. Mom made sure I was clear that having money does not make you a good person, nor does it shield you from rest of the world. She instilled in me that it was my responsibility to do what I could for the next generation because that's what my ancestors did for me. She taught me to live with honor, integrity, empathy, and generosity. And she made sure I knew that even though she loved me and believed I was special, I wasn't better than anybody else. I just had many more opportunities.

I'll never forget the lesson, and I am glad to be able to repeat it with conviction: Know that you are special, but understand that we are all one. Be grateful that others sacrificed so you could be where you are, and be willing to do the same. Everything you do to help someone else heals the universe in some way and is a profound act of spirituality. Think about leaving the world a better place than it was when you got here, and you will forever be connected to your higher power.

Always . . .

- **Practice tolerance.** Accept that not all people believe what you believe. Understand that their beliefs are as worthy as yours.
- **Have faith.** Remember that we all have a destiny. When life gets challenging, know that you are here for a reason and that everything will work out.
- **Attune to your own power.** Understand that you have the power of creation within you—not just to create life, but to create any experience you want.
- **Be humble.** You are a great person—but you already know that. So will everyone else. No need to show off or act superior. Because as wonderful as you are, you're just a human being, the same as anyone else.
- **Be centered.** Make room for meditation or prayer in your daily routine. Some days, finding that fifteen minutes may seem almost impossible, but you will be that much more productive and happy if you feel grounded and calm.
- **Give thanks.** If you are able to take a breath, you have much to be grateful for. Never take anything for granted.

10 WAYS TO HEAL THE UNIVERSE

This is your world—treat it right!

1. **Revere the planet.** Recycle—every little piece of plastic you separate from every little piece of paper means a lot. Don't litter, and if you see a piece of trash on the street, don't think of it as "not my problem"—pick it up and dispose of it properly.

2. **Work with kids.** Be a Big Sister, read to children at your local library, volunteer at a nearby school—and don't forget the kids in your own family. They are the future.

3. **Respect your elders.** Give up your seat on the bus to an older person, volunteer at a senior center, be attentive to your older family members and listen to their stories. Remember, they paved the way for you.

4. **Donate what you can.** Give to the charities of your choice. How much? A good rule of thumb is to donate 1 to 5 percent of your gross annual salary.

5. **Build your community, or your world.** Get involved in building homes for low-income families. Habitat for Humanity can help you figure out how (www.habitat.org).

6. **Go for the green.** Plant a tree. Visit sites like www.greenbelt.org (founded by Wangari Maathai, the first African woman to win the Nobel Peace Prize), www.sustainableharvest.org, or www.arborday.org for information.

7. **Feed the world.** Donate money or volunteer for Meals on Wheels (www.mowaa.org), spend time at a local soup kitchen, organize a canned-food drive. Prepare a nutritious dinner for someone you know who doesn't get a home-cooked meal very often.

8. **Comfort creatures.** Animals need love, too! Become a member of The Humane Society, help out at a local animal shelter, adopt and/or foster a shelter dog or cat. Treat your own pets with love—be sure to neuter your animals and don't allow them to roam.

9. **Create beauty.** Do your art! Fill the world with the purity of your vision, your voice, your words, your ideas.

10. **Practice random acts of kindness.** It's not just a bumper sticker, it's a way of life. Be there for a friend in times of trouble and smile at a stranger, just because.

INDIA.ARIE ON SPIRITUALITY

I remember hearing the buzz first. The whisperings of industry insiders that India. Arie could be the next big thing. But because India was so unconventional, few people were willing to make a bold prediction about her future. Curious about this soulful sister who clearly had a lot to say, I invited her to perform in our conference room at Vanguarde Media. I'll never forget that day: the throng of editors packed in tight, eager to see this new sensation; and India, with thick long locks, in a colorful flowing skirt, sitting on a stool holding only her guitar. And then she launched into "Video," the initial single off her first CD, Acoustic Soul. *We were all transfixed by her deep gorgeous voice and empowered by her words: "But, I learned to love myself unconditionally / Because I am a queen . . ."*

I decided that day to give her a cover, her first ever. Next thing I knew, Acoustic Soul *earned seven Grammy nominations and sold more than two million copies.*

Since making her amazing debut in 2001, India has been helping us connect with who we really are—physically, intellectually, and spiritually. Her second album, Voyage to India, *was as insightful as her first, and her most recent release,* Testimony: Vol.1, Life & Relationship, *solidifies India's position as an R&B Earth Mother who just wants us to love ourselves already! Here, she and I speak about what it means to connect with one's higher power while staying grounded and down-to-earth.*

Amy: **What does spirituality mean to you?**
India: When I speak about spirituality, it is the unseen energy of things. Everything has an unseen side. Dogs have a spiritual energy. Colors have a spiritual energy.

AB: **Do you consider yourself to be a spiritual person?**
IA: Of course I do. For me, I think it comes along with being an artist, because I seek to perceive more than what someone is showing me in everything. I want to have a deeper understanding. The process of making music and continuing to develop what my spiritual ideals are is completely connected. Music is the way that I express my spirituality; it is my connection and my outlet.

AB: **How do you define a higher power?**
IA: The unseen energy of something is its higher power. I believe in a

higher power of the universe and I also believe there is a higher power that exists in everything. That is why I make the kind of music that I make. I'm seeking to use the higher power of music, words, and what a voice can do to express the higher power of what a woman is, what a black woman is, what young black America is.

AB: *Do you think your music will help people bring forth their own higher power?*

IA: That is my intention. I don't know if it happens or not, but I believe in the power of intention.

AB: *Can you explain a bit more what you mean by the power of intention?*

IA: The power of intention is more that just saying, "This is what I want"—it's believing that you can have it. You can't be so detailed in your desires that you don't let God act, but it is knowing clearly what you want. I'm an unlikely celebrity just from the songs that I sing, the way that I look, the kind of voice that I have, the kind of clothes that I wear—everything. Technically, it's not supposed to work. But I don't let anyone tell me no. I know there is a higher power in me that can do anything. I think praying is a way of setting intention.

AB: *How so?*

IA: I believe that prayers are answered. I was in a long-term relationship, and the day after I broke up I remember saying a prayer to learn the lesson in this relationship instead of trying to blame [my ex] for what he did. "He has all his T-shirts in my closet and I'm so mad at him, and I'm the victim . . ." I had those feelings, but instead of living them, I chose to ask God to show me what the lesson was so that I could be a better person and be prepared to be a wife and a mother and all those things that are part of the higher vision I have for my own life. And when I find myself trying to blame [my ex] or talking bad about him, I remember that is not what I said I wanted. That's not what I prayed for.

AB: *Do you need to be in a place of worship when you speak to God?*

IA: It is a powerful aspect of the human experience if you can feel God when you are out walking in the woods. You are missing out on something really beautiful if you can't feel God in the scent of a rose.

Choose to feel from your spirit no matter where you are. If you go swimming, feel the water with your spirit. If you go to a wedding, feel it with your spirit. Or when you have a moment in your office, open up the window and play your favorite song and put your feet on the desk, just for a second, just to connect to your spirit. If it's a church for you, that's cool, but it doesn't have to always be at church.

AB: *Do you think that it's important to be tolerant of other people's be-liefs?*

IA: I see the benefit in being open-minded about spirituality. I have a song called "Gift of Acceptance." It says, "Give the world a present, and give the gift of your acceptance." This has been said so many times, but that is one of the biggest problems. We can't just live and let live. I understand the effectiveness of religion, but I don't agree with not being able to understand that everyone has a different way of expressing it. I don't think there is anything wrong with a person who is a devout Christian, but I personally think there is something wrong with a devout Christian who says everyone else is wrong.

AB: *How do you stay spiritually grounded, especially in your industry? I know it's got to be hard at times.*

IA: That is one of my biggest challenges. Being in the music industry is a big test of your spirituality. The most successful people in the music industry are mercenaries. You have to lie, you have to tell people what they want to hear, you have to act like you are happy when you are not happy, you have to wear makeup on TV and look totally different. It is all a lie. When I am just being myself and I'm happy, I look great. When I'm *acting* happy and I smile, it looks crazy. I'm always doing a balancing act of trying to be successful in a business that I know is not spiritual at all.

AB: *How can we all stay spiritually grounded?*

IA: One of the things I do is make decisions based on what feels right. I took four years off [between albums]. A lot of people would be afraid to do that, but there was a lot of work I needed to do on myself. I could have made myself ill by not addressing that stuff, by being on the road, and facilitating all the energy you need to have when you are a celebrity. I took the time that I needed and I trusted that things were going to work out.

Also, I definitely feel it's important for people to take time every day to pay attention to that [spiritual] aspect of life. The same way that you would work out or brush your teeth, you have to do whatever your spiritual practice is. Personally, I believe in prayer and I pray a lot. I pray before the plane takes off that we land safe. I pray for the purity of the food that I'm about to eat. I pray for everything.

AB: *What have been some of your most important life lessons?*
IA: Self-love was the biggest lesson in my life. I had to learn to define myself outside of anyone else's opinion of me. This is starting from elementary school, when the little white kids would ask, "What's wrong with your hair?" I'm a woman who does not fit into [traditional] standards of beauty. I'm not saying that I don't think I'm beautiful, but there is no standard for my look in the music industry at all. I'm the standard. I would not be able to stand up with the look I have and say "Hey, this is what I am" without self-love. That is why the song "Video" exists. That is something that has been very hard-earned for me and something that I still work on every day.

AB: *What is the best piece of advice you've received?*
IA: My mom always says, "Why be ordinary when you can be extraordinary?" I always remember that—it always gives me the courage to say the things that I want to say. In March 2005, I went to South Africa and I met Nelson Mandela. He said, "Be bold—be bold in talking against AIDS and violence against women." So I also took that and applied it to my life.

Why be ordinary when you can be extraordinary, and be bold. I like those two pieces of advice best. I tell everyone: Just be bold and stand behind what you believe.

PROMISE PAGE

My dreams and goals to enrich my spiritual
life are:

_____
_____
_____
_____
_____
_____

I promise that today I will:

_____
_____
_____
_____
_____

This year I promise to:

_____
_____
_____
_____
_____

I will always:

_____
_____
_____
_____
_____
_____

NOW, GO GET YOURS...

After having read this book, I hope you feel inspired and empowered—but I really don't want you to think that I have all the answers. No, girl-friend, not even close. All I've done is live a little! I've had a ton of experiences, made many mistakes, picked myself up, and in the process achieved some real successes. My life has been an interesting ride so far, and I fully anticipate learning many more profound lessons—both the easy way and the hard way. What I do know for sure is that life is truly an ongoing adventure, and that the only way to make the most of it is to be an active participant. Your dreams will never become reality un-less you envision the life you truly want and take real steps toward making it happen. At the same time, you've also got to stay open to the unpredictable stuff that can guarantee your life will never be boring. In other words, being happy and fulfilled is a balancing act between work-ing hard to realize your dreams while still taking advantage of com-pelling opportunities that may present themselves when you least expect it.

I'm doing that myself. As I finish this book, I'm considering my op-tions for my next big challenge. I could write more books, go back into magazine publishing, work on an Internet venture, or even take my mission and my message to radio and television. Or I could do all of those things! I'm both actively pursuing cool opportunities and wait-ing to see what will emerge in the coming year. Every day, I schedule meetings, contact people, and work on my action plan. And every day I also get calls and e-mails regarding projects I never would have thought of on my own. On the home front, my son, Max, is getting bigger and smarter all the time—and my husband and I are trying to come up with new ways to help him realize his full potential. Max has brought us closer than ever to our respective families. I'm especially en-joying watching my dad interact with his grandson, whom he loves more than anything! And Jeff and I are also thinking about what we want our lives to look like as Max grows up—and figuring out how we can move toward our dreams as a family. This is a really exciting time! And it just reaffirms that the more thoughtful and productive and open you are, the more possibilities you will have to be happy.

Just keep in mind that to "get yours," you've got to give as much as you get. Life is not easy, but that's okay. The more effort you put in to creating the adventure you want, the more fun and rewarding it will be. Accomplishing your goals by working hard and playing hard will give you fulfillment like nothing else. If you get stuck, just remember my seven "rules" for getting yours:

Always . . .

- **Embrace fear as growth.** The more you challenge yourself and reach outside your comfort zone, the more you are growing as a person and becoming the woman you were meant to be. Open your mind to new ideas and your eyes to new sights. Believe that you can do anything.
- **Be true to yourself.** Never let anyone else tell you what to do, whom to hang out with, what to wear, how to think. You know yourself best; this is your life. Identify your passions, embrace who you are, and get comfortable in your own skin.
- **Realize your value and demand the best.** No one will treat you properly or give you the opportunities you seek unless they feel your confidence. Expect your dreams to become reality and they will!
- **Put into the universe what you want to get back.** Make people feel your positive energy. Be generous and loving. Try to help others be all they can be. Contribute to your community. Obnoxious, petty, greedy people will never feel as fulfilled as people who strive to make the world a better place.
- **Have integrity.** Do what you say you are going to do. It's as simple as that. Whether it's your friend, your brother, your boss, or your neighbor—make good on your commitments. Most important, keep your promises to yourself. Use the "promise pages" at the end of each chapter to identify your dreams and list what steps you will take today, this year, and forever to make them reality. Then do it!

- **Stay independent.** Again, this is your life and no one can live it for you. Be your own woman—even as a wife, mother, girlfriend, daughter, friend. When you create the life you want, love and protect it as your most valuable asset. Don't let anyone convince you to give up something that makes you feel good in the guise of "taking care of you." Take care of yourself.
- **Do something meaningful every day.** Your life is happening right now, as you read this. Yes, I want you to dream big and work toward your goals. But please remember that nothing is worth more than today. And this day will never happen again. Make it count.

I know every one of you reading this book is beautiful and special and capable—and you deserve the absolute best in your life. Expect it and work for it, and whatever you want will be yours. I'm confident you will get yours, and have everything you ever dreamed of . . . and more! Please log on to my Web site (www.amyduboisbarnett.com) to let me know what adventures you are having and how you are working to create the life you truly want.

ACKNOWLEDGMENTS

It would have been impossible for me to write this book without an amazing group of girls who are more like family than friends. Kara LeGeros, my oldest friend and voice of reason, has been my rock for a quarter of a century. Maitrayee Bhattacharyya, my moral center, has literally gotten me through some of the most difficult times of my life. Alicia Felder, my partner-in-crime and style council, has been a trusted member of my inner circle since our days in retail. I miss you, Leesh! Lisa Gelobter is my black/Jewish/Francophile/ex-smoking cosmic sister. It was an honor to go through pregnancy with Jodie Patterson, who is a wonderful example of how possible it is to be a caring mom and still be *yourself.* Dawanna Williams has been a great friend from day one. Stefan Andemicael has never let being a guy stand in the way of a good girlchat (I mean that in the most manly way, of course!). They, and many others, have cheerfully let me write about them for years. Thanks for having a sense of humor about it!

Though my friends have provided me with invaluable support (and crazy stories!) over the years, if it weren't for my mother's example and influence, this book would simply not be. I have never met a woman more determined to "get hers" than Marguerite Ross Barnett. I've talked a lot about how strong, fearless, and driven my mom was. But she was also silly and warm and generous. She loved to cook spicy food, had a not-so-secret crush on Smokey Robinson, collected matching shoes, gloves, and purses in every color, developed a killer golf game in her forties—and was so determined to enjoy life that a week before she died, she flew to Hawaii so she could spend her last few days in paradise. Mom was a pioneer and a role model, but most importantly, she was my best friend.

Through good and bad times, my dad, Steve Barnett, has always made me feel precious and loved. He's also a wonderful grandpa. Maxie is so lucky to have you, Daddy! Liz Barnett is a gift from the universe. Thank you so much for being a really cool sister; we're going to keep getting closer every year. Many thanks to JoAnn Magdoff for endless talks about life—and for being my dad's best friend. I'm blessed to have a caring and insightful aunt like Emily Barnett, and my cousin Jessica Sbarsky is a talented, beautiful person who deserves all the best this life has to offer. At eighty-eight years old, my grandfather, Murray Barnett, made the eleven-hour journey from California to a cliff in Jamaica to witness my wedding; his strength of will and intellectual curiosity continue to be an inspiration. Laura Magdoff has a truly lovely and pure spirit. I miss my grandmothers, Mary Eubanks and Mary Barnett.

The entire Brown family welcomed me into their circle without hesitation, and in them, I have an unparalleled extended support system. I could not have asked for more generous and loving in-laws. Malcolm and Ernestine's warm house in Ohio is like home base! I'm so happy that Malcolm, Vanessa, and Salma live within walking distance. I get to eat Malcolm's cooking, chat with Vanessa about the joys of being a Brown graduate, and hear Salma ask for "Ahmee" and "Mac" on the regular. Rhonda Saffold has been my sistergirl sounding board, and I'm looking forward to Avery and Isaac showing Max how it's done on the basketball court.

Not many people can say they have "work family," but I'm truly fortunate. Angela Burt-Murray is one of the most creative and gifted editors I've ever encountered. Ang, you are a tremendous example for black women across the country. The eerily gifted Nina Malkin could make the *Farmer's Almanac* sound like Tolstoy. Really. And the incomparable Doreen Arriaga has held more important roles in my life than I can enumerate (including right hand, project manager, and personal cheerleader). Many thanks for always having my back, Dee. You are so special to me and I have no idea what I would do without you! To Sharan, the newest member of my work family, your wicked sense of humor made every day fun (and you are an excellent example of how to get yours, Miss Homeowner!). To Keith Clinkscales, the visionary behind Vanguarde Media, I would not be where I am today had you not given me the opportunity of a lifetime. And thank you to Isolde Motley for allowing me to kick down a door at Time Inc.—and remaining supportive through the fun and the shite!

I have had the best team in the world work on this book. My literary agent, Elyse Cheney, is a wonderful partner. She possesses vision, energy, and a truly good soul. My editor, Janet Hill, is brilliant, patient, and kind. Elyse and Janet: Many, many thanks . . . I'm also grateful to Julia Coblentz and Joanna Pinsker for getting the word out, and to Courtney Mauk, Clarence Haynes, and Christian Nwachukwu for keeping everything on track. Thanks to the Doubleday Broadway art department, especially Marlyn Dantes and Jean Traina, for creating a beautiful cover. Last but not least, Roberto Ligresti took a killer picture (I wish I could walk around with the cover shot taped to my head so I never have a pimple or bad hair day again!).

Special thanks to the smart, honest, funny, cool women who participated in this book (and, of course, to their managers and PR reps who *really* made the interview possible): Sanaa Lathan, Gayle King, Gabrielle Union, Mellody Hobson, Sarah Jones, Venus Williams, Courtney Sloane, Mo'Nique, India.Arie, Kelly Rowland, and Kelis. My friend Hill Harper gave the book its only—and a very much needed—male perspective.

Last but definitely never least, I am profoundly grateful for my husband, Jeffrey Brown, and my son, Max Robeson Brown. Jeff, you have the biggest heart of any man I've ever met and I know you always have my back. Max, you are my greatest treasure—you've been the love of my life from the minute you kicked me in the bladder. There is nothing in the world I wouldn't do for my family.

ABOUT THE AUTHOR

AMY DuBOIS BARNETT is an award-winning journalist, fiction writer, and television commentator. As the former managing editor of *Teen People*, Amy became the first African American woman in the country to head a major mainstream magazine. Before that, she was the editor-in-chief and driving force behind *Honey* magazine. Most recently, she was the deputy editor-in-chief of *Harper's Bazaar*. Amy has also been a weekly pop-culture commentator on CNN's *American Morning*, a regular panelist on NPR's *News and Notes*, and has been featured on numerous national television shows including *The Today Show*, *Good Morning America*, and *The Early Show*. She continues to make frequent television and radio appearances as an expert on social issues, pop culture, and professional development. In addition, Amy is an active board member of Girls Inc. of New York and is a motivational speaker at professional and educational organizations across the country. She received her B.A. from Brown University and an M.F.A. in creative writing from Columbia University. She lives in New York City with her husband and son.

Get Yours! was nominated for a 2008 NAACP Image Award in the Outstanding Instructional Literary Work category.

HEY, GIRLFRIEND, LET'S STAY IN TOUCH

For more valuable advice and tips on how to get yours, including information about the Get Yours coaching programs, don't forget to visit my Web site: www.amydubois barnett.com. Can't wait to hear from you!